MAKE THRIFT MEND

MAKE THRIFT MEND

Stitch, Patch,
Darn, Plant-Dye
& Love Your
Wardrobe

KATRINA RODABAUGH

Photography by KAREN PEARSON

ABRAMS, NEW YORK

TO CAROL,
MARY & LEONA,
FOR THIS
LINEAGE OF STITCHES.

AND TO DAVID,
MAXWELL & JUDE,
FOR THIS
HOPE FOR THE FUTURE.

"It is not enough to weep for our lost landscapes;
we have to put our hands in the earth to make ourselves
whole again. Even a wounded world is feeding us.
Even a wounded world holds us, giving us moments of
wonder and joy. I choose joy over despair. Not because
I have my head in the sand, but because joy is what
the earth gives me daily and I must return the gift."

ROBIN WALL KIMMERER
Braiding Sweetgrass: Indigenous Wisdom,
Scientific Knowledge, and the Teachings of Plants

CONTENTS

———

foreword

Katrina's first mending book, *Mending Matters*, matters to me enormously: It lives between my studio, my bedroom, and my sitting room, depending on whether I want to have a quick dip for a momentary inspiration, or I am looking for something really specific as a working reference. My copy is well thumbed, and full of page markers that I keep going back to—and I literally cannot wait to place *Make Thrift Mend*, the book you are holding in your hands, right next to it.

Let's face it: We all have to do something, because we can't carry on as we have, and our clothes, our wardrobes, are a comforting and impactful place to start; we have been fed overproduction and quantity over quality for so long now that many of us wouldn't know the difference between a good hemline and a shoddy one, a well-constructed garment and a flimsy piece of something to wear for a minute.

Katrina belongs to a category of individuals (and I consider myself to be cut from that same cloth) who love clothes and see their value, both as our chosen skin and as a powerful vehicle for self-expression, celebrating pieces where each tear is a memory of use, and each repair is a statement of intent.

In an industry that has been hell-bent on overproducing well over a hundred billion garments per year, we need to install balance, and that is prosperity over growth and adequacy instead of excess—our wardrobes and the clothes we choose to put in them (and how we care for them) have a huge part to play.

Katrina's concept of a fashion fast to antagonize fast fashion, and embarking on a journey that speaks of luxury, artistry, craft, and passion, make her a true pioneer for a fashion system that cherishes its roots and places them firmly at the forefront of our most relevant conversation: how to make fashion responsible and sustainable. And a fashion fast need not be as painful as a strict diet, after all; in fact quite the opposite—it can lead to a burst of creativity, awaken new curiosities, be the start of something new. We are so programmed to think that happiness is the next new, cheap online bargain that we don't bother to imagine that "newness" could be achieved with a little bit of a rethink of the things we already own.

Katrina provides the inspiration, the motivation, and the techniques to put daydreams into practice, whether you want to DIY it or ask a professional to do it for you, and the more you delve into her universe, the more you are compelled to do as she does.

—Orsola de Castro,
co-founder and global creative director, Fashion Revolution

introduction

This book is my hope for the future. It's my hope for the future of fashion, sustainable or conscious living, fiber arts, and the intersection where they create incredible opportunity for change. It's my attempt to share a written version of my personal art project, Make Thrift Mend, expanding my original fashion fast with tutorials, essays, quotes, photographs, and extensive resources. It's a follow-up to my last book, *Mending Matters*, which resulted from teaching dozens, if not hundreds, of mending workshops across the country and wanting to offer my techniques to folks anywhere books are available.

But in many ways this book, *Make Thrift Mend*, is about turning back to my instinct as an artist. It's about honoring that impulse to create a personal practice that fused my passion for the environment with my love of fiber arts and fashion. It's that willful spirit of many artists that persists despite the odds—to make art because we must. But in that space of necessary creativity, we shift our habits to consider our impact on the planet. And still make beautiful things.

If I've learned anything from teaching and working in sustainable fashion, it's that the solutions are infinite and individual. Our solutions for living sustainably should include our various budgets, lifestyles, cultures, geographies, aesthetics, technical skills, and more. It shouldn't look the same from person to person. Instead, it should include a myriad of solutions. It should also include the preservation of textile skills and the retention of the ability to simply make things with our hands.

If we are going to create a Slow Fashion future, it's not going to look like any fashion trend of the past. It will embrace circularity and invention. Yet it will heed the limits of nonrenewable resources and recognize when we've used enough. Or too much. It will look to upcycle, recycle, and reuse whenever possible. It will be low-waste and zero-waste. It will prioritize fibers that biodegrade, support local fibersheds and farms, and go beyond carbon-neutral to carbon-beneficial. Circularity will become the new norm—designers and makers will conceive of garments with the intention of using the materials again.

It will also consider the people making our garments. It will assume that ethical labor and fair working conditions are a mandate—all over the world. It will better utilize technology for design solutions and community-building. It will be committed to diversity, equity, and inclusion. It will consider and celebrate all bodies. It will be collaborative. It will be respectful. It will honor traditional textile techniques and expertise to make garments for today's citizens while paying deep homage to where, when, and how the techniques were developed.

But one thing that will also direct the Slow Fashion future is fierce creativity. Bold invention. Striking innovation. The best art and design are wildly inspired. The shifts will be necessary in policy, law, and among individuals. Collectively, we'll need to turn open-hearted to the plants, animals, and people of the earth who have been mindfully making garments using sustainable techniques for centuries. They hold the wisdom and the knowledge for the future. Before fast fashion there was another way. For all of us.

My great-grandmother Leona features prominently in this book. Though I never met her, I've learned so much about textiles through her work. Through her quilts and stitches, I study her techniques for repairing and repurposing fibers—not because it was fashionable but because it's just what she would have done. I reach back for her wisdom as much as I reach forward to the future I hope to create for my children. In many ways, this book is my hope for that future. May we be mindful. May we be respectful. May we be wildly inspired.

I hope you use the ideas and techniques in this book to stitch, sew, patch, darn, plant-dye and ultimately love your Slow Fashion wardrobe. Lastly, I hope you make beautiful things.

Xoxo,
Katrina

author's note

This book is inspired by my personal art project and fast-fashion fast of the same name, Make Thrift Mend. Started in August 2013, the project was conceived to create solutions in my personal wardrobe regarding the environmental crisis in the fashion industry. Make Thrift Mend was launched four months after the Rana Plaza garment factory collapsed in Dhaka, Bangladesh, killing 1,134 people and injuring 2,500 more. This disaster was a wakeup call. And I was determined to create an alternative. I had no idea this personal art project would become the center of my studio work or radically deepen my commitment to sustainable living. I gave up convenience in fashion and started a relationship with commitment instead.

For the first year of Make Thrift Mend I staved off all new clothing—I focused on mending what I owned, buying secondhand, and making simple garments. The next year I decided to buy new clothing only if it was locally made or handmade. The third year I added new clothing if it was organic, sustainable, and ethically made (mostly because I needed new underwear, bras, and leggings). The fourth year I turned to my studio materials—buying tools and fibers that were biodegradable, low-plastic, and heirloom quality. The fifth year I missed making things with my hands so I turned back toward handmade garments and taught myself basic knitting.

Each year of the project, I shifted the parameters to challenge myself in new directions. I learned that paying attention to my consumption was paramount, but creativity was paramount too. I've never returned to fast fashion but I've come to understand the multiplicity of challenges and solutions in conscious clothing. As my Make Thrift Mend project progressed—alongside my passion for secondhand clothing, simple sewing patterns, and mending just about everything—I realized that sustainability is not one-size-fits-all. It's a journey, not a fixed destination. This book is meant to share my journey in hopes it might support yours.

CHAPTER 1
BUILD

build

START WHERE YOU ARE

If I had to give one piece of advice on what turned my wardrobe into a Slow Fashion wardrobe, I'd say "pause." If we could just pause our shopping habits, slow down our consumption, and pay attention to the clothes we bring into our homes, we'd collectively make a huge shift. Consumption has accelerated to such a furious pace that most of us don't thoroughly consider what we purchase. It's not just some of us. It's all of us.

But if we can just pause before we purchase something—in this case, clothing—and confirm that we need it, love it, and might wear it for years, then I think we'd be in a different situation with consumption. This takes a shift in mindset that may take months or years. Awareness is key to a conscious or sustainable wardrobe. There are no perfect pathways in sustainable living—just better-informed choices for the individual and collective. Remember: progress, not perfection. While on the following pages I've listed ten ways to organize your thinking (and actions) for Slow Fashion, there could have been many more steps. Just start where you are and do the best you can. This is a journey that will deepen as you practice.

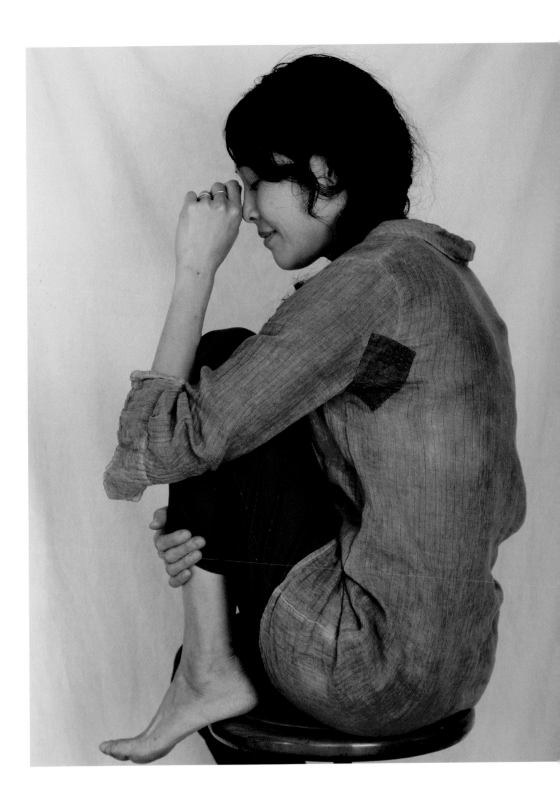

PAUSE

Before you do anything, do nothing. Just pause. The most sustainable clothes are the ones already in your closet. The first thing you need to do is to take a break from shopping, so make a commitment to a fashion fast. You could make it just a weeklong fast. But I'd encourage you to make it a little longer than feels comfortable yet just shy of feeling impossible. Maybe thirty days, three months, or even a year.

ASSESS

Acknowledge what you love to wear. Look at what is coming out of the clean laundry. See what's hanging at the front of your closet or folded on the top in your drawers. Or snap a photo of yourself each day for a week. It's helpful to gain insights about your personal uniform. This is also a good time to note anything that you're missing, like a long-sleeved T-shirt to wear under your favorite sweater.

ORGANIZE

Take inventory of the garments you own. Do you have eight black dresses? Four blue sweaters? Or six pairs of jeans, three of which need mending? Set them aside before you buy new jeans—we'll get to repairs. If you come across garments you aren't wearing, put them aside too. Sort your clothes into three piles: yes, no, and maybe. The pile you love should stay. The "no" pile should go, but thoughtfully (see "Donate," page 27). And the "maybe" pile could be a place where you experiment with styling, repurposing, dyeing, or patchwork. The goal is to shift your habits toward more intentional purchases that you'll tend, mend, and love to wear.

INSPIRE

Find your fashion inspirations. Who are your style icons? They can be famous or your best friends. Try to identify what you love about their look and name their styles: glamorous, artsy, executive, etc. Let your inspiration come from anywhere and everywhere: Train rides, magazines, books, movies, social gatherings, and social media can be great sources for fashion inspiration. Take notes, collect images, or create a digital inspiration board. I collect fashion images online for sewing, mending, dyeing, styling, and more. Sometimes all it takes is a simple shift in fashion styling to feel inspired. Now, what could you reimagine with what you already own?

RESEARCH

Let's look at the bigger picture and identify where to focus time and money and build community. Are you a maker and love visible mending or patchwork? Check out hashtags like #mendingmatters or #visiblemending on Instagram. If you're passionate about fiber, find ways to support fiber farms in your region or study the benefits of organic cotton. Decide where to buy secondhand and where to make local donations. Research where to take sewing, mending, or knitting classes; sign up for newsletters from ethical brands and independent artists; follow inspiring folks on Instagram, and just keep going.

GATHER

It's time for a party. Bring folks together in the name of Slow Fashion by hosting a clothing swap, mending circle, or DIY plant-dye party in person or online. Organize a swap with the families at your school, join a local repair group, or work with a nearby farmer to organize a community dye day with wilted dye flowers from their farm. There's a rich sustainable fashion community online, so be sure to reach out virtually too. There are great online activist organizations like Fashion Revolution. Regardless, find folks to support your Slow Fashion journey.

DONATE

This may be one of the hardest aspects of Slow Fashion. So many of our donated clothes ultimately end up bailed and shipped overseas, incinerated, or added to a landfill. Why? It's supply and demand. We toss off more secondhand clothing than we buy. However, with the rise in popularity of online secondhand shops, I hope we'll see this shift. Yet it's still hard to recycle fiber blends, torn clothing is not valuable for resale, and the cheap synthetics are clogging up our resale markets.

Before you donate, try to swap, gift, reuse, or redesign. Dye white clothes with plants (see the Thrift section, page 86) and overdye light-colored garments. Save unwearable clothes for patchwork, mending, or future craft projects. You can even tuck some tiny biodegradable, undyed textile scraps into a kitchen compost bin. Try to resell clothes with consignment shops or online sellers. Otherwise, donate clean, wearable clothes to charities, thrift stores, or resellers. Collect unwearable garments in a box and do some research to find a textile recycler near you. Just keep those textiles from the garbage—there are so many options to recycle, repurpose, reuse, resell, or donate.

CARE

Think before you wash and dry. A sizeable aspect to the environmental impact of our garments is how we care for them, mostly from overuse of hot water and overuse of machine drying. Wash less: Much of our clothing (such as jeans) can be worn several times before being washed. Just spot clean. Wash laundry with a full load typically in cool water with eco-friendly soap. Hang as much as you can on a drying rack or clothesline. When clothes do go into the dryer, use lower heat for less time, add wool dryer balls, and remove any dryer lint from the lint trap before starting a new load. Avoid dry cleaners whenever possible or choose eco-friendly cleaners. Eventually, you might find it perfectly natural to wash less, forgo your dryer, and spot clean regularly.

BOUNDARIES

Setting and honoring boundaries is a great way to hold space for your priorities in sustainable fashion. Whatever you decide your intention is going forward, name that right now and set some boundaries so you can be clear. Consider the following: If you need something new, where will you look first? Can you borrow from a family member or friend? Can you make your clothes? Can you take a class? Knowing where you'll buy, from which brands, and what fibers you'll prioritize will be so helpful. Lastly, what will you splurge on and where will you save money in your annual clothing budget?

CONNECTION

Let's find one inspirational word to help ground our Slow Fashion journey. What's your goal in your future wardrobe? What do you hope to embolden or embrace? Mine is *connection*. I want my wardrobe to create opportunities for connection with myself, my community, and the land. I try to consider how I'm connecting through making, mending, and preserving my clothes. Focus on what you really need or love and follow your instincts. It takes all of us making small shifts to create a collective action.

"As we turn to face the enormous destruction we humans are causing the Earth and its inhabitants, including ourselves, we must have faith and knowledge that we humans also have the capacity for healing and repair, for mending and making amends.

In the past we believed that to be an environmental activist you needed to partake in grand heroic acts: blocking oil trains, tree-sitting, protesting at the capitol. And while these acts are very important and must continue, we've come to see that there is also great importance in the very way we choose to live our lives, and in the small, everyday acts, like mending. As Dr. Clarissa Pinkola Estes put it so well, 'Ours is not the task of fixing the entire world all at once, but of stretching out to mend the part of the world that is within our reach.'"

NINA & SONYA MONTENEGRO
The Far Woods

"Working with pre-loved garments is an opportunity for conversation with many unseen forces; with the energies of the garment's previous owner, with the elements of nature it endured, and with the creative process. Some garments come to me like a blank canvas, mild in nature. Quiet. Understated. As though the stitches breathe life into these mass-produced garments, shining a light on their fibers.

Other pieces come to me with a life of their own. They speak through flaws, evidence of a prior owner like a hand leading to their evolution. I may not immediately notice. They may sit on my clothing rack for weeks, months, with a mild discontent, before I hear the whispers of their desires. Nothing seems to fit until one day . . . My white pencil, whittled to a stub, suddenly finds itself dancing across the garment, following curves over the shoulder, winding around the hips, telling stories I'd never heard, illustrating scenes never seen.

The garment becomes a canvas onto which dreams are channeled. This discarded arrangement of cloth once again finds value in our commodified world, discovering its purpose in a collaborative act that joins past, present, and future owner through the fibers of our daily lives."

CHRISTI JOHNSON
Mixed Color

CHAPTER 2
MAKE

make

HOW TO MAKE:
TOOLS, MATERIALS, AND TECHNIQUES

TOOLS

My sewing tools are fairly simple, but they are the ones I reach for time and time again. I prefer to hand stitch much of my finishing work on garments (hems, neck facings, bias tapes, etc.) and use a sewing machine for construction. My sewing machine is very simple—I use an old Singer that my mother gifted me soon after I graduated from college. It's a portable machine that's traveled around the country with me, and while it's quite basic, it still works just fine.

When choosing threads, needles, and other sewing tools, such as fabric pencils and scissors, I reach for higher-quality items because they last forever. That said, choose the tools you can easily access and that you'll use and love. My preference for tools and materials evolves as my studio practice evolves. And when basic tools and materials do the job, that's great by me. Use what you have. Make what you love. The rest will follow.

STITCHING LETTERS ACROSS THE
PAGES NOT LIKE PAPER BUT LIKE
A SOFTER WEARABLE BOOK. HELD
TOGETHER BY THE STRINGS. AND
SEEDS. AND PLANT OR ANIMAL
FIBER. STALKS PUSH THROUGH
SOIL BECAUSE OF SUNLIGHT. WE
REACH BECAUSE WE MUST. OR WE
REACH BECAUSE THE SEEDS DO

MENDER'S
MUSINGS

needles

I use sturdy metal Sashiko needles for much of my hand stitching because I'm using mostly Sashiko thread—even for decorative embroidery. If I'm using thinner thread, such as a few strands of embroidery thread, then I'll use thinner embroidery needles. For mending, I also use Sashiko needles, especially when mending denim. I match the width of my needle to the weave of the fabric, the width of the thread, and the demands of the project. Trust your instinct—if the thread feels too thick for the fabric, try a thinner thread and needle.

scissors

I have several pairs of high-quality sharp metal fabric scissors. I keep snips and small embroidery scissors in my hand-sewing and mending kits. I also have pinking shears I use on the edges of denim patches for mending. Invest in a quality pair of fabric scissors and they will last you a very long time.

tape measure or ruler

Tape measures are best for working with yardage, and rulers for stitching by hand. I keep both in my sewing kits because they are small and portable. I like to keep a small 6-inch wooden ruler in my stitch kit so that I can make straight lines when working with patches. That said, almost any ruler will do for stitching and mending.

pins

Fabric pins with a large pinhead are easier to pull out when I'm machine sewing. I also find them easier to locate when I predictably drop one on the floor. Choose pins that work for you. I also use safety pins to hold patches in place without the risk of sticking my fingers.

embroidery hoops

Although I rarely use embroidery hoops when I mend, they're handy when I'm working with embroidery thread and more decorative work. A few of the stitching projects in the "Make" section call for a hoop. Basic wooden hoops are my preference, but use what works for you. If you do use a hoop when mending, be sure that the garment is not so frayed that the edges of the hoop could make a tear.

washable fabric pens and pencils

I use a fabric pencil to make straight lines for stitches and mending. After trying more than a dozen different fabric pencils, I'm hooked on the Clover Chaco chalk liners, which are often found in the quilting section of craft stores—they make beautiful lines, dust off easily, and draw with just a little pressure. I also regularly use several wooden fabric pencils. Any quality pencil is fine as long as it's fiber safe.

thimbles

I ignored the beauty of thimbles for too many years. Then I started mending heavy denim and canvas and my fingers protested. So I started experimenting with thimbles and now I'm a believer. I have several thimbles, but I always seem to reach for the same two: a quality metal thimble and a soft leather one. That said, thimbles are fairly personal, so use what works for you.

pliers

Sometimes fabric is too dense or heavy for hand stitching. In this case, a simple set of needle-nose pliers is a great help. I keep them on my studio desk and if I know I'll be stitching heavy-duty fabric, I toss them in my stitch kit if I'm on the go. Being able to pull the threaded needle with the pliers truly saves my hands and wrists. Push with a thimble, pull with pliers.

beeswax

I use 100 percent natural beeswax on my Sashiko and linen thread as needed. I once dyed cotton thread with avocado pits, but when it dried it was too brittle and swollen for my needle. A few coats of beeswax coated the thread and it was perfect for stitching again.

bone folder or point turner

A point turner or bone folder can be a great tool when sewing. They help turn corners and create a lovely smooth angle on sewn fabrics. If I don't have a bone folder nearby, I tend to use whatever small tool is within reach. Taping over the sharpened end of a pencil works in a pinch, but take care not to get pencil marks on your fabric.

MATERIALS

There's such a joy in handling and selecting fibers and designing a project with the most beautiful materials in mind. At times, the most stunning materials might be handwoven linen with visible slubs or expensive organic-cotton and hemp-blended denim. Other times, the most valuable materials are secondhand garments, vintage textiles, or other thrifted fibers just waiting for a new life through plant dyes, thoughtful repairs, or patchwork.

I have a patchwork quilt of my great-grandmother's that needs some basic mending. Made with simple vintage cottons and entirely hand-pieced and hand-stitched, the quilt is absolutely one of the most treasured textiles in my home. Value is personal and subjective. Yet when we choose valuable materials or repair valuable textiles we are more likely to tend them with great care and attention.

fabric

There are several factors to consider when buying new materials like fabric. I prioritize biodegradable materials such as cotton, linen, hemp, wool, and silk whenever possible. Yet the environmental impact of conventional cotton—which requires ample irrigation and pesticides to grow—is significant. It has a tremendous impact on the earth and on the farmers who grow the cotton. Yet it's still biodegradable at the end of its life cycle. Organic cotton is a much healthier choice, though it comes at a higher financial cost. In the end, I still choose cotton over synthetics.

Other plant-based fibers like linen and hemp require a fraction of the water and pesticides to grow and they have rich histories in textiles dating back several centuries. Plant-based fibers can be dyed, sewn, mended, and ultimately composted. I especially love linen because of its weave, texture, drape, and the way it takes plant dyes. I wear it year-round.

If choosing synthetics, I try to select recycled fabrics. My synthetics mostly make up athletic or performance wear like my down winter coat, a bathing suit made from recycled fibers, and my son's mandatory soccer uniforms. It's very hard to completely eradicate plastics from our lives, but we can reduce them significantly by choosing biodegradable fibers when available. I apply this approach to my studio too—biodegradable new materials, recycled fabrics, or secondhand textiles. Remember, there is no perfect sustainable lifestyle.

Wool and silk are great fibers for dyeing and sewing. If you're worried about the ethics of silk farming, there's also Peace Silk (silk breeding and harvesting that adheres to strict environmental and social standards). As for wool, many of us have access to regional wool for yarns, and some mills are starting to integrate local or regional wool into fabric yardage. If you're interested in the carbon footprint of fabric, check out some of the books in the Resources section (page 215), such as *Fibershed* and *The Conscious Closet,* or websites like Fashion Revolution.

thread

For hand stitching I typically work with cotton Sashiko thread. It's beautiful, sturdy, soft, rustic, 100 percent cotton, has a nice hand, pairs wonderfully with denim and linen, and also lacks sheen. I love this thread for mending denim and adding stitches to handmade garments.

I sometimes work with 100 percent cotton embroidery thread for decorative stitching. It's available in hundreds of colors. White or light-colored threads could also be dyed with plants, as long as they are truly 100 percent biodegradable materials like cotton or linen.

My thread choice depends on the fabric and the stitching project. That said, I do sometimes use linen thread or silk thread when stitching or mending—if I want to match the fiber to the garment, my choice depends on the fiber content of the garment. For machine sewing, I typically use an all-purpose 100 percent cotton machine-sewing thread. With some exceptions, I usually shy away from vintage threads as they can be brittle, breakable, or damaged.

TECHNIQUES

Stitches

I try to keep my stitches very simple so that they are accessible to the largest group of people. There are just a handful of stitches that I use throughout my mending, sewing, and making. If you are familiar with more decorative stitches and you'd like to use those for any of the projects, please do. These are just my tried-and-true hand-stitching techniques that I use to repair and decorate my garments and also the ones I teach in my classes. I've tried to be as thorough as possible, but if you need a step-by-step visual, do a quick search online for dozens of videos.

straight stitch

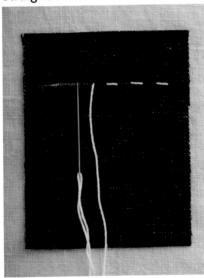

The **straight stitch** is the most basic hand stitch. This is an individual stitch that comes up from underneath the fabric and inserts back under the fabric about ¼ inch (6 mm) away. Stitch length will vary from person to person, but I keep my straight stitches between ⅛ and ¼ inch (3 and 6 mm). I keep my stitches less than ½ inch (1.3 cm) apart so I won't accidentally pull a stitch with a finger, toe, key, or any other small object that might catch a longer stitch.

The straight stitch allows for great versatility. You can stitch in any direction to make a row of horizontal, vertical, or diagonal stitches. You can easily pivot directions between stitches, which can be very useful for an odd-shaped patch. This is a great stitch if you're mending several layers of bulky fabric, such as denim, or if you're tidying up the end of your mending lines to make them equal in length.

whipstitch

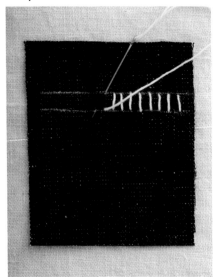

running stitch

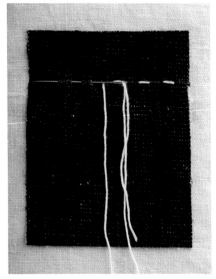

The **whipstitch**, like the straight stitch, results in a singular stitch each time you insert the needle. Whipstitches are particularly useful when you need to stitch the edge of the fabric, like a torn knee, or tack down the edges of a hole on an interior patch. To make a whipstitch, insert your needle from underneath the fabric—say, from the top side of a torn knee with a patch pinned behind—and then insert the stitch vertically about ¼ inch (6 mm) below where you started. Make a diagonal stitch of the same length behind the fabric to begin your second stitch just next to the top of your first. This will result in a row of stitches that is vertical on the right side of the garment and diagonal on the underside.

The **running stitch** is my favorite for mending clothing. This is a collection of straight stitches, but instead of making one individual stitch each time you insert the needle, you can make three to five stitches at a time. You weave your needle up and down through the fabric three to five times before you remove the needle completely to make the next stitch. These stitches are small and fairly uniform, and they head in the same direction without overlapping. They result in a short line of stitches each time.

Running stitches maximize the needle length and result in straight rows of stitches, although you can also use them to make a circle, a square, or another simple shape—especially if you've marked your stitch line with a fabric pencil. You can complete running stitches from one side of the fabric: Keep your hands on top of the fabric and make the stitches from the top

chain stitch

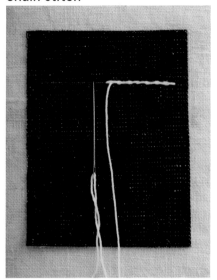

backstitch

instead of pulling the thread out from the underside with each stitch.

The running stitch is great for patching knees, elbows, or other hard-to-reach spots on garments. It is also ideal when covering a larger surface of fabric, like a quilt or the jacket. I use the running stitch when making lines of stitches on various fabrics.

The **chain stitch** is a very basic embroidery stitch that I often use to hand stitch text. Just as it sounds, the chain stitch creates a chain, or links, of thread that can make a continuous line. This is easier with embroidery thread than with Sashiko thread, as embroidery thread typically has a six-ply structure that allows you to single out the strands with your needle in the chain stitch. Sashiko threads aren't as easily split for chain stitches. If using Sashiko thread, I'd probably use a back-stitch instead, to get a continuous line.

For the chain stitch, insert your needle from underneath the fabric and exit through the front. Make one small stitch and reinsert your needle from underneath again. On your second stitch, come up from underneath to the top through your previous stitch—you'll split the length of that first stitch in half. Then reinsert the needle a stitch's length in front of the last stitch. In this way, you'll continue making stitches until you've completed your line.

The **backstitch** is another very useful stitch for creating a continuous line of text. Unlike the chain stitch, the back-stitch works well with Sashiko thread. Because of Sashiko's single-ply struc-ture, it doesn't split as easily as embroi-dery thread. While the backstitch is a very basic stitch, it takes me a moment to wrap my brain around it before I begin. Online videos are very helpful in clarifying the how-to.

42

french seam

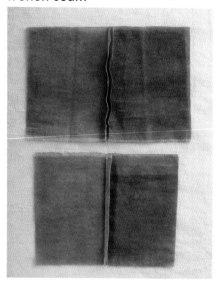

For a basic backstitch, start on the underside of your fabric and pull the threaded needle to the top. Make a larger stitch than usual. Now, go in the reverse direction from the way your stitches are headed—make one stitch to the left of the knot if you're stitching to the right of the knot. Insert the needle back toward the knot but pass it by and make a stitch twice as long as your top stitches. Pull the thread through on the top side and reinsert the needle where your last stitch ended. Continue in this manner until all your stitches are complete. This, quite literally, is taking two steps forward and one step back, but it does make a lovely continuous line.

The **French seam** has long been a workhorse in my simple sewing toolkit. It's a beautiful finished seam that keeps all the loose edges on the inside and is wonderful when working with loosely woven fibers like linen. When I make a garment, I want it to feel like an heirloom—even if it isn't—so I almost always try to make French seams. This can mean cutting the pattern a size larger to allow for larger seam allowances. (Be sure to alter the pattern accordingly for the best fit.)

To make a French seam—whether sewing by machine or by hand—start by sewing the wrong sides of the fabric together. This is counterintuitive to most of us, but it's just the first step. After you've made the first seam, trim your seam allowance to just ¼ or ⅛ inch (3 or 6 mm) from the seam. I leave larger seam allowances on fibers that more easily unravel or fray, like linen. With a tight-weave cotton, I'm comfortable with a very tiny seam allowance like ⅛ inch. Also, this differs from pattern to pattern.

Press the seam with an iron, and turn the sewn fabric so right sides are now facing. Make a second seam to enclose that first seam. I typically make my first seam at ¼ inch (6 mm) and then trim it to about ⅛ inch (3 mm), flip, and add another ¼-inch (6-mm) seam. That depends on the pattern, as some patterns call for a ⅜- or ⅝-inch (9.5 or 16 mm) seam allowance. Be sure to follow the pattern directions.

43

MAKE: PROJECTS

As an artist, I'm naturally drawn to experimenting with various materials and learning new techniques. I experiment with methods and materials until the approach feels like my own—until it looks like me. If I can't see my aesthetic reflected in a finished project then I haven't fully incorporated the techniques into my work yet. As artists and makers, we have to take the time to study, experiment, iterate, and ultimately refine our aesthetics and clarify our voices until the work becomes a mirror through which we can see ourselves reflected.

Through this process of making I've learned about the quality of materials and tools. I've learned how different materials respond to alterations and when a material pushes me out of my comfort zone in the best possible way versus when I'm not getting hoped-for results and need to pivot. I've also come to realize that sometimes the most valuable materials are vintage, antique, or secondhand. The quality of a vintage linen tablecloth is truly remarkable—the heavy linen slubs, the weight of the fiber, and the craftsmanship of the edging.

As we witness the effects of fast fashion and overconsumption, we can be inspired to shift our personal habits and to also make shifts in our studios and creative spaces. How can we use offcuts, scraps, and remnants as the sources of new designs? How can we design using small pieces of gorgeous fibers? What if we dye a few yards of linen with flowers from the garden and make a one-of-a-kind garment? This shift in material selection can strengthen our creative process to result in handmade clothes that are meaningful, innovative, and better for the planet.

It's thrilling to think of design projects being inspired by offcuts or otherwise "undesirable" materials like worn, torn, or imperfect garments. This is more time-consuming and more complicated than beginning with new yardage or yarn. But it also results in a truly unique fiber object that cannot be replicated or mass-produced. This might not be a solution for large-scale manufacturing, or not yet, but it's a wonderful way for artists, makers, and designers to honor the potential in existing materials; push outside our comfort zones; and really embrace slow design to make something truly original.

STITCHED SENTIMENT: **moon neck lining**

There's something magical about having the moon phases secretly stitched to the inside of a handmade garment. From the outside, we see a simple indigo dress. But from the inside, it's a handmade treasure lined with moon power. I like to think of this dress as my secret weapon. When I wear it to meetings and events, I get an added dose of courage and confidence from these secret stitches.

For millennia our ancestors have charted moon phases for everything from farming and concocting herbal medicine to charting seasons, recording events, and marveling at the cosmos. Noticing the nightly moon phase—from any urban, suburban, or rural environment—connects us to the rhythms of nature. So why not keep those phases close to our chests with stitched moons? Don't worry, it can still be our secret. (Note: This is the Washi Dress pattern by Made by Rae with various pattern alterations like skirt pleats in front and back, forgoing the interfacing, lengthening the bodice, lengthening the skirt, and adding oversized pockets.)

Project 1

MATERIALS

Garment to be embroidered

Tape measure or ruler

Washable fabric pen/pencil

Coin, for tracing

Fabric scissors

Fabric for neck facing or lining

Straight pins

Embroidery thread

Embroidery needle

Embroidery scissors or snips

Thimble (optional)

Iron (optional)

Sewing machine (optional)

1 Choose a pattern with linings or facings to which you can add stitches. Necklines are a great place for moon phases because they are naturally curved, gesturing toward a cyclical pattern. Select design elements that support your vision, such as coordinating fabric and thread. Here I've used linen hand-dyed by Jessica Lewis Stevens with a fermented indigo vat.

2 Use a tape measure or ruler to find the center of the neck facing or lining to help guide the moon sketches (or fold the facing/lining in half) and use a pin to mark the center. You can also measure and add a pin to mark the first quarter and last quarter, if you like. Any marking that indicates space, symmetry, and balance can improve the overall design.

3

4

3 With your washable fabric pen/pencil, trace nine moons onto your neckline, beginning with the one in the center and adding four on each side. My nine-part moon phase includes: New Moon, Waxing Crescent, First Quarter Moon, Waxing Gibbous, Full Moon, Waning Gibbous, Last Quarter Moon, Waning Crescent, and back to a New Moon. Technically, there are eight parts to the moon cycle, but because this design forms a U-shape and not a circle, I added a New Moon on both ends.

4 Thread a needle, knot the thread about ½ inch (1.3 cm) from the end, insert the needle from the underside of the fabric, and pull it through to the knot. Begin sewing a straight stitch (page 40) or running stitch (page 41), as you prefer. Complete one moon at a time. I typically leave only about ½ inch (1.3 cm) between stitches. Tie off the thread as needed.

5 Continue stitching until all moons are complete. Tie off on the underside of the fabric as needed. Iron if needed.

6 Sew the neck facing or lining into place as designated in the garment pattern. I tend to cut all my fabric pieces and create all my hand-stitched embellishments before I machine stitch the garment seams. Whatever method you choose to build your garment, enjoy this sweet secret between you, me, and the moon.

"When my children were younger, I would buy secondhand clothes for them as a way to save money. For myself, I had difficulty finding things I wanted to wear in sizes that would fit my body, though this didn't bother me as much in thrift stores. It was always a bit of a thrill when something turned up on the racks. Impulsively buying these finds, resulted in a full closet, but not a lot of things I loved. It wasn't until I started making my clothes, that I felt motivated to patch up holes or redo a popped seam. My caring about these garments enough to repair them, stems from knowing firsthand the effort put into their construction. I have a connection to the process. The fabric and print reflect my particular taste and the stiches holding the pieces together are a result of my skill. My mending is almost always a hasty machine darn. But even still, the garments have value, because they were made by me, for me and with their repairs, can continue to be worn again and again."

SONYA PHILIP
100 Acts of Sewing

STITCHED SENTIMENT: illustrated plant pocket

The more I build a relationship with local plants through gardening and foraging, the more I push myself to correctly identify them and learn their dyes and uses. Plant identification is essential to foraging—I want to be certain I'm gathering the correct plant before I prepare it for dyes, foods, or teas. Plants can be sorted by branching patterns, flower petals, shapes of leaves, fruit, seeds, nuts, smells, habitats, and more. But one of my favorite ways to get to know a plant is to sketch it in my notebook.

Many dye plants double as medicinal plants or triple as edibles, so I prioritize these powerful allies and grow them in my gardens. Stinging nettle is one example that offers dye color as well as nutrients and healing properties. It's also a plant to (figuratively) keep in my pocket as a reminder of the protection of the natural world. Stinging nettle is something of a guard plant—when fresh, it has a powerful sting, but when dried or blanched the sting vanishes, resulting in a soft, beautiful leaf with tremendous potential. (Note: This garment is a vintage French linen tunic, dyed with fermented indigo; stitched pockets were added for utility and embellishment.)

MATERIALS

Garment to be embellished

Fabric to be used for pockets

Fabric scissors

Washable fabric pen/pencil

Tape measure or ruler

Cotton embroidery thread

Embroidery hoop

Embroidery scissors

Embroidery needle

Straight pins

Iron

Sewing machine

Project 2

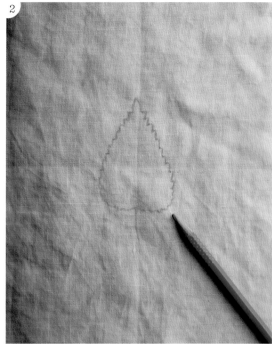

1 Choose an existing garment or a garment pattern with ample pockets. If using an existing garment, choose contrasting or coordinating fabric for your patch pockets. Like the linen tunic, the pockets are also dyed with indigo, but I've left the linen used for the pocket linings undyed. The thread is 100 percent cotton.

2 Cut two pockets and two pocket linings. Choose one pocket lining to use for this project. Fold the pocket lining in half in both directions to find the center of the fabric. This is a useful design guide before you start sketching. Using your washable fabric pen/pencil, sketch the herb of your choice. Don't worry about the image being perfect—focus on sentiment and connection, not photographic realism. This should feel fun!

3

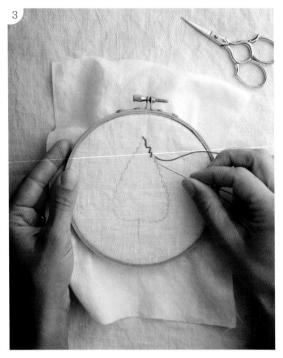

4

3 For this project, I'm using an embroidery hoop. Thread the needle, knot about ½ inch (1.3 cm) from the end of the thread, and insert the needle from the underside of the fabric. Begin sewing straight stitches (page 40) or running stitches (page 41), as you prefer. Tie off and rethread the needle as needed.

4 Continue stitching until you've finished your design. Tie off thread on the underside of the fabric; this lining will be sandwiched inside the pocket. Iron if needed.

5

6

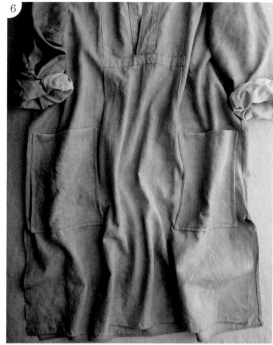

5 Place the pocket and the pocket lining with right sides facing. Sew the lining to the pocket front on the top and two sides, leaving the bottom hem open—or sew two-thirds of the bottom hem as well, leaving just a few inches open to turn the pocket right side out. Cut the seam allowance corners on a diagonal to allow for easier turning. Turn the pocket right side out. Iron seams so sides lie flat.

6 Pin the pocket to the garment. Check the position in a mirror to be certain it's where your hand naturally falls. Turn the pocket's bottom opening under ¼ inch (6 mm) or ⅝ inch (1.5 cm) and pin in place. You'll catch and close this opening when you sew the pocket to the garment. With your sewing machine, or using a hand stitch of your choice, stitch the pocket to the garment: Start at the top of one side, continue across the bottom, then stitch up the other side until finished. Enjoy!

"I have always unabashedly loved clothes. But I come from a family that always believed in buying the best quality we could afford, even if that meant having far fewer things than our peers. So, although I grew up with very nice, well-made clothes, I didn't have a huge closet (and, honestly, having to wear a school uniform for twelve years meant I didn't usually feel deprived).

I didn't learn to sew until my 30s, right around the same time that I learned to print fabric. Sewing is the perfect hobby for me; I do still love a uniform, and will often use the same pattern over and over again, satisfying my need for variety by using (and, often, making) different fabric.

The pleasure that I felt as a young adult when I'd shop for clothes at the mall has been replaced by the pleasure of selecting a pattern, choosing my fabric, and sewing a garment that fits perfectly. And the best thing about this process is that the pleasure is prolonged. I'm not engaging in a quick transaction. Rather, I'm spending days creating my clothing, enjoying the process as much as I enjoy wearing the finished garment."

JEN HEWETT
artist & author

STITCHED SENTIMENT: embroidered poem pocket

For years I've been embroidering words into pocket linings, hemlines, and necklines of handmade garments. I've stitched everything from poems, quotes, and single words to recipes and remedies into my clothes. You can stitch any words you like, and make them visible if you choose, but I treasure the private moments when the words, illustrations, or sentiments are just for me.

Here I've stitched one of my favorite herbal remedies for staving off anxiety and fostering calm: skullcap, motherwort, milky oats, tulsi, and rose. Frayed nerves need support to sustain the work we demand—and when I glance down at this remedy in my pockets, I remember to take a deep breath and reach for that inner calm. (Note: The pattern in this project is the Forager Vest designed by Meg McElwee of Sew Liberated. The model, Katharine Daugherty, wears her own handmade dress. This remedy is for the "Big Calm" created by Fat of the Land Apothecary, in Catskill, New York. It's not meant to treat, cure, or otherwise heal any existing medical condition, of course. Work with a certified herbalist, acupuncturist, or naturopathic medical care provider to find an herbal remedy that is right for you.)

MATERIALS

Garment to be embellished

Fabric for pockets

Fabric scissors

Tape measure or ruler

Straight pins

Washable fabric pen/pencil

Embroidery thread

Embroidery needle

Embroidery scissors or snips

Thimble (optional)

Iron (optional)

Sewing machine

Project 3

1 Choose a pattern with space on linings or facings for text. Collect materials that support your design, such as coordinating fabric and thread. When possible, use treasured fabrics handmade by people you love or admire—these handmade sentiments not only add to the garment's value but also make it feel like a collaborative art project.

2 Select the space for the text you'll stitch to the garment lining or facing. This pattern calls for a generous 2-inch (5-cm) fold at the top of the pocket, making it an ideal spot. Using a tape measure or ruler, find the center of the area to be stitched, and mark with a pin or fabric pen/pencil for a guide. Count the letters to be stitched (I had thirty-six letters) and then divide the letters over the space, to spread the words evenly. I'll add eighteen letters on each pocket.

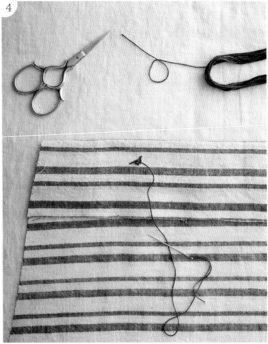

3 Using the center guide you marked, and knowing the number of letters you need, use a pin to mark the start and finish of the space for each word. This might seem tedious, but it helps with the overall design. Sometimes I mark the start, middle, and finish of each word if I want to be more precise. Once marked, use your washable fabric pen/pencil to write the words freehand within the space allotted.

4 Thread a needle, knot the thread about ½ inch (1.3 cm) from the end, and insert the needle from the underside of the fabric. Begin stitching at the start of the first letter. I like to use a chain stitch (page 42) and basic cursive text—allowing the end of one letter to join the start of the next—and to leave clear spaces between words. Tie off on the underside of the fabric as needed.

5

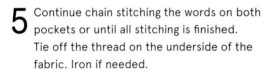

6

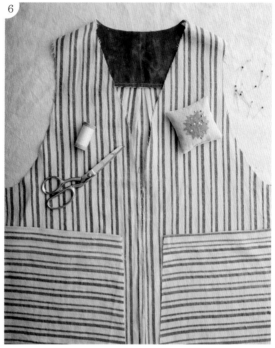

5 Continue chain stitching the words on both pockets or until all stitching is finished. Tie off the thread on the underside of the fabric. Iron if needed.

6 Sew the embroidered pieces into place and continue with the garment construction following the pattern instructions. I typically cut all my garment pieces, hand stitch my secret notes to the linings, and then use my trusty machine to sew the rest of the garment as directed. Of course, you can hand stitch the seams too, if you like. Remember, reach for that inner calm.

"Many of us travel our life path owning far too many clothes that simply don't last the distance, often soothing our consciences by remaking pre-loved garments; but clothes sourced from thrift stores are increasingly compromised by dry-cleaning, heavily perfumed laundering agents or simply the cloying fragrances worn by their former owners, while natural fibres are becoming harder to find.

My solution has been to sew my clothing using natural fibre fabrics sourced sustainably and fairly from artisans, made to wear well and ready to absorb natural colour directly infused into the cloth by means of the bundled ecoprint. It's a technique I discovered in the 1990s that requires far less botanical matter than other dyeing methods, needs no mordants, can mask stains and imbue cloth with memories of time and place.

These are durable and timeless clothes for the journeywoman that can be stitched into and mended as required, that will develop a rich patina (along with a lifetime of embedded stories) as they age. The shapes are simple and comfortable. They can be worn in multiple combinations, layered for warmth, even slept in at night. I see them as a second skin, and know my foremothers would approve."

INDIA FLINT
Prophet of Bloom

REDESIGN VINTAGE: **tablecloth top**

There's a wonderful opportunity to upcycle fabrics by using household linens, secondhand textiles, or salvaged yardage. I'm drawn to the vintage prints on linen tablecloths and daydream about the previous lives those textiles lived. If you're lucky enough to find a vintage tablecloth while perusing thrift stores, consider it as a fabric choice for a simple garment. This tablecloth easily transitioned into a three-quarter-sleeve shirt with floral pockets. I particularly love the juxtaposition of busy fabric prints paired with a simple, modern garment pattern.

When using secondhand textiles or upcycling household linens, let the fabric dictate the design. In this case, I put the bold central flowers on the bodice; the sleeve length was decided by the amount of fabric that remained. I imagine this shirt topped with a straw hat, worn in a garden, while fresh flowers are collected in vases. It's an homage to the endless inspiration we receive from beautiful blooms. (Note: The pattern in this project is the Wiksten Shift Dress + Top designed by Jenny Gordy. Flowers designed by model and floral designer Yuko Yamamoto.)

MATERIALS

Vintage tablecloth

Pattern for garment

Straight pins

Fabric scissors

Tape measure or ruler

Washable fabric pen/pencil

Thread

Sewing machine

Iron

Embroidery thread (optional)

Embroidery scissors or snips (optional)

Thimble (optional)

Personalized garment label (optional)

Project 4

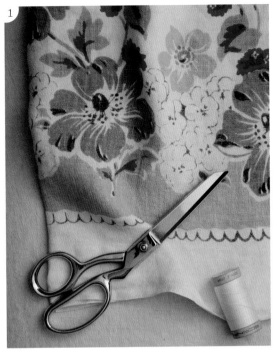

1 Gather your design elements, starting with a secondhand textile like a vintage tablecloth. Choose a pattern that complements the fabric.

2 Decide how best to lay out the pattern on the fabric to take advantage of the fabric's design. Make a sketch of the garment as part of your design process or gather images and materials into an inspiration board. Consider where the print might fall on the body once the garment is constructed. For example, I knew that scalloped edging would look sweet along the cuffs of this top. I often use my children's colored pencils and a simple notebook for this stage of the design.

3 Cut the pattern from the fabric. If you need to patch fabric together to attain the correct size, go ahead and piece with pride. Otherwise, cut the fabric according to the pattern guidelines and the design you sketched in Step 2.

4 Add elements to enhance the design; allow the fabric to dictate this process. Is there an offcut that would make a nice patch pocket? Could you cover buttons with fabric scraps to incorporate more vintage elements? Add stitches or embroidered text to any linings or facings? Now is the time to really slow down and make this garment special.

5 Sew the fabric pieces together according to the pattern. Step back to pause and amend the design as you go. There's no need to rush—enjoy this making process. I like to add French seams (see page 43) to my garments whenever possible, as they make such lovely finished seams. You will need to consider the seam allowance of a French seam before cutting the fabric, but I find it's worth it to take this extra step.

6 Complete sewing of the garment. Consider adding sentimental details like printed labels, stitched poems, or illustrated herbs to the inside of your garment. If you don't have labels, just stitch your initials to a scrap of fabric and sew it to the back of the neckline. Like finding the artist's name at the corner of a quilt, these handmade tags are like little love notes from the maker.

"Putting my hands to work on my clothing is a way for me to stay connected as a mother of three young children—connected to myself, connected to the web of life that keeps me clothed, and connected to my ancestors. I could easily get swept up in family logistics and the to-do lists of my small business, but the feeling of needle and thread slipping through fabric is my practical form of meditation—it keeps me grounded. It anchors me to what is happening right now—the making moment. That moment is inextricably woven into the garment fibers, magically conjured each time I wear the piece. Whether I am mending a store-bought garment, altering a thrift store find, or designing and sewing an entire garment, I am always grateful for the reminder to breathe deeply and slow down, and for the fiber-forged, timeless connection between the moment and the maker."

MEG McELWEE
Sew Liberated

REDESIGN PATCHWORK: **zero-waste top**

The zero-waste movement has inspired me to give more thought to my fabric offcuts and textile scraps. How can I incorporate these by-products to reduce waste, while putting them at the center of new design? Traditional garment patterns often prioritize yardage, drape, grain, etc. But what of those pretty bits relegated to the waste pile? I've started amending pattern-cutting guides to maximize my fabric use, to add seams or embrace patchwork. Although minimal waste is a natural, if not inevitable, part of the making process, let's start viewing our offcuts as an opportunity for innovation.

I have several baskets of scraps in my studio. One basket is for tiny offcuts destined for pillow and pouf stuffing. Another basket contains larger pieces that might be mending patches, quilt squares, or piecework. And a third basket holds even larger scraps that can be incorporated into household objects or new garments like this top. Who says garments have to be made from all one fabric, especially when you can turn hand-dyed fabrics, gorgeous ikats, and handwoven textiles into a patchwork shirt? (Note: This top is made using the Top No. 1 pattern designed by Sonya Philip of 100 Acts of Sewing, with various fabrics.)

MATERIALS
Pattern for garment
Fabrics for garment patchwork
Fabric scissors
Ruler
Calculator
Straight pins
Thread
Sewing machine

Project 5

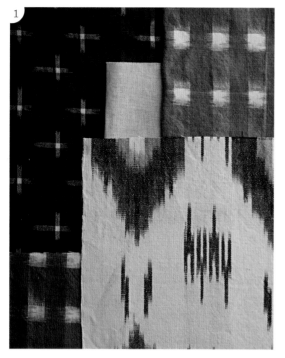

1 Choose a garment pattern that will allow for patchwork (just consider how many pieces the pattern uses, where the seams fall, and so on). Choose design elements, such as fabric and thread. I created patchwork from pieces of handwoven ikat fabrics and one cotton fabric I dyed with flowering quince branches. The seams are all stitched by machine for this project.

2 Decide where best to cut the pattern into patches. Notice where the lines will fall on your body and where they will fall in relation to the construction seams. I chose to make patches at the top of this pattern, and, because I wanted to add French seams (see page 43), I avoided any extra bulk in the armholes. I also oriented my patches vertically to keep the extra French seams from adding bulk to the side seams. If you like, sketch out the design in patchwork first—it can be very helpful.

3

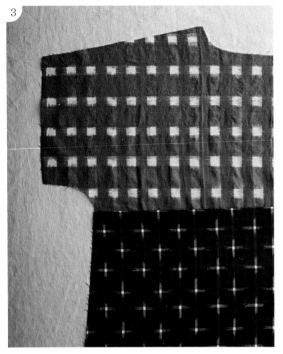

4

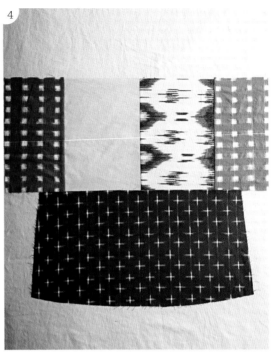

3 Cut the fabric into squares or rectangles as you wish, keeping the pattern shapes nearby for reference. Remember, you'll have to add fabric for seam allowances in creating the patchwork. This math can get tricky if you're adding many patches. Just lay out the design as you like so you can see the composition.

4 Sew patches together to make the garment piece. If I'm working with several patches, I'll often sew them into a grid and then cut the garment from the sewn grid. This is to ensure I've left enough space for the patchwork's French seams. If you're trying to make a zero-waste garment, keep comparing the sewn patchwork to the pattern piece to be sure you're meeting the measurements. Otherwise, get your calculator and make careful measurements, adding ⅝-inch (1.5-cm) seam allowances to each patch. Try to be patient. It's a shirt. You can do it.

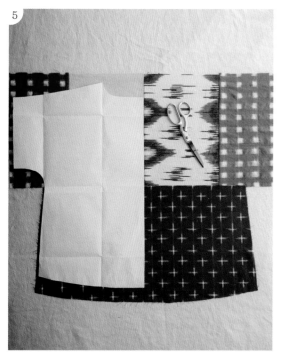

5 Once you've finished the patchwork, make any necessary changes before cutting the garment into the pattern shape. You can remove any extra fabric and save that for another project.

6 Now sew the garment according to the pattern directions as instructed. I like to use minimalist patterns for this type of work because it means fewer pieces to create. Sonya Philip is a master of minimalist patterns in basic, geometric shapes that result in very wearable and simple garments, making them perfect for patchwork.

"The process of making something, beginning with raw materials, engaging our senses and abilities—and our limitations—and following through until we have a finished piece is itself a kind of spiritual inquiry into the nature of reality and the nature of the self. Put more straightforwardly, when I make something, I discover more about who I am, which includes a deeper understanding of the world in which I live. That this knowledge is usually intuitive and implicit rather than explicit makes it no less transformative."

AIDAN OWEN
The Knitting Monk

UPCYLCED OFFCUTS: **patchwork tote**

Patchwork allows us to use beloved scraps; experiment with design elements of composition, line, scale, and color; and make a truly unique textile. Often the contents of my scrap bin determine the pattern I'll use. If I only have a tiny amount of beautiful hand-dyed fabric from dye tests or from sewing projects, I can use those precious scraps in a patchwork pocket, handmade tag, or small detail like a cuff or collar.

This project was inspired by a few special scraps from my natural-dyed fiber basket—a swatch of indigo-dyed linen, a madder-dyed linen, and two ikat offcuts. It was just enough for a large patch pocket. (Note: The tote pattern in this project is the Portsmith Tote designed by Klum House with corresponding leather handles and hardware kit; the patch pocket is a simple amendment to the pattern. The model, Denise Bayron, wears her own handmade and hand-dyed dress.)

MATERIALS
Pattern for tote
Fabric for tote
Fabrics for patchwork
Straight pins
Tape measure or ruler
Fabric scissors
Washable fabric pen/pencil
Sewing machine
Thread
Iron

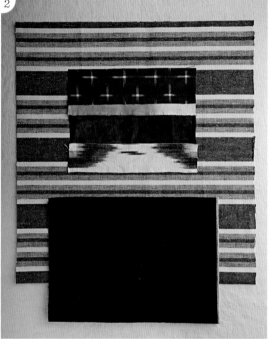

1 Choose a pattern that allows for patchwork—most do. Also remember that, even if the pattern doesn't call for details, patchwork pockets, linings, or other embellishments can easily be added to most standard patterns. Gather all your materials before you begin.

Decide how best to use the fabrics and patchwork in your design. If you like, sketch the tote bag in your notebook with the added pocket. It helps me to see what I'm making in sketched form before I start to sew.

2 Cut the patchwork fabric into squares, rectangles, or other shapes that easily fit together for a pocket. If you're feeling ambitious, you could use triangles or circles too. For this pocket, I stuck with rectangles as my design feature and let the rectangles mirror the horizontal lines in the main fabric.

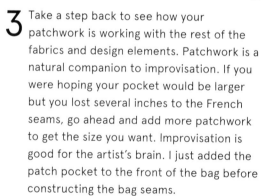

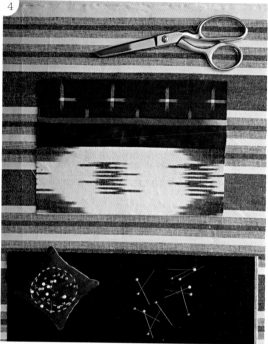

3 Take a step back to see how your patchwork is working with the rest of the fabrics and design elements. Patchwork is a natural companion to improvisation. If you were hoping your pocket would be larger but you lost several inches to the French seams, go ahead and add more patchwork to get the size you want. Improvisation is good for the artist's brain. I just added the patch pocket to the front of the bag before constructing the bag seams.

Sew the pieces together to make your patchwork. If, like me, you're obsessed with French seams (see page 43), start by sewing wrong sides together and then flip right sides together to sew a second seam so all raw seams are contained inside the finished seam. Then repeat this French seam technique on all the rectangles until they are sewn together with finished horizontal seams.

4 Continue sewing according to the pattern guidelines. I lined my patchwork pocket so that all the seams, even side seams, would be finished. I also created a simple binding on the interior seams of the tote to finish those raw seams. Or consider adding a lining to the pattern if you wish. Now add books, yarn, and knitting needles, and take that beautiful tote to the park.

Connection with Our Ancestors: The Lineage of Stitches and Sketches

In working with traditional crafts or handwork there's an incredible opportunity to connect with our ancestors. It might be a literal connection—sitting with an elder as they teach us to sew, knit, or stitch—or it might be a metaphorical connection. As we develop sewing skills, we reconnect with the techniques our ancestors used to make clothing. We remember that at some point, most households sewed, knit, and mended. Before fabric was readily available as yardage, most households also spun, wove, and made cloth. It's easy to imagine how cloth might have so much more value if we had to tend the sheep, then shear, card, spin, dye, and weave or knit the wool into fabric.

These basic fiber techniques resulted in necessary garments and also kept those garments in rotation. We mended cloth because it had value. We can connect to this sense of value, and to generations before us, when engaging in the act of making dresses, mending pants, and darning sweaters. We use the same tools our grandparents used—needle, thread, yarn, fabric. We make or mend textiles and gain self-sufficiency, technical skill, and creative expression. There's tremendous opportunity for customization as we improve our craftmanship and learn to make a garment from the fabric we choose by selecting the fiber, weight, and color. Suddenly, we can make one-of-a-kind treasures. But for our ancestors, this was common.

My maternal great-grandmother, Leona, died many years before I was born, though she is still considered the family matriarch and family fiber artist. Her daughter, my mother's mother, Mary, also passed before I was born. I've longed to connect to these women on my mother's side of the family—wondering what it might be like to learn from their creative practice. Yet I've felt connected to my grandmothers my entire life, through their quilts and drawings.

My mother comes from a family of makers and artists, though they never would have described themselves as such. Like many women of their generations, they were homemakers, gardeners, cooks, cleaners, social organizers, and full-time parents, although Leona earned an income for her family too. Mary was a hobbyist painter and illustrator. Leona was a quilter and stitcher. Leona was also a backyard homesteader, though that's not a term she would have used to describe tending chickens and gardens or foraging for herbs.

My opportunity to actually speak with these women about how to mend my clothes or tend my gardens never arrived. Yet they are a constant presence in my studio. Leona's fiber crafts were dotted throughout my childhood home: handmade footstools with elaborate needlework, crocheted afghans, and beloved patchwork quilts, completely handstitched. My mother displayed drawings and paintings by Mary and reminded us of the few pieces of furniture that were handed down from these ancestors—a dresser, a desk, a table. In these ways, I felt the presence of the women who came before me. I felt my place in their lineage of stitches and drawings and fiber arts. I also knew they had inspired my mother to stitch, sew, knit, and work with textiles, which resulted in her teaching me.

I never met Leona, nor Mary, yet each time I stitch I feel Leona's presence. One of her pieced quilts now hangs over the back of my living room chair, and I often trace my fingers over her stitches, trying to imagine what she daydreamed when she sewed. I open the folded quilt and marvel at her colorwork—the instinctive balance of warm and cool colors, dark and light tones, and tiny cotton prints juxtaposed against solid white cottons.

I have a few of Mary's drawings and I gaze at them while I imagine her hands generating each line—the way fragile dashes contrast with heavy, thick marks that create balance and movement. I wonder what she thought as she worked, if she imagined that my mother might have children—me and my siblings—or if she ever imagined how her lineage would persist to my sons. It's as if she left these gifts for us—simple line drawings that now grace the walls of our contemporary homes.

Through their creative work my grandmothers offer connection and anchor me in my creative practice. Sometimes I imagine they are accompanying me as I work—nudging me toward certain fabrics, colors, or designs. Urging me to mend my clothing and sew simple garments to continue the legacy of making. My hands generate marks across denim with cotton thread like Mary made marks across the page with ink pens. My patchwork uses scrap fabrics in the most basic sense of upcycling—inspiration for new garments in the spirit of Leona's quilts.

As I continue the lineage of making, accessing their knowledge through doing, building technical skills, strengthening design impulses, and familiarizing myself with materials, I also do the basic acts they were doing—I sketch, I stitch, I patch, I make. Our lives are separated by births, deaths, inconceivable technology, impossible industry, and so much more. Yet the simple acts of sketching and stitching connect us.

My mother also taught me to notice color, pattern, scale, line, and texture. She wouldn't call these "design elements," nor would she have identified herself as an artist, but that's what she was teaching me—how to look at the world more closely. Technically, my mother taught me to sew and stitch, but she also gave me access to imagination. She normalized creativity. She nudged me toward expression. Regardless of our identities as artists or makers, most of us can pick up the simple tools of needle and thread and learn to make basic repairs. Through this work we engage in artmaking and we connect with the experience of building something with our hands.

Even if our parents weren't makers, or our grandparents weren't living when we were young, we can still connect to them through these traditional crafts. We can use our hands to make similar objects to the ones they created, with similar tools. Maybe we can seek out stories and photographs from other family members or research the daily activities of the region of the world where our ancestors lived. We can connect our rituals to their rituals—the ceremonies of needle and thread.

I hem a skirt by hand, the way my mother taught me, like a family recipe passed through multiple kitchens. I don't worry if the technique is accurate, I know it works and it's what my mother found effective. In this way, I honor the folk traditions of our family. I can also choose to push this tradition into a new space by making it relevant in my fiber arts practice—I choose to celebrate the repairs of my clothing with high-contrast thread, whereas my grandmothers aimed for invisible repairs. If I reach back further, my English ancestors would've darned their sweaters with one technique and my German relatives with another.

I think of Leona when I stitch, but I also think of her when I pull dandelions from my yard in the early spring—plucking the tender leaves before the flowerheads open, as that's when they're the sweetest. Allegedly, Leona had two buckets of weeds as she gardened—one was the edibles for the chickens. I wonder if she knew she could make yellow and green plant dyes with the dandelions. I didn't grow up knowing my grandmothers, but I knew they were creative. I knew they were makers. I knew they died young. And I knew their lives were quite similar and yet entirely different from mine. I never questioned their relevance in my life—Leona taught Mary to sew, then Mary taught my mother, and then my mother taught me.

We can connect to the craftwork of our ancestors in any culture, region, or century even if we don't know much about them. What did the people of that region use for dyes before synthetics? What motifs or symbols did they traditionally embroider on clothing? How did they upcycle fabrics into patchwork or piecework? Someday my great-grandchildren might trace their fingers over my stitches and wonder what I thought as I sewed garments, dyed cloths, or mended blue jeans. I hope I'll get to meet them. Regardless, I know we can connect through this lineage of stitches, threading us together through several generations of art and design.

THRIFT
(&DYE)

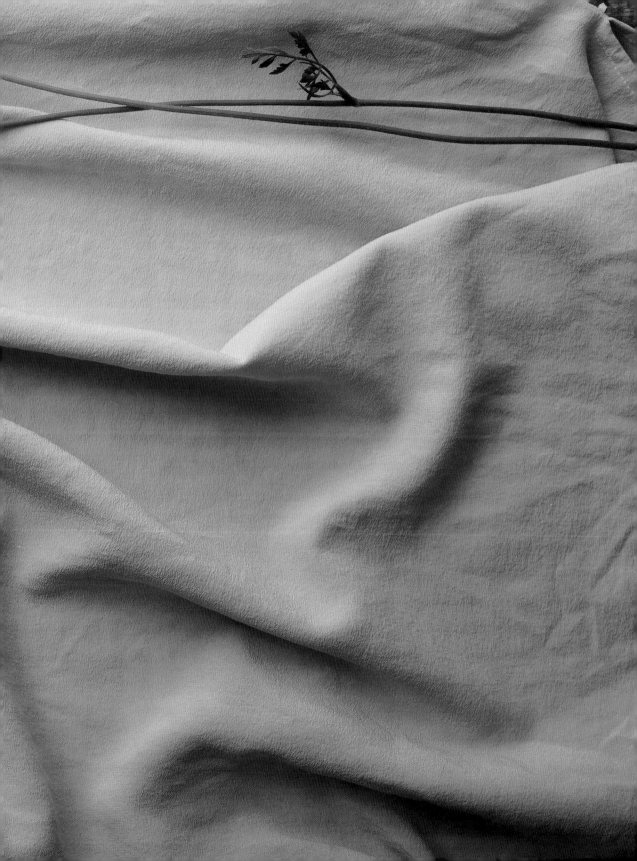

thrift (& dye)

HOW TO DYE: TOOLS, MATERIALS,
AND TECHNIQUES

TOOLS

I'm fairly forgiving in my classes regarding preferred techniques, but here's where I insist: All dye tools must be reserved for dyeing only—never use your dye pots to cook or prepare food. It's not safe. Never mix mordants, dye plants, or dyed cloth with your kitchen tools or items you intend to eat or ingest. Always dye in a well-ventilated area with fans, open windows, and/or vents. Wear gloves, an apron, a dust mask, and any other necessary protective material to be sure your skin, lungs, and clothes are kept safe from dye materials. I use my outdoor studio in the warmer months—it's forgiving to wet materials, separate from my kitchen, and has great ventilation. That said, I dye from my kitchen stove in the winter months but I never (ever) mix my dye tools with food prep.

Having experimented with dyes for the past eight years, I've amassed a collection of dye tools. It can seem overwhelming to purchase or find all these materials at once, so don't. When you begin dyeing, just find the very basic essential tools. You can build your collection as you dye. Some of these items may be found secondhand. Remember, start where you are and build from there.

pots

Find stainless-steel pots with tight-fitting lids if you don't want your pots to interfere with dye colors. When I started using plant dyes, I just had one pot for dyeing. As my space and interest grew, so did my collection of dye tools. I use almost exclusively stainless-steel pots for dyeing.

Some folks use pots or vessels as mordants. This means that they want the pots to interact with the dye colors. For this, try aluminum pots, copper pots, or cast iron, as these metals can alter dye colors. It is not safe to use these metals in powder form, only to use the pot as the mordant for these metals. For more information on this technique, check out India Flint's website and book *Eco Colour* (see Resources, page 215).

bowls

I have a few large stainless-steel mixing bowls that I use for dyeing. These are great when I'm straining plant materials from the dye pot. A large bowl with a lip is best, though any vessel will do.

strainer

You'll need a large strainer for dyeing. This will be important when you've soaked your dye plants and want to extract them from the dye liquid before adding the cloth or garment. I have two large strainers, both stainless steel. Cheesecloth or another straining device can also be used.

spoons

Large wooden or stainless-steel spoons are useful for stirring dye pots. Some folks prefer to use metal tongs.

measuring spoons and cups

Glass measuring cups let you see the mordant and dye liquid through the vessel. I also have stainless-steel measuring spoons for accurately measuring mordants.

jars with lids

Basic glass canning jars with tight-fitting lids do the job of mixing mordants.

kitchen scale

A basic kitchen scale is very helpful for weighing fabrics, garments, or other fibers before dyeing, as well as for weighing dye plants. Mine is a very basic kitchen scale that converts grams to ounces.

rags/towels

A few basic rags or hand towels will allow you to wipe off spoons, clean up spills, and keep your dye space tidy and dry. Again, to be safe, I never use my dye rags for household spills or kitchen rags. I keep dye rags for dyeing purposes only.

dust mask, rubber gloves, and a protective apron

When using mordants, wear these items to protect your eyes, nasal passages, hands, and clothing from potential irritants, especially when handling aluminum acetate or iron. I always wear an apron when I'm working with dyes, at any stage of the dyeing process, to be sure I'm protecting my clothes from unwanted stains or splatters.

eco-friendly mild detergent

Using an eco-friendly mild detergent is the best choice for your fiber art projects, dye experiments, and your wardrobe. Look for a pH-neutral laundry soap that's nontoxic and gentle on your fibers.

heat source

Dyes require a heat source. I have portable electric burners and propane stoves in my outdoor dye studio. These are great for traveling to teach classes and for adding several burners to a simple outdoor space. In the winter months, I experiment with small dye pots on my kitchen stove, but I'm always careful to isolate my dye tools from any other kitchen tools.

The sun is also a wonderful heat source. In the warmer months I often use solar energy to heat glass jars of dye experiments or leave lidded pots in the sun for a few days to absorb color. It's slower than a propane, gas, or electric burner but can lend beautiful results. Be careful of any animals or children in your area and secure lids to keep everybody safe.

dye journal

My dye journal is just a simple notebook where I staple small samples of dye fibers to the pages and note the plant, mordant, date, and fiber sample. Sometimes I'll even list the location where I foraged the plants. I can look back through my journal and see how the dyes differed depending on fiber, season, mordant, etc. It's the most useful tool in my dye studio and I can't recommend it enough. It's also a very beautiful way to narrate your dye journey through color, fiber, and text.

MATERIALS

fabric

When working with natural dyes, use only biodegradable fabrics. I prefer cotton, linen, hemp, wool, and silk fabrics for dyeing. I always test my dye colors on fiber scraps before submerging an entire garment or textile. I keep scraps of various fabrics in my studio; I'll cut them into strips for dye experiments. This way I can readily compare the difference of fibers and colors using the same plant, mordant, and dye circumstances. It's amazing how one dye plant will yield variations across fibers when all other variables are the same. I also keep small skeins of yarn for dye experiments.

Plant fibers typically yield a lighter hue than animal fibers when working with plant-based dyes. The animal fibers create a better bond to the plant dyes, whereas the plant fibers typically need a bridge or a mordant to create that bond. (An exception is indigo, a fermentation process that results in blue tones on plant-based fibers. Indigo is not covered in this book.)

garments

Dyeing secondhand garments is one of the best ways to reinvigorate existing clothes that have faded or lost their luster. It's also a magical way to transform thrift store finds with color. I adore finding white and light-colored secondhand garments in linen, cotton, wool, or silk and wearing them as is before turning them into a color experiment.

When considering garments for dyes, I think about four factors: fiber content, color, weight, and texture. The fiber content needs to be plant- or animal-based. I check the content tag to see the fiber details. If there's no tag I often pass it by unless I'm certain it's silk or linen, which I've become adept at identifying by sight and touch—a side effect of so much time in secondhand shops. If it's white or cream-colored, awesome. But even if it's a light color like pale yellow, green, or pink, I can always overdye it for a new hue. Use basic color theory to better understand how this works. See Lisa Solomon's *A Field Guide to Color* for more information.

When I've found the fiber and color that will work for dyeing, I move on to fiber weight and texture. If it's a heavy wool sweater with a cable pattern, I know I'll need quite a bit of plant dye to get a 1:1 ratio of fiber to dye. For example, the wool sweater dyed with goldenrod flowers (see page 98) weighs about 500 grams, so I needed to forage a large pot of flowers. Light garments such as silk tank tops typically weigh around 100 grams so they are much easier to dye with a small amount of plant material. Lastly, texture can be a boon when dyeing garments, because variations help conceal inconsistencies in dye. On the other hand, if I'm looking to highlight my inconsistencies for a mottled effect, bundle dyeing, or surface design, then a smoother texture might be best.

thread

Any natural-fiber thread can also be used for dyes. I've had great results dyeing 100 percent cotton Sashiko thread with plants. Any cotton, linen, hemp, silk, or wool thread will work. Just remember to unwind thread back into a hank and loosely tie that hank with loops of thread for best results.

yarn

Natural dyes are wonderful on plant- and animal-based yarns. If you're planning a special project for knitting, crocheting, weaving, or other fiber arts, these yarns can be dyed incredible colors. You can also dye smaller bits of yarn, or leftover yarn, for darning, as it requires so little fiber for smaller projects. I've had great results dyeing 100 percent wool yarn with plant dyes. Any cotton, linen, hemp, silk, or wool yarn also work well. Just remember to unwind the yarn back into a hank, and loosely tie that hank with loops of thread, for best results.

mordants

A mordant allows plant dyes to bind to fiber. It helps with colorfastness and lightfastness and typically yields more intense, bold colors. There are numerous mordants, but I tend to use only two, and then one modifier. For mordants on plant-based fibers, I use aluminum acetate; for mordants on animal fibers, I use aluminum potassium sulfate. These are nontoxic mordants found in the baking section of grocery stores or the soil-amending section of gardening stores, though I prefer to buy my mordants from reputable dye suppliers such as Botanical Colors or others listed in the Resources section (see page 215). See the specific dye projects for measurements of aluminum acetate or aluminum potassium sulfate.

I sometimes use an iron modifier to shift colors after dyeing. The saying goes that aluminum brightens colors and iron saddens them. In short, aluminum will typically make colors richer and iron will make them darker. I use iron sparingly, as it's very potent and when wet can spot any other dyed fibers. If I'm using iron, I keep it isolated from all other fibers, then rinse it well and let it dry completely before it touches other fabrics or yarns.

Iron can be purchased in powder form as ferrous sulfate or you can make your own. To make a simple homebrew iron solution, add some small rusty objects (like a large handful of rusty nails) to a glass jar with a tight-fitting lid, and then add water to fill the jar (some folks add vinegar, but I usually don't). Place the jar in a sunny windowsill until the water turns orange from rust. Use the liquid as a post-modifier on dyed cloth and rinse the cloth well. Use as much iron as you need to get the color result you desire.

Typically, iron doesn't need more than ten or fifteen minutes to shift color. Some folks say iron makes fibers (particularly animal fibers) brittle, so you might think twice before using it on heirloom fibers. That said, I've found cotton is very hardy and even linen, silk, and wool can be modified with iron as long as they are rinsed well and handled with care. Always keep iron away from children and pets.

dye plants

The list of dye plants is seemingly endless. Because so much information about working with plant dyes was passed down orally, learned informally, or shared among families and communities, there will probably never be a comprehensive list of dye plants. Keep this in mind when experimenting, and be sure you can properly identify what you are harvesting to avoid any irritants, toxins, or endangered species. There are dozens of plants that are popular with dyers because they are known to give consistent results and be fairly colorfast and lightfast, and can be grown or foraged in a large enough quantity to dye various amounts of cloth.

Each region and culture will have its local and native plants that produce a range of color—those that adapted and thrived in that region with its particular temperature, sunlight, water, soil, nutrients, and other environmental conditions. Some dye plants are considered sacred plants, religious plants, healing plants, or otherwise significant plants to specific cultures around the world. Please do your research and never forage a plant that is protected, endangered, or sacred to a culture other than your own. There is so much knowledge and wisdom to be gained regarding plants and textiles and we must always approach this work with honor, reverence, and deep listening.

Here is a short list of plant dyes that I have used for color and that can be grown or found in various regions of the United States (roughly ordered on a rainbow spectrum, moving from red to pink, orange, yellow, green, blue, purple and then toward brown or gray, often with the cooler green and gray colors achieved by the addition of iron or ferrous sulfate): madder root; rose petals; flowering quince branches; avocado pits and skins; onion skins; eucalyptus leaves; coreopsis flowers; calendula flowers; zinnia flowers; marigold flowers; goldenrod flowers; wild fennel fronds; sour grass (*Oxalis*) flowers; Queen Anne's lace (wild carrot) flowers; dandelion flowers, leaves, and stems; willow branches; apple branches; rose petals, leaves, and branches; yarrow flowers; peppermint leaves; spearmint leaves; rudbeckia (black-eyed Susan) flowers; indigo leaves; Hopi black dye sunflower seeds; acorns; rosemary leaves; lavender leaves; black walnut hulls; staghorn sumac fruit and leaves.

THRIFT/DYE: PROJECTS

Working with natural dyes is one of the most magical acts I've experienced as an artist. The way plant-based dyes can transform cloth is nothing short of alchemy. Of course, it's also chemistry. But you don't need to be a chemist to make beautiful colors on textiles. You do need to pay attention to your plants, dyes, and fibers to create the best dyes and to transform secondhand garments into colorful creations.

I work with whole-plant dyes almost exclusively, though I do work with extracts for my fermented indigo vat. This means that I work with the root, bark, leaves, flowers, seeds, or fruits of the plant instead of working with the dye in powder or extract form. This also means I am regularly harvesting dye plants from my garden, foraging from my surroundings, and saving food scraps from my kitchen. Whether you live in an urban, suburban, or rural environment you can grow or forage plants or save food scraps for dyeing.

When I first started working with natural dyes I lived in a small apartment in Oakland, California, with a tiny, shared yard. I used mostly foraged sour grass, eucalyptus, and wild fennel; kitchen scraps of onion skins and avocado pits; and garden-grown rosemary, lavender, and lemons from my neighbors. That's the magic of a Mediterranean climate like the San Francisco Bay Area—fruit falls from the trees nearly year-round.

Now that I live in the Hudson Valley of New York, with an acre of land, I have large gardens for vegetables, herbs, fruit trees, and dye plants. But I still forage for dye plants in my surrounding parks, fields, forests, and roadsides. I've also collected coffee grounds from cafés and food scraps from restaurants. Many restaurants are happy to save the scraps as long as you provide a lidded container and pick it up when you promised. If you're near a flower farm, ask if you can gather seconds or if you can help weed and take broken plants from the ground—you'd be surprised how many beautiful dye flowers like marigolds, zinnias, or coreopsis can't be sold by farmers because they are imperfect, though they are perfectly suited for our dye pots.

Note on foraging and harvesting: It's essential that you properly identify plants before using them for any purpose. Ask a gardener, botanist, or herbalist if you're uncertain. Field guides that specialize in plants in your region are a tremendous tool for identification. When foraging, be sure to harvest responsibly. Never take all of one plant; you need to leave some for the animals, insects, and ecosystem that depend on it, so spread your foraging out over a larger area. Also, never harvest on private land without permission. Use caution when harvesting in any location, but never harvest medicinal or edible plants near roadsides or other pollutants. It is typically permissible to use dye plants found in those locations, as you will not be ingesting them, but be mindful when foraging. As for harvesting from your garden—do your homework and then get familiar with the cultivation preferences for your plants.

When selecting secondhand garments for dyeing, remember to consider fiber content, color, weight, and texture, as discussed on page 92. This will help you to make the strongest choices in fiber to result in beautiful experiments in your dye pots. Remember, working with whole plants is like cooking. You'll want to start with basic recipes using common ingredients, then build confidence and skill as you progress. When you're ready for more dye recipes, check out the various dye books in the Resources section. And remember, embrace the process and enjoy the relationship you're building with plants.

(Note: The activities and materials discussed in this book may be potentially toxic, hazardous, or dangerous. *Please take all safety precautions and follow all instructions. Handle dyes, mordants, and foraged plants with the utmost care.* The author has made every effort to provide well researched, sufficient and up-to-date information; however, we also urge caution in the use of this information. The author and publisher do not accept liability for any accidents, injuries, loss, legal consequences, or incidental or consequential damage incurred by any reader for the mishandling or misuse of these materials or in reliance on the information or advice provided in this book. Readers should seek health and safety advice from physicians and safety and medical professionals.)

GOLDENROD FLOWERS: **wool sweater**
SOLIDAGO CANADENSIS

Goldenrod dye is one of my favorite shades of yellow—particularly on wool. The more I work with natural dyes, the more I love to discover rich combinations of whole plants and fibers. In my region of Upstate New York, we have a rich history of fiber farms and an abundance of the native goldenrod plant; perhaps not incidentally, they make a marvelous combination.

Goldenrod flowers create a rich and rather predictable lightfast and colorfast dye. One secondhand wool cardigan I dyed years ago is still as vibrant now as it was then. Natural dyes offer exceptional complexity of color because the dye is made with a whole plant and not extracted from a single color source. I swear goldenrod dye almost vibrates on fiber as if it were electric.

Project 7

MATERIALS

Garment to be dyed

Kitchen scale

Eco-friendly mild laundry
    detergent

Measuring spoons

Large stainless-steel lidded pot

Mordant (aluminum potassium
    sulfate)

Lidded jar for mixing mordant

Goldenrod flowers

Large stainless-steel pot
    for dye

98

1 *Weigh and Wash*. Weigh the dry garment with a standard kitchen scale. This is the weight you'll use to prepare the mordant and plant materials. Wash and dry the garment according to the care label. If the garment doesn't have a care label, consider washing it by hand with warm or cool water, being careful to minimize irritating the fibers to avoid felting, and use mild soap. Lay the garment flat to air-dry if you're not dyeing it right away.

2 *Scour*. Most wool garments can be scoured if the temperature shift in the water is gradual and there is no irritating of the fibers by stirring, twisting, or otherwise felting. If you're working with an antique or fragile garment, be sure to use extra care or check with an expert. Fill a stainless-steel pot with enough room-temperature water for the garment to move freely. Add a teaspoon of mild eco-friendly laundry detergent. Swish around before adding the garment. Then, carefully add the garment. Slowly bring the pot up to a simmer. Let it simmer for about 15 minutes. Turn the heat off and let it gradually return to room temperature. Once completely cooled, rinse the garment carefully with room-temperature water until the soap is thoroughly removed.

3

3 *Mordant.* Using the weight of the dry garment or fiber from Step 1, use 1 tablespoon of aluminum potassium sulfate to each 100 grams of fiber. (If, for example, the garment is 400 grams, add 4 tablespoons of mordant.) I fill a pint-size canning jar about one-third full with hot tap water, add the powdered mordant, fasten the lid securely on the jar, and (wearing an oven mitt if the water is too hot) shake until the mordant has dissolved completely. This helps to avoid unnecessary steam or vapors.

Next, fill a stainless-steel pot with enough water to cover the garment, add the dissolved mordant, stir, and then add the wet garment. (The garment should soak for up to 1 hour in tap water before mordanting or dyeing for best absorption.)

Cover the pot with a tight-fitting lid, bring the water up to a low simmer, then remove it from the heat and let it cool completely. To avoid any unnecessary mordant steam entering the room where you're working, do not take the lid off the pot during this phase. The water does not need to boil, just simmer or stay just below simmering.

4 *Collect Dye Plants and Make Dyes.* Now comes the fun part. Collect enough goldenrod flowers to fill a large stainless-steel pot. Ideally, you'd collect a 1:1 ratio of dry fiber weight to plant material. If, for example, you're dyeing a 400-gram wool sweater, collect about 400 grams of goldenrod flowers. In my region, goldenrod is plentiful and I don't have to worry about overharvesting. Keep in mind that you might need to forage from more than one place to collect enough flowers.

Once you've collected the flowers, put them in the pot you'll use to make the dye. Don't be concerned if there are some stems or a few rogue leaves. Add enough water to cover the flowers. Put the full pot on the burner over high heat and bring it to a simmer. Let it simmer for 30 to 60 minutes or until you notice the color start to drain from the flowers. Turn off the heat and let sit overnight, if possible. The dye should be truly golden when it's ready to use.

5

6

5 *Strain and Dye Garments*. Strain the flowers from the dye bath, keeping the dye liquid for your project. You can compost the flowers in almost any plant compost. That said, I keep my wildflower compost separate from my kitchen compost so I don't inadvertently sprout wildflower seeds when adding the compost to my garden.

Return the dye liquid to the dye pot. Add the wet garment or fibers. (If you are mordanting and dyeing on different days, make sure to soak fibers thoroughly in tap water before adding them to the dye pot.) Ideally, all liquid will be at room temperature to avoid shocking wool with a sudden change of temperature. Bring the dye to a simmer, then allow it to simmer for about an hour. Remove from the heat and let the garment soak in the dye overnight.

6 *Rinse Garment and Let Dry*. When you've achieved the desired color—plus a shade or two, as the colors will dry lighter—remove the garment from the pot. Rinse well with room-temperature water until the water runs clear. For future washes, use eco-friendly soap, hand-wash with room-temperature water, and lay flat to dry. Let that glorious electrifying color shine.

BLACK WALNUT HULLS: **linen pants**

JUGLANS NIGRA

Black walnut hulls are another very potent source of natural color. They have a long history of being used as inks and paints (they're even said to be found in the works of Leonardo da Vinci and Rembrandt). Black walnut makes a stunning warm, rich shade of brown. It's one of my favorite dyes for overdyeing—dyeing a fiber a second, third, or subsequent time to alter or darken the color or add an overtone. If I've experimented with a new plant dye and it's underwhelming, resulting in a shade of beige I hadn't predicted, I find that an overdye of black walnut will usually result in a deeper, more pleasing brown. Linen, especially in beige or white, is a wonderful fiber for black walnut— it can be transformed to charcoal gray or almost black with a modifier of iron.

Project 8

MATERIALS

Garment to be dyed

Kitchen scale

Eco-friendly mild laundry
   detergent

Measuring spoons

Large stainless-steel lidded pot

Dust mask, rubber gloves, and
   protective apron (for working
   with aluminum acetate)

Mordant (aluminum acetate)

Lidded jar for mixing mordant

Black walnut hulls

Large stainless-steel pot
   for dye

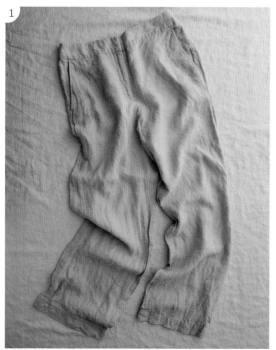

1 *Weigh and Wash.* You'll want to weigh the dry garment on a standard kitchen scale. This is the weight you'll use to measure the mordant and plant materials. Wash and dry the garment according to the care label. If the garment doesn't have a care label, consider washing by hand with warm or cool water and mild soap. Hang the garment and allow to air-dry if you are not dyeing right away.

2 *Scour.* Most linen garments can tolerate scouring. If you're working with an antique or fragile garment, be sure to use extra care or check with an expert. Fill the stainless-steel pot with enough water for the garment to move freely. Add a teaspoon of mild eco-friendly laundry detergent. Swish around before adding the garment. Carefully add the garment. Bring the water to a boil. Let it simmer for about 30 minutes. Turn the heat off and let it gradually return to room temperature. Rinse in room-temperature water until the soap is thoroughly removed.

3 *Mordant.* Wear a dust mask, rubber gloves, and protective apron. Using the weight of the dry garment or fiber from Step 1, use 1 teaspoon of aluminum acetate to each 100 grams of fiber. (If, for example, the garment is 300 grams, add 3 teaspoons of mordant.) I fill a pint-size canning jar about one-third full with hot tap water, add the mordant, fasten the lid securely on the jar, and (wearing an oven mitt if the water is too hot) shake until the mordant has dissolved completely.

Next, fill a stainless-steel pot with enough hot tap water to cover the garment, add the dissolved mordant, stir, then add the wet garment. (The garment should soak for up to 1 hour before mordanting or dyeing for best absorption.)

Cover the pot with a tight-fitting lid, bring the water up to a low simmer, then remove from the heat and let it cool completely. To avoid any unnecessary mordant steam entering the room where you're working, do not take the lid off the pot during this phase. The water does not need to boil, just simmer or stay just below simmering.

4

4 *Collect Dye Plants and Make Dyes*. My kids and I love this part—children are great at foraging for plants, and especially good at collecting hulls. Collect enough black walnut hulls to fill a large stainless-steel pot. Ideally, collect a 1:1 ratio of dry fiber weight to plant material. If, for example, you're dyeing linen pants that are 200 grams, collect about 200 grams of black walnut hulls. In Upstate New York, these hulls are abundant in late summer and autumn, and I don't worry about overharvesting. Keep in mind you might need to forage from more than one place to collect enough hulls. (Black walnut hulls are easy to dry and use all winter long. I just leave mine in a basket on the porch until they've dried completely—although sometimes I have to be smarter than the squirrels.)

Once you've collected the hulls, put them in the pot you'll use to make the dye. Add enough water to cover the plant material. Put the full pot on the burner and bring it to a boil. Let it simmer for 30 to 60 minutes or until you notice the color of the liquid is a dark brown. Continue to simmer until you reach the color you desire. Turn off the heat and let it sit overnight, if possible. Sometimes the liquid is very dark—the color of black coffee.

5

6

5 *Strain and Dye Garments*. Strain the hulls and any residual powder from the dye bath, keeping the dye liquid for your project. I toss the hulls with yard compost on the edge of our property—I don't add these hulls to my compost bin; although they are biodegradable, they can inhibit the growth of other plants and I don't want them mixed with my garden soil.

Return the dye liquid to the dye pot. Add the wet garment or fibers. (If you are mordanting and dyeing on different days, make sure to soak fibers thoroughly in tap water before adding them to the dye pot.) Linen is a hardy fiber, so you don't have to worry about shocking the fibers with hot or cold water. Bring the dye to a simmer, then simmer for about an hour. Remove from the heat and let the garment soak in the dye overnight.

6 *Rinse Garment and Let Dry*. When you've achieved the desired dye color—plus a shade or two, as the colors will dry lighter— remove the garment from the pot. Rinse well with room-temperature water until the water runs clear. For a darker shade of brown, simply repeat Steps 4 to 6. For future washes, use eco-friendly soap, hand-wash with warm water, and air-dry or lay flat to dry. This can be a great dye to cover stains or fading, too—black walnut hulls and indigo are typically my favorites for overdyeing.

"I started Botanical Colors to change the way clothes were made. We offered a natural dye option to large brands and retailers that was innovative, proven, and scalable. My early efforts were met with skepticism and it didn't feel like it was going to go anywhere. I did a lot of Internet searches on the definition of insanity! Eventually some forward-thinking brands embraced the idea of natural dyes and local manufacturing.

Now awareness is steadily growing and brands are naturally dyeing deadstock or takeback clothes to extend their life. But the emergence of regional textile economies uses plant-based colors as its foundation. It literally blossoms into a solution: Purchase local fiber and dye it with local plants.

I never dreamed that natural dyes would capture such prominence in regenerative and sustainable economies. And it makes us happy: Growing, nurturing, the benefits of carbon-busting and supporting local farmers, and a bit of technical nerdiness to process and dye. The result is a beautiful color and you feel like an alchemist. Now I can't imagine doing anything different. Every plant, every color is fresh and exciting and I'm always eager to see what's in the dye pot."

KATHY HATTORI
Botanical Colors

"Brilliant hues can be found in our everyday surroundings—from colors made from a dinner with friends, to a rainbow produced from the weeds we pass by every day without a second thought. Upcycling and refreshing our clothing and textiles with natural palettes can add abundant benefits, from dye gardens that attract pollinators, to healing hues made from medicinal herbs that have the ability both to soothe and please our eyes as well as our skin.

As a natural dyer, there is endless potential in 'cooking with color,' knowing a plant from root to stalk, and the opportunities that can be found in a discarded peel. The biodiversity and vibrancy of a color palette made from leftovers from a favorite meal before hitting the compost pile can be astounding.

'Refreshing' our clothing and textiles with hues created from the seasonal sweepings on our sidewalks, the byproducts of a summer picnic, the leftovers of a sweet-smelling bouquet, or even the weeds in our very own backyards, are just a few examples of how authentic ingredients and experiences can help us to create more meaningful wardrobes—beginning with what we have—and fully savoring all that emerges in the process."

SASHA DUERR
artist & author

QUEEN ANNE'S LACE FLOWERS: silk tank top

DAUCUS CAROTA

I have such fond memories of wildflowers swaying along the road-sides of my childhood summers. So for me, the return of flowers after a harsh Upstate New York winter is often a true dose of optimism and renewal. And the array of wildflowers in the Northeast in late summer is truly breathtaking. Queen Anne's lace, goldenrod, chicory, ironweed, and rudbeckia collide in playful bouquets that make my heart sing. Queen Anne's lace, also known as wild carrot, is a delicate, lacy plant that makes beautiful dyes. The yellow from this plant is typically a bright, light, clear shade that hints toward chartreuse. It's spectacular on secondhand silk.

Note that Queen Anne's lace has a vicious lookalike in poison hemlock—this toxic plant, another member of the parsley family, has a spotted stem and lacks the wispy bracts at the base of the flower-head. The Queen Anne's lace umbel is sometimes maroon, though not always, so be sure to reference other plant parts for identification. It's important to do your research before foraging. The USDA's Agricultural Research Service is a good place to start.

Fun fact: The plant and its maroon umbel (the flat cluster of flowers at the bloom's center) gained its common name after the legend that England's Queen Anne pricked her finger while tatting exquisite lace and a droplet of her blood fell to the center of the lace pattern.

MATERIALS

Garment to be dyed

Kitchen scale

Eco-friendly mild laundry
    detergent

Measuring spoons

Large stainless-steel lidded pot

Mordant (aluminum potassium
    sulfate)

Lidded jar for mixing mordant

Queen Anne's lace flowers

Large stainless-steel pot
    for dye

Project 9

112

1 *Weigh and Wash*. Weigh the dry garment with a standard kitchen scale. This is the weight you'll use to prepare the mordant and plant materials. Wash and dry the garment according to the care label. If the garment doesn't have a care label, consider washing it by hand with warm or cool water and mild soap. Let it air-dry if not dyeing right away.

2 *Scour*. Most silk garments can tolerate scouring. If you're working with an antique or fragile garment, be sure to use extra care or check with an expert. Fill a stainless-steel pot with enough room-temperature water for the garment to move freely. Add a teaspoon of mild eco-friendly laundry detergent. Swish around. Add the garment. Bring the water to a boil. Let it simmer for about 30 minutes. Turn the heat off and let it return to room temperature. Once completely cooled, rinse carefully with room-temperature water until the soap is thoroughly removed.

3 *Mordant*. Using the weight of the dry garment or fiber from Step 1, use 1 tablespoon of aluminum potassium sulfate to each 100 grams of fiber. (If, for example, the garment is 300 grams, add 3 tablespoons of the mordant.) I fill a pint-size canning jar about one-third full with hot tap water, add the mordant, fasten the lid securely on the jar, and (wearing an oven mitt if the water is too hot) shake. This helps to avoid unnecessary steam or vapors. Repeat shaking until the mordant has dissolved completely

Fill a stainless-steel pot with enough water to cover the garment, add the dissolved mordant, stir, then add the wet garment. (The garment should soak for up to 1 hour before mordanting or dyeing for best absorption.) Cover the pot with a tight-fitting lid, bring the water up to a simmer, then remove from the heat and let it cool completely. To avoid any unnecessary mordant steam entering the room where you're working, do not take the lid off the pot during this phase. The water does not need to boil, just simmer or stay just below simmering.

4 *Collect Dye Plants and Make Dyes.* Collect enough Queen Anne's lace flowers to fill a large stainless-steel pot. Ideally, you'd collect a 1:1 ratio of dry fiber weight to plant material. If, for example, you're dyeing a 100-gram silk shirt, collect about 100 grams of Queen Anne's lace flowers. In the Hudson Valley, where I live, Queen Anne's lace is plentiful through summer and fall, so overharvesting isn't an issue. Keep in mind that you might need to forage from more than one place to collect enough flowers. (Make sure to correctly identify Queen Anne's lace by the hairy stem, red center flower it often presents, and wispy bracts, or consult a field guide for your region.)

Once you've collected the flowers, put them in the pot you'll use to make the dye. Don't be concerned if there are a few stems or bracts included. Add enough water to cover the flowers. Put the full pot on the burner and bring it to a simmer. Let it simmer for 30 to 45 minutes or until you notice the dye color starting to shift to a bright yellow—flowers don't typically need to simmer for very long to extract color, so use your best judgment. Turn off the heat and let it sit overnight, if possible.

5 *Strain and Dye Garments*. Next, strain the flowers from the dye bath, keeping the dye liquid for your project. You can compost the flowers in almost any plant compost. That said, I keep my wildflower compost separate from my kitchen compost so I don't inadvertently sprout wildflower seeds when adding the compost to my garden.

Return the dye liquid to the dye pot. Add the wet garment or fibers. (If you are mordanting and dyeing on different days, make sure to soak fibers thoroughly in tap water before adding them to the dye pot.) Bring the dye to a simmer, allow it to simmer for 15 to 30 minutes, then soak on low heat for about an hour. Remove from the heat and let the garment or fibers soak overnight or until you've achieved the desired color.

6 *Rinse Garment and Let Dry*. When you've achieved the desired color—plus a shade or two, as the colors will dry lighter—remove the garment from the pot. Rinse it well with room-temperature water, until the water runs clear. For future washes, use eco-friendly soap, hand-wash with warm water, and hang or lay flat to dry. Silk will dry quickly on a dry, breezy day. Then watch as the yellow from the Queen Anne's lace seems to dance across the texture of your silk garment.

117

FLOWERING QUINCE BRANCHES: linen top

CHAENOMELES SPECIOSA

There are many challenges that come with renovating and tending our family's two-hundred-year-old farmhouse in a climate that ranges from hot summers to frigid winters, but the charms of this bicentennial beauty far outweigh the burdens. One of those charms is the bevy of trees, bushes, and flowers that have been planted on the property by former owners. I was delighted to find an ancient flowering quince in our yard alongside established lilacs, forsythia, pussy willows, silver maples, and more.

Many fruit trees and bushes can make lovely dyes. At times, the leaves, fruit, berries, or nuts are used, but often it's the bark. (A quick search will yield dye recipes for quince, apple, cherry, plum, apricot, elderberry, raspberry, and many others.) So imagine my joy when I realized this gorgeous flowering quince could make dyes in addition to producing edible fruits perfect for homegrown jams. For this recipe I used cuttings from our overgrown flowering quince, the branches trimmed into small pieces to fit easily inside the dye pot. I often use the dye more than once as it's so potent.

MATERIALS

Garment to be dyed

Kitchen scale

Eco-friendly mild laundry
   detergent

Measuring spoons

Large stainless-steel lidded pot

Dust mask, rubber gloves,
   and protective apron
   (for working with
   aluminum acetate)

Mordant (aluminum acetate)

Lidded jar for mixing mordant

Hand-pruners

Flowering quince branches

Large stainless-steel pot
   for dye

118

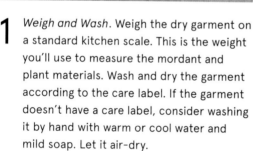

1 *Weigh and Wash.* Weigh the dry garment on a standard kitchen scale. This is the weight you'll use to measure the mordant and plant materials. Wash and dry the garment according to the care label. If the garment doesn't have a care label, consider washing it by hand with warm or cool water and mild soap. Let it air-dry.

2 *Scour.* Most linen garments can handle scouring. If you're working with an antique or fragile garment, be sure to use extra care or check with an expert. Fill a stainless-steel pot with enough room-temperature water for the garment to move freely. Add a teaspoon of mild eco-friendly laundry detergent. Swish around. Add the garment. Bring the water to a boil. Let it simmer for about 30 minutes. Turn the heat off and let it return to room temperature. Once completely cooled, rinse with room-temperature water until the soap is thoroughly removed.

3 *Mordant.* Wear a dust mask, rubber gloves, and protective apron. Using the weight of the garment or fiber from Step 1, use 1 teaspoon of aluminum acetate to each 100 grams of fiber. (If, for example, the garment is 300 grams, then add 3 teaspoons of mordant.) Fill a pint-size canning jar about one-third full with hot tap water, add the mordant, fasten the lid securely on the jar, and (wearing an oven mitt if the water is too hot) shake until the mordant has dissolved. This helps to avoid unnecessary steam or vapors.

Fill a stainless-steel pot with enough hot tap water to cover the garment, add the dissolved mordant, stir, and then add the wet garment. (The garment should soak for up to 1 hour before mordanting or dyeing for best absorption.) Cover the pot with a tight-fitting lid, bring the water up to a simmer, then remove it from the heat and let it cool completely. To avoid any unnecessary mordant steam entering the room where you're working, do not take the lid off the pot during this phase. The water does not need to boil, just simmer or stay just below simmering. Use a dust mask and proper ventilation.

121

4 *Collect Dye Plants and Make Dyes.* Collect enough flowering quince branches (or other fruit tree branches, especially after pruning season) to fill a large stainless-steel pot. Ideally, you'd collect a 1:1 ratio of dry fiber weight to plant material. If, for example, you're dyeing a 200-gram linen top, you'd collect about 200 grams of flowering quince branches. (Most orchards prune their fruit trees on an annual basis; check with the owner or farm manager to see if you can collect the trimmed branches when the pruning is done.)

Once you've collected the branches, remove the leaves, then use hand-pruners to cut them into smaller pieces so they can easily fit into a pot. Add them to the pot you'll use to make the dye. Add enough water to cover the chopped branches. Put the full pot on the burner and bring to a boil. Reduce the heat and let it simmer until you notice the color start to appear in the liquid, about 30 to 60 minutes. Turn off the heat and let it sit overnight, if possible. Sometimes I have to repeat this process over two or three days. It can take that amount of time (or longer) of soaking, or repeatedly bringing up to a boil and simmering, to coax the color from bark.

122

5 *Strain and Dye Garments*. Strain the bark from the dye bath, keeping the dye liquid for your project. You can compost the bark in almost any plant compost or in a pile of yard scraps at the edge of your yard.

Return the dye liquid to the dye pot. Add the wet garment or fibers. (If you are mordanting and dyeing on different days, make sure to soak fibers thoroughly in tap water before adding them to the dye pot.) Bring the dye to a simmer, allow it to simmer for 15 to 30 minutes, then reduce to low heat for up to an hour. Linen is a hardy fiber and can take a low boil or long simmer. Remove from the heat and let the garment soak in the dye overnight.

6 *Rinse Garment and Let Dry*. When you've achieved the desired color—plus a shade or two, as the colors will dry lighter—remove the garment from the pot. Rinse it well with room-temperature water until the water runs clear. For future washes, use eco-friendly soap, hand-wash with warm water, and hang or lay flat to dry. You now have exquisite shade of coral, as beautiful as the blossoms of a flowering quince.

GARDEN FLOWER MIX: **wool sweater**

COREOPSIS (COREOPSIS TINCTORIA), MARIGOLD (TAGETES), AND CALENDULA (CALENDULA)

A great joy of working with natural dyes is sharing information with other dyers. Like gardening, foraging, or homesteading, the knowledge I've gathered has been derived as much from informal learning with friends as from books, internet searches, and ongoing research. During one January artist's residency with my dear friend and local artist Brece Honeycutt, she enlightened me with the idea that dye materials could be combined to make color. The possibilities blew my mind. So I often adoringly call this dye Brece's Flower Blend.

While it might not offer as potent or predictable a shade as a single-source color, blending dye sources is a great way to experiment with whole plants, especially when each plant typically yields a similar hue—in this case, warm yellows and oranges. It also gives you a reason to dry that small harvest of garden flowers—you can add it to other handfuls of dye flowers to have enough for a pot, come winter. The flowers in this blend are coreopsis (also known as tickseed), marigold, and calendula. They all dry beautifully for winter color—simply put the fresh flowers on a towel, screen, or countertop to dry completely; store them in canning jars with proper labels and then bring them out for some color therapy during the winter. (Note: The model, Katharine Daugherty, wears her own handmade dress.)

MATERIALS

Garment to be dyed

Kitchen scale

Eco-friendly mild laundry detergent

Measuring spoons

Large stainless-steel lidded pot

Mordant
  (aluminum potassium sulfate)

Lidded jar for mixing mordant

Mixed flower blooms
  (fresh or dried)

Large stainless-steel pot for dye

124

1 *Weigh and Wash.* Weigh the dry garment on a standard kitchen scale. This is the weight you'll use to measure the mordant and plant materials. Wash and dry the garment according to care label. If the garment doesn't have a care label, consider washing by hand with warm or cool water, being careful to minimize irritating the fibers to avoid felting, and use mild soap. Lay the garment flat to air-dry if you're not dyeing it right away.

2 *Scour.* Most wool garments can be scoured if the temperature shift in the water is gradual and there is no irritation of the fibers by stirring, twisting, or otherwise felting. If you're working with an antique or fragile garment, be sure to use extra care or check with an expert. Fill a stainless-steel pot with enough room-temperature water for the garment to move freely. Add a teaspoon of mild eco-friendly laundry detergent. Swish around, then add the garment. Slowly bring the pot to a simmer. Let it simmer for about 15 minutes or less. Turn the heat off and let it gradually return to room temperature. Once completely cooled, rinse carefully with room-temperature water until the soap is thoroughly removed.

126

3 *Mordant.* Using the weight of the dry garment or fiber from Step 1, use 1 tablespoon of aluminum potassium sulfate to each 100 grams of fiber. (If, for example, the garment is 400 grams then add 4 tablespoons of mordant.) I fill a pint-size canning jar about one-third full with hot tap water, add the mordant, fasten the lid securely, and (wearing an oven mitt if the water is too hot) shake until the mordant has dissolved completely. This helps to avoid unnecessary steam or vapors.

Fill a stainless-steel pot with enough water to cover the garment, add the dissolved mordant, stir, and then add the wet garment. (The garment should soak for up to 1 hour before mordanting or dyeing for best absorption.) Put a tight-fitting lid on the pot, bring the water up to a simmer, then remove it from the heat and let it cool completely. To avoid any unnecessary mordant steam entering the room where you're working, do not take the lid off the pot during this phase. The water does not need to boil, just simmer or stay just below simmering.

4

4 *Collect Dye Plants and Make Dyes.* Collect enough dye flowers for this project—you can use fresh or dried. Ideally, you'd collect a 1:1 ratio of dry fiber weight to plant material. If, for example, you're dyeing a 400-gram wool sweater, collect about 400 grams of garden dye flowers. In my region, our gardening season runs from about June through October so I dry many dye flowers to use in the colder months.

Once you've collected the flowers, put them in the pot you'll use to make the dye. Add enough water to cover the flowers. Put the full pot on the burner and bring to a simmer. Let it simmer until you notice the color starting to drain from the flowers, about 30 to 45 minutes. Turn off the heat and let it sit overnight, if possible. Unlike bark or stems, flowers can be delicate, so your simmer time might be less; just experiment and keep checking the plants to see if the color has been extracted.

5

6

5 *Strain and Dye Garments*. Strain the flowers from the dye bath, keeping the dye liquid for your project. You can compost the flowers in almost any plant compost—I add mine to my kitchen compost and turn it into my garden soil when it's ready. I don't mind a few random flowers poking out of my vegetable garden if the seeds germinate.

Return the dye liquid to the dye pot. Add the wet garment or fibers. (If you are mordanting and dyeing on different days, make sure to soak fibers thoroughly in tap water before adding them to the dye pot.) Ideally, all the liquid will be room temperature to avoid shocking the wool with a sudden change of temperature. Bring the dye up to a simmer, allow it to simmer for about 30 minutes, then keep on low heat for about an hour. Remove from the heat and let the garment soak in the dye overnight.

6 *Rinse Garment and Let Dry*. When you've achieved the desired color—plus a shade or two, as the colors will dry lighter—remove the garment from the pot. Rinse well with room-temperature water until the water runs clear. For future washes, use eco-friendly soap, hand-wash with lukewarm water, and lay flat to dry. Bask in your gorgeous garden color all year long.

129

"The earth remembers, it recalls beauty, suffering, and everything in between. We cannot forget, there were bodies, minds, and spirits silenced, surrendered, and subjugated in the name of color. I am actively working to remember. My time serving as a farmer and artist-in-residence on the Baltimore Natural Dye Initiative has allowed me to connect deeply to what the soil has seen.

The daily cultivation, ritual, and communion in growing dye plants has awakened in me an ancestral spirit of honor, care, and protection. I come from farmers and a diaspora rich in cloth traditions. The more I rest in these truths the more I am empowered to remember the wisdom, ingenuity, experimentation, and resourcefulness of elders. What was lost can be regained, what has been broken can be brought to the light and healed.

My personal practice in natural dyes continues to be ignited and illuminated through engagement with students, quilters, farmers, activists, and youth. I am pushed to leave things better than when I came, to expect the best in myself and others, to show up with open hands and an empty heart. We are the seekers. What we find, use, and return is up to us."

KENYA MILES
artist & Blue Light Junction director

"My life has changed drastically by becoming a natural dyer. Before learning dye could come from nature, I admired the landscape as I would a photograph—a flat portrait, more or less. Desiring to make a particular color, or seeing a plant and wondering if it could create a color, led me to learn how to identify plants, mushrooms, trees, cacti, and flowers. Now, the stress of my daily life melts away as I wander through the forest, fully present, taking in shapes, textures, and smells. Being in nature and understanding it more has greatly awakened my sense of gratitude for the bioregion in which I live and continues to enrich my care and respect for the earth. The clothing I naturally dye is imbued with fond memories of walking through the forest and with the love I feel for the Earth."

KRISTINE VEJAR
A Verb for Keeping Warm

PEPPERMINT LEAVES: cotton top

MENTHA X PIPERITA

Another edible, medicinal, and dye plant from my backyard garden, is the common peppermint. Joined in this power-plant category by such herbs as lavender, rosemary, calendula, rose, nettle, sage, dandelion, and more, the mint family offers subtle color that can shift to more dramatic tones with iron. Truthfully, I don't work often with iron as a modifier because it's so potent. If not rinsed or separated from other dye samples, it leaves spots, makes stains, and modifies almost any other natural dye it touches. Yet just small amounts of iron can shift mediocre yellows to glorious greens, and bland beiges to lovely silvers. Be sure to isolate iron-dyed textiles from other dyed fabrics, rinse thoroughly, and let them dry completely before touching other fibers.

Iron is also thought to be harsh on fibers like wool, silk, or even linen. It's known to make the fibers brittle, or even break, with time. When I say "time" I mean centuries. I haven't heard of iron decaying fibers in just a decade or two, nor that it takes a toll on cotton the way it does on other fibers. So, this cotton top is the perfect canvas for experimentation. Use iron sparingly and with great respect, keep it away from other dyes, children, and pets and enjoy the alteration it brings.

MATERIALS

Garment to be dyed

Kitchen scale

Eco-friendly mild laundry
   detergent

Measuring spoons

Large stainless-steel lidded pot

Dust mask, rubber gloves, and
   protective apron (for working
   with aluminum acetate)

Mordant (aluminum acetate)

Lidded jar for mixing mordant

Peppermint leaves

Large stainless-steel pot for dye

Iron modifier (ferrous sulfate)

Project 12

132

1 *Weigh and Wash.* Weigh the dry garment on a standard kitchen scale. This is the weight you'll use to measure the mordant and plant materials. Wash and dry the garment according to the care label. If the garment doesn't have a care label, consider washing it by hand with warm or cool water and mild soap, and then air-dry.

2 *Scour.* Most cotton garments can handle scouring. If you're working with an antique or fragile garment, be sure to use extra care or check with an expert. Fill a stainless-steel pot with enough water for the garment to move freely. Add a teaspoon of mild eco-friendly laundry detergent. Swish around. Add the garment. Bring the water to a boil. Let it simmer for about 30 minutes. Turn the heat off and let it return to room temperature. Once completely cooled, rinse the garment with room-temperature water until the soap is thoroughly removed.

3 *Mordant.* Wear a dust mask, rubber gloves, and protective apron. Using the weight of the dry garment or fiber from Step 1, use 1 teaspoon of aluminum acetate to each 100 grams of fiber. (If, for example, the garment is 200 grams, add 2 teaspoons of mordant.) I fill a pint-size canning jar about one-third full with hot tap water, add the mordant, fasten the lid securely on the jar, and (wearing an oven mitt if the water is too hot) shake until the mordant has dissolved completely. This helps to avoid unnecessary steam or vapors.

Fill a stainless-steel pot with enough hot tap water to cover the garment, add dissolved mordant, stir, and then add the wet garment. (The garment should soak for up to 1 hour before mordanting or dyeing for best absorption.) Put a tight-fitting lid on the pot, bring the water up to a simmer, then remove it from the heat and let it cool completely. To avoid any unnecessary mordant steam entering the room where you're working, do not take the lid off the pot during this phase. The water does not need to boil, just simmer or stay just below simmering. Use a dust mask and proper ventilation.

4 *Collect Dye Plants and Make Dyes*. Collect enough peppermint leaves to fill a large stainless-steel pot. Ideally, you'd collect a 1:1 ratio of dry fiber weight to plant material. If, for example, you're dyeing a 200-gram cotton shirt, you'd collect about 200 grams of peppermint leaves. In my region, peppermint grows fervently in my garden and is plentiful from spring through fall. You can try this recipe with any mint leaves, but you'll get slightly different results, depending on the type of mint—I've found spearmint results in warmer beiges and peppermint cooler yellows, but you'll have to experiment with your water, fibers, and mordants to test the mints.

Once you've collected the leaves, put them in the pot you'll use to make the dye. Add enough water to cover the leaves. Put the full pot on the burner and bring to a

simmer. Let it simmer until you notice the color start to drain from the leaves and into the liquid, about 30 to 45 minutes. Turn off the heat and let sit overnight, if possible. Enjoy the aroma—this dye plant makes the entire room smell divine!

5 *Strain and Dye Garments*. Strain the leaves from the dye bath, keeping the dye liquid for your project. You can compost the leaves in almost any plant or kitchen compost.

Return the liquid to the dye pot. Add the wet garment or fibers. (If you are mordanting and dyeing on different days, make sure to soak fibers thoroughly in tap water before adding them to the dye pot.) Bring the dye to a simmer, allow it to simmer about 30 minutes, then keep on low heat for about an hour. Remove from

6

the heat and let the garment soak in the dye overnight.

Prepare the iron modifier according to the instructions. If using iron in powder form as ferrous sulfate, add a small amount of powder, about ½ teaspoon per 100 grams, to about 1 cup of hot tap water in a pint-size canning jar, securely fasten the lid on the jar, and shake the jar until the powder has dissolved. If using a homebrew iron (made of rusty objects added to water then left to soak until the water turns orange), you can add that brew very gradually and directly to the dye liquid—a little goes a long way, so start small with as little as ½ cup. Either way, you'll slowly add iron modifier until you achieve the color you desire. Keep all other fibers, pots, and tools away from the iron and wash everything well when you're finished. Iron is

very potent in shifting dyes. Also, store iron modifier in a safe place away from children and pets. Be sure to wash your pots very well after using iron to prevent staining future dye projects.

6 *Rinse Garment and Let Dry.* When you've achieved the desired color—plus a shade or two, as the colors will dry lighter—remove the dyed garment from the pot. Rinse very well with room-temperature water until the water runs clear. For future washes, use eco-friendly soap, hand-wash with warm water, and lay flat to dry. Relish your moody shade of green.

YELLOW ONION SKINS: **cotton top**

ALLIUM CEPA

Onion skins are probably one of the most common kitchen scraps for creating natural dyes. Even if you live in an apartment building in a big city, with no backyard garden or even herbs growing in window boxes, you can still collect enough onion skins for dyes. Just store them in a paper bag once they're dry, building your collection until you have enough for your fiber project. You can also ask to collect extra onion skins from grocery stores, farmer's markets, or local farms. I've found folks give them to me generously and happily, as they have little use for them otherwise. But I put them to use making glorious shades of amber, orange, and nearly red on cellulose and animal fibers. You can use any type of onion skin for dyes, but for this project I use yellow onion skins.

MATERIALS

Garment to be dyed

Kitchen scale

Eco-friendly mild laundry
    detergent

Measuring spoons

Large stainless-steel lidded pot

Dust mask, rubber gloves,
    and protective apron
    (for working with
    aluminum acetate)

Mordant (aluminum acetate)

Lidded jar for mixing mordant

Yellow onion skins

Large stainless-steel pot for dye

138

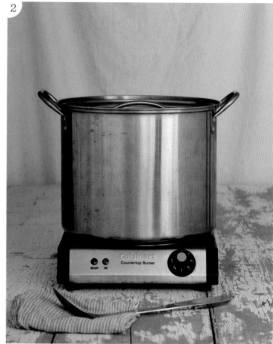

1 *Weigh and Wash.* Weigh the dry garment on a standard kitchen scale. This is the weight you'll use to measure the mordant and plant materials. Wash and dry the garment according to the care label. If the garment doesn't have a care label, consider washing it by hand with warm or cool water and mild soap, and letting it air-dry.

2 *Scour.* Most cotton garments can handle a good scouring. If you're working with an antique or fragile garment, be sure to use extra care or consult an expert. Fill a stainless-steel pot with enough water for the garment to move freely. Add a teaspoon of mild eco-friendly detergent. Swish around. Add the garment. Bring the water to a boil. Let it simmer for about 30 minutes. Turn the heat off and let it return to room temperature. Once completely cooled, rinse the garment with room-temperature water until the soap is thoroughly removed.

3 *Mordant.* Wear a dust mask, rubber gloves, and protective apron. Using the weight of the dry garment from Step 1, use 1 teaspoon of aluminum acetate to each 100 grams of fiber. (If, for example, the garment is 200 grams then add 2 teaspoons of mordant). I fill a pint-size canning jar roughly one-third full with hot tap water, add the mordant, fasten the lid securely on the jar, and (wearing an oven mitt if the water is too hot) shake until the mordant has dissolved completely. This helps to avoid unnecessary vapors.

Fill a stainless-steel pot with enough hot tap water to cover the garment, add the dissolved mordant, stir, then add the wet garment. (The garment should soak for up to 1 hour before mordanting or dyeing for best absorption.) Cover the pot with a tight-fitting lid, bring the water up to a simmer, then remove it from the heat and let it cool completely. To avoid any unnecessary mordant steam entering the room where you're working, do not take the lid off the pot during this phase. The water does not need to boil, just simmer or stay just below simmering. Use a dust mask and proper ventilation.

4

4 *Collect Dye Plants and Make Dyes.* Collect enough onion skins to fill a large stainless-steel pot. Ideally, you'd collect a 1:1 ratio of dry fiber weight to plant material. (If, for example, you're dyeing a 200-gram cotton top, you'd collect about 200 grams of onion skins.) If you're saving onion skins from your kitchen, just wait until you've amassed enough materials. If you're collecting from local farms, grocery stores, or markets you can collect from more than one place to get the amount needed. Though be sure you're collecting just one type of onion, in this case yellow onion skins, as different onion skins will result in different dye colors.

Once you've collected the onion skins, put them in the pot you'll use to make the dye. Add enough water to cover the plant material. Put the full pot on the burner and bring it to a boil. Reduce to a simmer for about 30 to 60 minutes or until you notice the color start to drain from the onion skins and the skins are translucent. Turn off the heat and let the dye materials soak overnight, if possible.

5

6

5 *Strain and Dye Garments.* Strain the onion skins from the dye bath, keeping the dye liquid for your project. Compost skins.

Return the liquid to the dye pot. Add the wet garment or fibers. (If you are mordanting and dyeing on different days, make sure to soak fibers in tap water before adding them to the dye pot.) Bring the dye up to a simmer, allow to simmer for about 30 to 45 minutes, then keep on low heat for about an hour. Remove the pot from the heat and let the garment soak overnight. This will yield a richer color.

6 *Rinse Garment and Let Dry.* When you've achieved the desired color—plus a shade or two, as the colors will dry lighter—remove the garment from the dye pot. Rinse well with room temperature water until the water runs clear. For future washes, use eco-friendly soap, hand-wash with warm water, and hang or lay flat to dry. Revel in the rich amber color.

AVOCADO PITS & SKINS: raw silk pants

PERSEA AMERICANA

I praise the avocado. As a vegetarian of twenty-five years, raising two vegetarian children alongside my vegetarian husband, I count on this nutrient-dense fruit for its combination of essential minerals, vitamins, and healthy fats. True, avocados are not grown anywhere in my region, but they are a beloved part of my diet, so the least I can do, if I'm buying this food grown in California, three thousand miles away, is use all of its parts. I'm thrilled to reduce food waste and save avocado pits and skins for dyeing. (You can also ask local restaurants for them. Kitchens are sometimes happy to set the skins and pits aside for you to pick up, if you provide them with a clean container with a fitted top.)

Many dyers keep avocado pits and skins in the freezer— swearing they retain the fats that help assist the dyes. But since my freezer is packed with preserved summer fruits and vegetables, I dry mine. I've had great luck drying the pits and skins on a saucer on the countertop, or in a cast-iron pan on the woodstove in winter, and later using them to create beautiful pink, peach, and even rose-colored dyes.

MATERIALS
Garment to be dyed
Kitchen scale
Eco-friendly mild laundry detergent
Measuring spoons
Large stainless-steel lidded pot
Mordant (aluminum potassium sulfate)
Lidded jar for mixing mordant
Avocado pits and/or skins
Large stainless-steel pot for dye

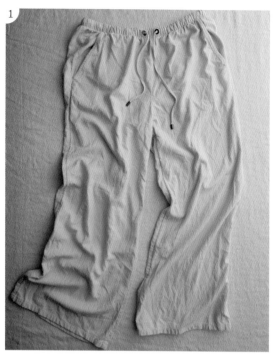

1 *Weigh and Wash*. Weigh the dry garment on a standard kitchen scale. This is the weight you'll use to measure the mordant and the plant materials. Wash and dry the garment according to the care label. If the garment doesn't have a care label, consider washing by hand with warm or cool water, mild soap, and then letting it air-dry.

2 *Scour*. Most silk garments can tolerate scouring. If you're working with antiques, use extra care. Fill a stainless-steel pot with enough water for the garment to move freely. Add a teaspoon of mild eco-friendly detergent. Swish around. Add the garment. Bring the water to a boil. Let it simmer for about 30 minutes. Turn the heat off and let it return to room temperature. Once completely cooled, rinse the garment until the soap is thoroughly removed.

3 *Mordant*. Using the weight of the dry garment or fiber from Step 1, use 1 tablespoon of aluminum potassium sulfate to each 100 grams of fiber. (If, for example, the garment is 300 grams, add 3 tablespoons of mordant.) I fill a pint-size canning jar about one-third full with hot tap water, add the mordant, fasten the lid securely on the jar, and (wearing an oven mitt if the water is too hot) shake until the mordant has dissolved completely. This helps to avoid unnecessary vapors.

Fill a stainless-steel pot with enough water to cover the garment, add the dissolved mordant, stir, then add the wet garment. (The garment should soak for up to 1 hour before mordanting or dyeing for best absorption.) Cover the pot with a tight-fitting lid, bring the water up to a simmer, then remove it from the heat

3

4

and let it cool completely. To avoid any unnecessary mordant steam entering the room where you're working, do not take the lid off the pot during this phase. The water does not need to boil, just simmer or stay just below simmering.

4 *Collect Dye Plants and Make Dyes.* Collect enough avocado pits and/or skins to fill a large stainless-steel pot. Ideally, you'd collect a 1:1 ratio of dry fiber weight to plant material. If, for example, you're dyeing 300 grams of raw silk pants, you'd collect about 300 grams of avocado pits and/or skins.

Once you've collected the avocado pits and/or skins, put them in the pot you'll use to make the dyes. Add enough water to cover the plant material. Put the full pot on the burner and bring it up to a boil.

Let it boil until you notice the color start to drain from the pits and/or skins and the water turns pink, beige, or even rose. Then reduce to a simmer for about 30 to 60 minutes. Sometimes I have to repeat this process several times to coax the color from avocado pits. Turn off the heat and let the dye sit overnight, if possible. You can repeat this process over two or three days if needed.

147

5

6

5 *Strain and Dye Garments*. Strain the plant material from the dye bath, keeping the dye liquid for your project. You can compost the avocado parts in almost any plant compost. (It's slow composting, though. My neighbor laments that her avocado pits and skins just get tossed from one compost pile to the next for several seasons—they can take a very long time to break down completely.)

Return the dye liquid to the dye pot. Add the wet garment or fibers. (If you are mordanting and dyeing on different days, make sure to soak fibers thoroughly in tap water before adding them to the dye pot.) Bring the dye to a simmer, allow it to simmer for about 30 minutes, then keep on low heat for about an hour. Remove the pot from the heat and let the garment soak in the dye overnight.

6 *Rinse Garment and Let Dry*. When you've achieved the desired color—plus a shade or two, as the colors will dry lighter—remove the garment from the pot. Rinse well with room-temperature water until the water runs clear. For future washes, use eco-friendly soap, hand-wash with warm water, and hang or lay flat to dry. These are by far my favorite shades of pink.

Deepening Our Connection with Nature: Dye Plants as Allies and Teachers

There's an incredible potential to connect with the natural world through the plants around us. If we can shift our gazes to see these living creatures as allies and teachers, we can start to develop a relationship that nourishes, inspires, and even heals. If we can remember that we are forever connected to the natural world and that we share this connection with other people, animals, and plants, we can build compassion and act as responsible citizens. Working with natural dyes allows me to witness the life cycle of local plants—noticing when the plant buds, blossoms, withers, and goes dormant before budding again. I notice how the weather, foot traffic, and even my kitchen compost impact a plant's growth and ability to survive or thrive.

Natural dyes are a powerful and joyful source of color. Plants like black walnut, brazilwood, indigo, logwood, madder, sumac, weld, and woad were recorded to create vibrant colors on cloths centuries ago—prior to the invention of synthetic dyes in the mid-1800s, all textile dyes were derived from plants, animals, or minerals. As plants are regionally and culturally specific, we can look across continents and identify various plants used as natural dyes in each location. Today, natural dyes can be used in extract, powder, or whole-plant forms. When we're creating dyes at home or in a studio as part of a creative or personal practice, we have the freedom to experiment. We can create one-of-a-kind textiles or build layers of color through overdyeing with whole plants. When dyeing just a handful of garments or just a few yards of fabric we can use foraged plants like black walnut hulls, homegrown dyes like coreopsis petals, or even kitchen scraps like avocado pits and skins.

By growing, foraging, or preserving plants for dyes we begin to deepen our relationship to the seasons, weather, landscape, and plant life cycles around us. I start calendula seeds in my kitchen window so they are ready to transplant into my garden beds in late May. If it's a cool spring, I'll wait until we're officially past our frost date to transplant fragile seedlings. But if it's a warm spring, I might plant a week or two earlier. Once the plants are established, I water, weed, and harvest on a weekly, then daily, schedule. With some plants, like chamomile, the more I harvest, the more the plant produces, so it benefits us both to tend with a daily rhythm. With a dye plant like madder, whose roots take several years to establish, I'll have to commit to tending that plant for years before I harvest color.

In foraging for dye materials there's a wonderful opportunity to identify, study, and map plants in my region. I know that goldenrod typically peaks in August and can maintain blooms until October, so I have secondhand clothing, skeins of wool, or yards of fabric I intend to dye that magical shade of yellow prepped and waiting by the end of July. I've come to locate staghorn sumac in the neighbor's field, goldenrod behind the nearby park, black walnut hulls along the edge of a parking lot, acorns on a favorite hiking path, Queen Anne's lace along my road, and the dandelions dotting my backyard throughout spring and summer. The list of foraged dye plants is long and, surprisingly, spans all four seasons—though the abundance is particularly dizzying in late summer and early fall.

There is significant overlap between foraged dye plants, edible plants, and medicinal plants. Indigenous communities have been interacting with local plants since the beginning of human civilization—we have much to learn about cultivating relationships with plants by honoring their longstanding connections with Indigenous peoples. Many of the dye plants we use today have significant cultural, or even spiritual, history in various communities where they originated. Pre-industrialization, our ancestors learned to identify plants for food, building materials, medicines, tools, fibers, dye plants, and more.

Each geographical region has its particular Triple Power Plants, as I like to call them—plants that offer dense nutrients, supportive healing properties, and potent dye color. Black walnuts, calendula, dandelions, lavender, peppermint, rose, rosemary, sage, and stinging nettles are just a few plants that I consider Triple Powers. Stinging nettle has been known to offer more nutritional density than many of the plants I grow in my garden—they far outperform my tomatoes. Yet they are often removed from yards with shocking fervor—the American trend towards a pristine green lawn has not helped our herbal allies so much as it's created a weather-intolerant monocrop coveted by our neighbors. Personally, I prefer a yard of red clover, dandelions, and purple violets.

We moved to our 1820s farmhouse in New York in the fall of 2015. At the time, we inherited one of those pristine green yards, an acre thick. We worked swiftly to establish a vegetable garden, flower garden, small fruit orchard, and large fenced area for the chickens to peck, forage, and play. Year by year, we create additional zones for composting, gardening, and tending our homestead while reducing grass. We grow native plants, pollinators, and edibles at every turn. Yet the most notable shift in our yard has been the diversity that's returned—dandelions, clovers, violets, purslane, nettles, and more. I cheer for the biodiversity in my yard even if some neighbors might raise an eyebrow at how our formerly green grass has turned into a collage of "weeds," or the term I prefer: "yard salad."

I plant my gardens to accommodate dye plants, vegetables, fruits, herbs, and pollinators. Sometimes the same plant, like lavender, works quadruple duty by providing dye color, honeybee food, herbal teas, and herbal medicine. In this case, I have to prioritize wisely, leaving some flowers for bees and drying some for winter teas, baths, and simple hydrosols. Plants like calendula span my dye pots and homemade salves, but because they produce so many flowers I don't have to choose between uses. Others, such as our beloved flowering quince tree, don't make me choose between beautiful flowers for the kitchen counter or bark for my dye pots—when the bouquets wilt, the barks can be turned into dyes.

Yard size doesn't need to determine access to dye plants either. Many plants can be grown in containers—such as peppermint, sage, and rosemary—and many others can be foraged from parks, sidewalks, and nearby fields or forests. We need to be vigilant in correctly identifying the plant and only taking what we need. We also need to be mindful of where we are foraging and not trample any fragile species. It's best to steer clear of roadsides and other areas of potential pollution if we plan to consume the plant. Dye plants, however, can be harvested from a roadside or ditch because they won't be eaten.

There isn't a one-size environmental solution when it comes to growing or foraging plants or preserving food scraps for natural color. Instead, like most attempts in sustainable living, we need to consider the local ecosystem and determine what makes the most sense for each individual based on location, geography, climate, budget, lifestyle, culture, and technical skill. We're all still learning, but a willingness to experiment goes a long way.

As with most practices, start where you are. If foraging dandelions from the local park is your annual attempt at local color—fantastic! Or if you're plotting out your large dye garden, hoping to get a rainbow of dyes from your backyard—marvelous! All these various attempts at sustainable living create a wonderful web. I'd like to imagine a beautiful weaving of sustainable or conscious lifestyles that intersect, diverge, overlap, and thread together to make the most incredible tapestry. We can begin to create plant color one dye pot, one garment, and one dye plant at a time, deepening our relationship to nature with each color we create.

CHAPTER 4
MEND

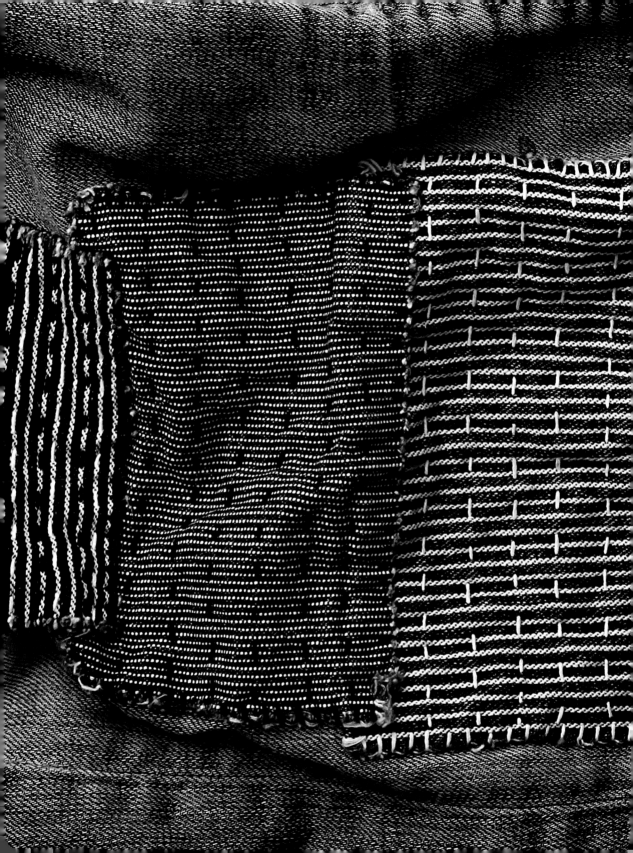

mend

HOW TO MEND: TOOLS, MATERIALS, AND TECHNIQUES

TOOLS

See page 34 for a complete list of tools for making and mending, including needles, thread, scissors, fabric pencils, ruler or measuring tape, embroidery hoops, and thimbles.

darning egg, mushroom, or tool
I have several vintage wooden darning tools and I love them as objects as much I as love them as practical tools. Darning eggs are great for darning socks and the handles can be useful for mending fingers on gloves. Darning mushrooms are best for mending larger flat surfaces on sweaters.

That said, I tend to go between darning tools with fluidity and I'm just grateful to have a handful in my studio. If you don't have a darning tool, there is no shortage of household objects that have been used instead: Potatoes, apples, onions, plastic Easter eggs, tennis balls, and wooden spoons (for glove darning) are just a few. Be sure to use a tool that is safe for you and your textiles. If you know a woodworker, they might make you a custom egg—my husband has made several.

MATERIALS

fabric

There are several factors to consider when mending garments or choosing fabric for patches. I prioritize biodegradable materials in my studio whenever possible: Cotton, linen, hemp, wool, and silk are my favorite fibers to wear, dye, and mend. If you are working with knit or stretch fabrics instead of woven fabrics, use stretch stitches. The whipstich (page 41) is a basic stretch stitch; you could also choose stitches from Natalie Chanin's book *The Geometry of Hand-Sewing*.

When mending woven garments, try to match the fiber and weight to the patch—medium-weight denim jeans are patched with medium-weight cotton patches, while lightweight linen shirts are mended with lightweight linen patches. You can use new fabric for repairs or you can use secondhand textiles or garments as patches—it's up to you and your project.

yarn

When mending knit sweaters and socks, I try to match the fiber and weight to the yarn for darning. For example, a cashmere sweater could be repaired with a thinner yarn like fingering or sport-weight cashmere or fine merino wool.

For darning, I typically use yarn from my stash, as only small amounts of yarn are needed for most repairs. I also keep a few skeins of white, or undyed cream, yarn in various weights for dye projects and darning. This way I can dye small amounts of yarn with home-grown or foraged dye materials and then use these special yarns to darn my garments. I prioritize 100 percent biodegradable yarns—mostly 100 percent wool—from independent farms, small yarn shops, and independent yarn designers. There is such a wealth of thoughtful and earth-friendly yarn lovers that there's no shortage of beautiful yarns. Choose thoughtfully and with love for the animals, farmers, and folks who make our fibers.

MEND: PROJECTS

Mending is central to my creative work and my advocacy for sustainability in fashion. The simple act of repairing clothes has transformed my textile work and altered the course of my life. It's not an overstatement to say that mending changed me. What started as a simple act of self-sufficiency—learning to repair my jeans—grew into an act of love, resistance, reclaiming, creative expression, self-acceptance, disruption, activism, and more. The huge turning point—my lightbulb moment—was when I realized I could use my background as an artist to apply simple design elements to the repairs on my jeans.

I use basic stitches in my repair work because I want the stitches to be accessible to all the students in my workshops, regardless of their experience with sewing or embroidery. I also use basic stitches because they are often all I need. Adding more decorative stitches is always an option, one I leave to the maker. But I like to remind folks that if your repairs are in hard-wearing places on your garment—like the upper thighs of your jeans—they are going to continue to receive friction and ultimately tear again. This is an opportunity to remember that mending is an ongoing process. Each repair is also an opportunity to strengthen our designs. Sometimes we might want to save decorative stitches for areas that receive less direct friction. But, again, that's up to you.

My visible mending on denim is largely influenced by traditional Japanese Boro and Sashiko. *Boro* translates to "rags," but has recently become synonymous with the patched, stitched, and mended garments of the Aomori Prefecture in Northern Japan during the Edo period. Boro evolved from the necessity to preserve the smallest scrap of fabric, add strength and warmth through patching, and use fibers like hemp and later cotton to withstand wide-ranging weather conditions. These Boro garments were mended with basic and utilitarian Sashiko stitches. While modern Sashiko has evolved into a more precise and highly skilled embroidery technique, traditional Sashiko stitches prioritized utility over precision—the stitches were meant to repair and patch garments while adding warmth. The history of Boro and Sashiko is very rich and beautifully documented in the gorgeous book *Boro: Rags and Tatters from the Far North of Japan.*

While my mending is inspired by Boro and Sashiko, particularly repairs on denim, I'm also influenced by the various darning techniques found throughout Europe. Each culture has its own history with making and repairing garments, and even a quick search for historic darning shows different examples in Sweden, Germany, Belgium, England, and so on. I'm fascinated by the culturally specific techniques and many variations for darning and mending clothing. My mending is also deeply inspired by the hand stitching and patchwork of my great-grandmother's quilts and my family's craft lineage. If we look across the globe, particularly before the rise of fast fashion, we can see various repair techniques across cultures, dating back to the beginning of textiles. Fibers were so valuable that we learned to repair our clothes. From this place of need, many beautiful techniques were developed that combined utility and design.

I use basic darning techniques to repair my sweaters, gloves, socks, and more. Based on the basic weave (sometimes called basic darn), my darning is often stitched in high-contrast color to the garment, drawing attention to the act of repair—much like the basic stitches I use to teach visible mending on denim, linen, and silk. But, if you are familiar with more decorative darning stitches—or if you knit, crochet, or weave and you'd like to use your favorite stitches to match the stitches in your knitted garment—please use what you have available to make a repair that is the most satisfying to you. After all, they are your clothes and I want you to feel 100 percent ownership of what makes you feel confident, expressive, and joyful.

BACK POCKET STITCHES

Denim has held an iconic place in our American wardrobes for ages, from the original Levi's work wear to Marilyn Monroe to seemingly every rock band. Some statistics claim the average American owns seven pairs of jeans. We love our denim. Yet it's not one of the most eco-friendly fabrics to produce, with its use of conventional cotton, high demand for water, and synthetic indigo dyes. Now, combined with synthetic fibers to get that popular stretch fit, it also breaks, tears, and frays rather quickly.

Yet I can't stop wearing it. What other fabric pairs so perfectly with linen tunics, wool sweaters, leather boots, clunky clogs, and strappy sandals? I try to shop as mindfully as possible when it comes to buying denim, supporting companies that produce sustainably, using organic cotton and/or natural indigo, or buying secondhand. For my older denim, however, mending is my solution. Luckily, denim is a gorgeous woven fabric that takes stitches and patches wonderfully, and grows more appealing with each repair. This simple back pocket mend uses reverse appliqué—the patch is on the inside and the stitches tack down the edges of the hole to prevent further damage. It's a favorite repair for knees, elbows, pockets, or any place a high-contrast mend is welcome.

Project 15

MATERIALS

Garment to be mended

Scrap fabric

Tape measure or ruler

Fabric scissors

Straight pins and safety pins

Washable fabric pen/pencil, such
   as tailor's chalk or a quilter's pen

Sashiko thread

Sashiko needles

Iron (optional)

Pinking shears (optional)

Needle-nose pliers (optional)

Embroidery scissors or snips for
   cutting thread (optional)

Thimble (optional)

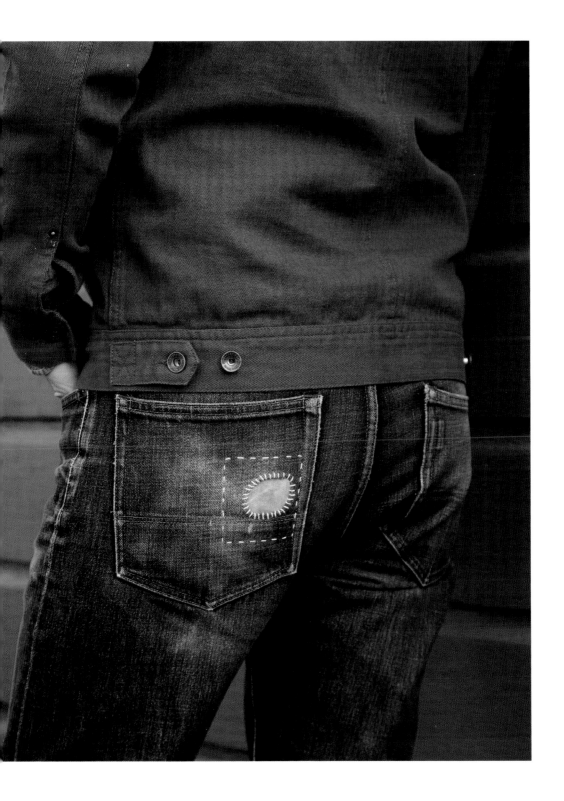

1 Lay the garment flat on your work surface. Iron if needed. Measure the hole or tear, adding ½ to 1 inch (1.3 cm to 2.5 cm) to all sides. Be generous: It's better to make a patch that's too big than too small. For example, if your tear is 1 inch (2.5 cm) wide, cut a patch that is 2 or 3 inches (5 or 7.5 cm) wide. This will allow you to cover the hole as well as the damaged, frayed, or weakened areas around it, and to sew your patch into strong fabric.

2 Cut the patch from your scrap fabric according to the measurements from Step 1. Use pinking shears if you want to help prevent the patch edges from fraying.

3

4

3 Trim the frayed edges of the hole or tear. This will give a clean edge for the upcoming stitches. I promise—your stitches will be prettier and more functional than that distressed fray.

4 Slip the patch inside the pocket. If you are repairing a hole or tear over a front pocket in a pair of jeans, be sure to slip the patch between the pocket lining and the hole so you don't sew the lining closed. Pin the patch in place with safety pins.

5 Using your washable fabric pen/pencil and a ruler, trace straight lines around the perimeter of the patch to mark its edges.

5

165

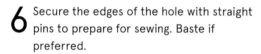

6 Secure the edges of the hole with straight pins to prepare for sewing. Baste if preferred.

7 Thread a needle, knot the thread at one end, and insert the needle from the garment's underside, keeping the knot hidden underneath. Take care not to sew the pocket body to the garment fabric underneath. Insert the needle just at the edge of the hole, and begin stitching with a whipstitch (page 41) around the perimeter of the hole, tacking the hole's edges to the patch, until all edges are sewn down. You can repeat with a second set of whipstitches if there are still visible areas of the hole to be sewn down. Remove pins as you sew.

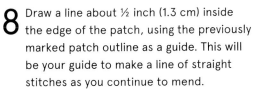

8 Draw a line about ½ inch (1.3 cm) inside the edge of the patch, using the previously marked patch outline as a guide. This will be your guide to make a line of straight stitches as you continue to mend.

9 Thread a needle, knot thread at one end, and insert the needle from the underside of the pocket, keeping the knot hidden underneath. Be careful not to sew the pocket body to the garment underneath. Using your marked guideline and a running stitch (page 41) or a straight stitch (page 40), stitch around the perimeter of the patch. Once you're finished, tie off the thread on the pocket's underside with a square knot, leaving a ½ inch (1.3 cm) tail on your thread.

UPPER THIGH/INSEAM STITCHES

Of all the repairs I teach in my classes, the most popular is the upper-thigh or crotch repair, particularly in denim. Our jeans are easily worn here because when most of us walk, run, dance, or otherwise move our beautiful legs, our thighs rub together. There are fairly simple ways to repair this area and get those pants back into rotation. My preferred method for the upper thighs of jeans is a subtle, low-contrast mend—although I love high-contrast visible mending on many parts of my clothes.

For this repair, I match the color, fiber, and weight of the patch and thread to the garment. And to keep the eye moving away from the upper-thigh mends, I add high-contrast stitches or patches to the back pocket, knee, belt loop, or other area of the pants. That said, if you do want to draw attention to the upper thighs of your jeans, by all means, use high-contrast materials and have fun.

Project 16

MATERIALS

Garment to be mended

Scrap fabric

Tape measure or ruler

Fabric scissors

Straight pins or safety pins

Washable fabric pen/pencil, such
     as tailor's chalk or a quilter's pen

Sashiko thread

Sashiko needles

Iron (optional)

Needle-nose pliers (optional)

Embroidery scissors or snips
     (optional)

Thimble (optional)

Pinking shears (optional)

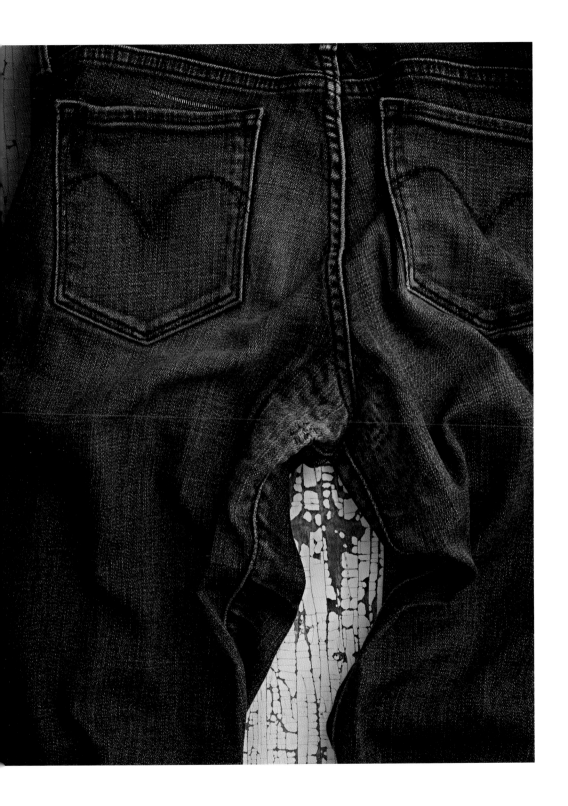

1 Lay the garment flat on your work surface. Iron if needed. Measure the tear or distressed area(s) at the upper-thigh inseams and crotch inseams, adding ½ to 1 inch (1.3 to 2.5 cm) to all sides. Be generous: It's better to make a patch that's too big than too small. This will allow you to cover the hole as well as the damaged, frayed, or weakened areas around it, and to sew your patch into strong fabric.

If the fabric on both front and back of each upper thigh's inseam needs mending, consider each side of the inseam a quadrant. You'll mend one side of each quadrant first, resulting in four separate but overlapping patches, if all quadrants need repairing.

2 Cut the patch from your fabric scrap according to the measurement in Step 1. Use pinking shears if using denim with a raw edge. (If repairing linen or other loosely woven fabrics with linen or loosely woven patches, finish the edges on the patch to prevent fraying.) Note: If desired, try to align the grain of the patch with the grain of the garment. If a less visible mend is desired, try to match all fiber weights, colors, and grainlines. For example, mend midweight, light denim jeans with a midweight, light denim patch and thread, with stitches following the same line as the garment's grain.

3 Trim frayed threads from the garment exterior. Turn the garment inside out. Trim frayed threads from the interior. This will give a clean edge for the upcoming stitches. I promise—your stitches will be prettier and more functional than that distressed fray.

Place the patch on the garment's underside and secure it with safety pins, or use basting stitches, if you prefer. Align the patch grainline and garment grainline as closely as possible, if desired. When the pins are in place, turn the garment right side out.

4 Using your washable fabric pen/pencil and a ruler, trace straight lines around the perimeter of the patch. This is your stitching guideline. You might want to switch to straight pins if that's easier.

5 With the patch edges pinned into place, use a fabric pencil to draw several straight lines approximately ¼ inch (6 mm) apart, parallel to each other. Draw enough lines to cover the whole patch. You can stitch along the grainline of the fabric if you're aiming for a less visible repair. (Note: If the garment is badly torn, you might want to use a whipstitch, as in the project Back Pocket Stitches on page 162, to first secure the edges of the holes before stitching the patch or secure the hole with darning stitches at the end of your mending.)

6 Thread a needle, knot the thread at one end, and insert the needle from the garment's underside, keeping the knot hidden underneath. Choose a marked guideline to sew the first line of running stitches (page 41). When you get to the next row, just drop vertical stitches down on the back side of the patch, inside garment. These vertical stitches won't show from the right side of the garment.

7 Continue sewing the running stitches until the patch is completely secured. Then tie off the thread on the underside of the garment with a knot, leaving a ½-inch (1.3-cm) tail on your thread.

8 To add darning stitches (page 194) for greater strength, sew stitches directly over the hole or most distressed area of the fabric. Align the stitches to one another, as you will use these as your warp when weaving in the next rows of stitches.

9 Make rows of stitches perpendicular to the warp stitches in Step 8 by weaving the thread in and out of the rows of vertical stitches. Keep weaving right to left, then left to right, until the stitches are tightly woven and hole or distressed area is completely secured with vertical and horizontal stitches.

PATCHWORK PANT LEGS

One of my favorite things about mending jeans is the possibility of continuing to mend them for years to come. Patches build layers and texture over time, offering an opportunity for a canvas of repairs—square and rectangular patches, vertical and horizontal stitches, adding color or print—to make the jeans more beautiful with each fix. Some of my first mending stitches are hidden under the knees of these jeans, and at this point I have repaired most of the original denim (I stopped counting after twenty-one mendings). They are now like a journal, a memoir, a record of each time I sat down to repair them so that I had the pleasure of wearing them again. And again.

This project offers the opportunity for patchwork as well as the chance to consider how layers hold the potential for experimenting with scale, composition, line, and color. These jeans are a wearable modern mending sampler—truly sharing my progress and documenting my mending memoir with each patch and stitch.

Project 17

MATERIALS
Garment to be mended
Scrap fabric
Tape measure or ruler
Fabric scissors
Straight pins or safety pins
Washable fabric pen/pencil, such
   as tailor's chalk or a quilter's pen
Sashiko thread
Sashiko needles
Iron (optional)
Pinking shears (optional)
Needle-nose pliers (optional)
Embroidery scissors or snips
   (optional)
Thimble (optional)

1 Lay the garment flat on your work surface. Iron if needed. Measure the hole or tear, adding ½ to 1 inch (1.3 to 2.5 cm) to all sides. Be generous: It's better to make a patch that's too big than too small. This will allow you to cover the hole as well as the damaged, frayed, or weakened areas around it, and to sew your patch into strong fabric.

Cut the patch from your scrap fabric according to the measurements from Step 1. Use pinking shears if you want to help prevent the patch edges from fraying.

2 Pin your chosen patch in place on top of the garment.

176

3 Using your washable fabric pen/pencil and a ruler, trace straight, parallel lines on top of the patch at approximately ¼ to ½ inch (6 mm to 1.3 cm) apart. Alternatively, if using striped fabric, use the lines on the patch as stitching guides.

4 Thread a needle, knot the thread at one end, and insert the needle from the underside of the garment, keeping the knot hidden underneath. Using your marked guidelines and a running stitch (page 41), stitch to the end of each marked line. When you get to the next row, simply drop down a vertical stitch down the back side of the patch, keeping these vertical lines on the garment's underside.

5 Continue sewing the running stitches until the patch is secured. Tie off the thread on the garment's underside, leaving a ½-inch (1.3-cm) tail on your thread to prevent unraveling.

6 Using your washable fabric pen/pencil and a ruler, draw a straight line ¼ inch (6 mm) from the edge of the patch on all sides. This will help you to create a tidy, even line when stitching.

7 Thread a needle, knot the thread at one end, and insert the needle from the underside of the garment. Using a whipstitch (page 41), secure all edges of the patch to the garment. Use a low-contrast thread if you like. If your hands get tired, use a thimble to push the needle and needle-nose pliers to pull the needle as you stitch.

8 Continue until the patch is secured, tie off the thread on the garment's underside, again leaving a ½-inch (1.3-cm) tail on your thread to prevent unraveling. Congratulations. You've given your jeans more patina, and even a bit of grace.

UNDERARM PATCHES

An elbow, pocket corner, button placket, or collar may be more fun than an underarm to patch, but the underarms are a typical place of distress. Even here there's still the creative opportunity of visible mending. In repairing this tunic, I used a patch that felt intentional and beautiful, adding to the overall design. Using plant-dyed patches, special threads, or favorite offcuts for patches is a good way to make the repair more meaningful.

In thinking about the tunic's design, I weighed the merits of putting a patch under just one arm or adding a second to make it symmetrical. To strengthen the design, I chose symmetry. But random patches on the torso, elbows, or collar would make the repair scheme seem part of the initial design too. I even consider where I'll add more external patches over time—creating a journal of mending stories.

Project 18

MATERIALS

Garment to be mended

Scrap fabric

Tape measure or ruler

Fabric scissors

Straight pins or safety pins

Washable fabric pen/pencil, such
   as tailor's chalk or a quilter's pen

Sashiko thread

Sashiko needles

Iron (optional)

Pinking shears (optional)

Embroidery scissors or snips
   (optional)

Thimble (optional)

1 Lay the garment flat on your work surface. Iron if needed. If the patch fabric is lightweight or frays easily, plan to finish its edges by turning them under to prevent fraying. Measure the hole or tear, adding ½ to 1 inch (1.3 to 2.5 cm) to all sides. You might add more if turning under the patch's edges. Consider the color of your patch, thread, and garment, and whether you want a high- or low-contrast repair. Cut the patch from your scrap fabric according to these measurements. Cut a second patch if mending both underarms, or if symmetry is part of the design.

2 Center the patch over the torn or damaged area of the garment. Turn the edges of the patch under by ¼ inch (6 mm) and press with an iron to create finished edges. Miter, square, or round the patch's corners as desired. Pin the patch in place, right side facing up. Try on the garment and check the patch placement in a mirror—is it at the right height on the armpit? Readjust if needed. Also, consider the drape of the arm and make sure the patch won't interrupt any draping or movement.

3

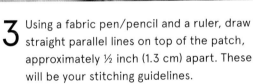

4

3 Using a fabric pen/pencil and a ruler, draw straight parallel lines on top of the patch, approximately ½ inch (1.3 cm) apart. These will be your stitching guidelines.

4 Thread a needle, knot the thread at one end, and insert the needle from the underside of the garment, keeping the knot hidden underneath. Sew a line of running stitches (page 41) along each marked line. When you get to the next row, simply drop down a vertical stitch down the back side of the patch, on the garment's underside.

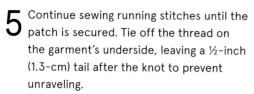

5 Continue sewing running stitches until the patch is secured. Tie off the thread on the garment's underside, leaving a ½-inch (1.3-cm) tail after the knot to prevent unraveling.

6 Check the tear from the underside of the garment to be certain the edges were secured by running stitches. If not, add stitches to the edges of the hole until they are secured to the patch. Keep adding stitches until you're satisfied that the repair is stable. Repeat on the second underarm if needed. Wear with pride!

"Darning can just be simple, practical mending activities as well as artistic or decorative needlework. You can enjoy this activity in your own style and at your own speed. It's not important to be neat or messy. It can be a private activity too. Moth holes, stains, and tears happen by accident, which I like. You might be surprised, sad, or shocked to see these damages, but those feelings become good energy to start to darn. Feeling that you can control your personal belonging's life by yourself is fantastic. Because we don't have many opportunities to fix something with our own hands these days. The quality of garments has declined compared to thirty years ago. Somehow, we have learned to throw away even slightly damaged garments. Garments become consumable products and people forget to respect each item and that doesn't help you to be happier."

HIKARU NOGUCHI
artist & author

COLLAR REPAIRS

Our ancestors treasured their clothing in ways that fast fashion has made nearly obsolete. As clothing has been made at faster speeds, with lower-quality fibers and unethical labor practices, the result is too often cheap clothing with a very short life. My great-grandmother would be aghast at the quality of today's clothes, and that her great-grandchildren might not darn their torn sweaters, stitch fallen hemlines, or turn button-down collars.

I try each year of my Make Thrift Mend project to make progress, but there is still much work to be done to honor and practice these traditional garment repairs. Luckily, there's an army of mindful makers, concerned designers, and conscious shoppers that want to turn the fast-fashion tide into a more sustainable, thoughtful future. A common spot for wear is our shirt collars. This repair offers a traditional fix for fraying in this vulnerable area. It's called "turning a collar" and it's exactly that—remove the collar from the shirt, mend it, and then turn it over when you sew it back down.

MATERIALS
Garment to be mended
Scrap fabric
Seam ripper
Tape measure or ruler
Fabric scissors
Straight pins
Washable fabric pen/pencil, such
   as tailor's chalk or a quilter's pen
Embroidery or Sashiko thread
Embroidery or Sashiko needles
Iron (optional)
Pinking shears (optional)
Embroidery scissors or snips
   (optional)
Thimble (optional)
Sewing machine (optional)

1 Lay the garment flat on your work surface. Iron if needed. Using a seam ripper or snips, remove the collar from the shirt by carefully ripping out existing stitches at the collar's base, where it joins the collar band.

2 Measure the hole in the collar, adding up to 1 inch (2.5 cm) on each side to cover the hole completely. Cut the patch from your scrap fabric according to this measurement. Slip the patch inside the hole. If the hole to be repaired is close to an intact seam (top or sides), trim the patch so it fits and lays flat between the layers; if it extends beyond the open edge, trim it flush so the excess doesn't get in the way when sewing the collar back on. Then, pin the patch's corners to the top of the collar so that you can open the collar along the bottom edge to stitch.

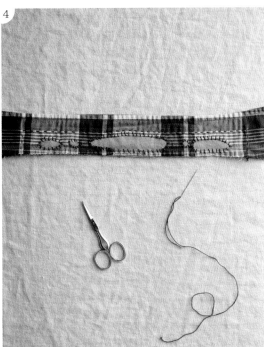

3 Fold under the edges of the hole and pin or baste to patch. Thread a needle, knot the thread at one end, slip the needle between the collar layers and insert the needle into the patch, keeping the knot hidden underneath the patch. Begin sewing whipstitches (page 41) from between the layers of the collar around the edge of the hole. These stitches will tack the edge of the hole into place. Continue stitching.

4 Once the edges of the hole are stitched in place, sew a few running stitches (page 41) around the perimeter of the entire patch to secure it in place. Use a fabric pen/pencil and ruler to trace straight lines for stitching guidelines.

5 Once the patch is stitched, slip the mended collar back into the top of the collar band, flipping the collar so that the mended side is on the underside of the collar when folded into place. The undamaged part of the collar is now on top and the mended side is hidden. Pin the collar into place.

6 Using running stitches, by hand or with a sewing machine, as you prefer, sew the collar back into place at the top of the collar band. Your repair will be your secret. Finding vintage shirts with these hand-sewn repairs is always such a pleasant surprise.

"Mending clothing is a type of detective work. Looking for clues in damage about the maker and wearer of the garment. Paying attention to where things fray and wear out. Then deciding what move you're going to make to repair it: Do you fill the hole, stitch the sides together, are you in a rush or do you have time to mend slowly? There are decisions about whether you make your repair in a similar or contrasting color, with rough or smooth yarn, or simply with what is at hand. The more you mend, the easier the decisions are. You are training your fingers to do the thinking."

CELIA PYM
artist & mender

DARN: **sweater**

The tight weave and fine threads of knitted cashmere result in soft, luxurious garments that beckon us to maintain them for many years. With very basic darning, holes or frays in fine knitwear can be repaired and adorned. Although it's important to match the weight of the darning yarn to the weight of the yarn in the garment, it's not essential to match the exact fiber (although it could add sentiment if repairing a handmade sweater and locating the original fiber or farm yarn). I like to add bright, contrasting repairs that punctuate the overall garment, so for this navy sweater I scanned my small yarn stash and chose a tiny skein of bright pink baby merino to cartwheel across the surface. (The knitters among you—who might have substantial stashes of yarn from finished projects—may be able to match color, weight, and fiber for your repairs.)

MATERIALS

Garment to be mended

Tape measure or ruler

Washable fabric marker pen/
    pencil, such as tailor's chalk or
    a quilter's pen

Yarn

Fabric or embroidery scissors for
    cutting yarn

Yarn/darning needles

Darning egg or mushroom
    (optional)

Thimble (optional)

Project 20

192

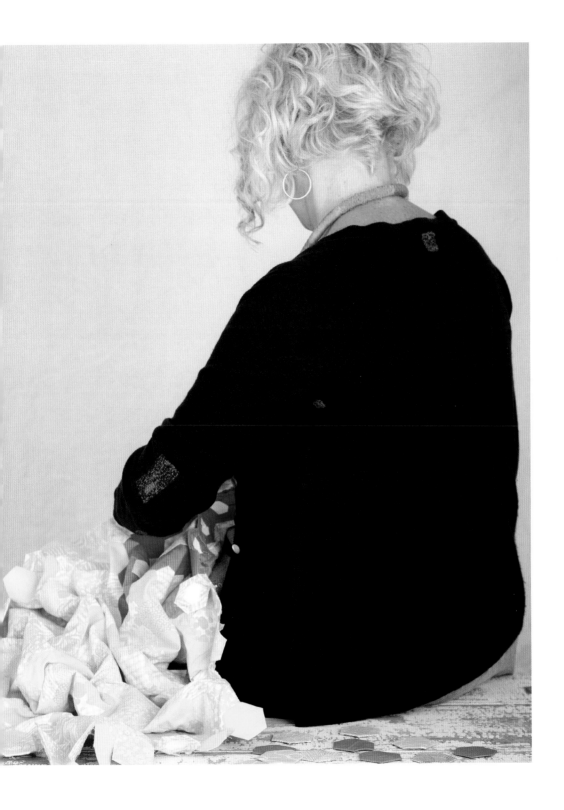

1 Lay the garment flat on your work surface. Choose contrasting or matching yarn. Cut approximately 18 inches (46 cm) of yarn from the skein. Thread your yarn needle. There's no need to knot the end of the yarn, as it will be woven in at the end. Leave 2- to 3-inch (5- to 7.5-cm) tail on your yarn for easy weaving later. (Note: I use darning eggs for socks and darning mushrooms for flat surfaces, but with a tiny hole like the one shown, I typically don't use a darning tool. But use one, if you prefer.)

2 Use your washable fabric pen/pencil or chalk to draw a square (or circle, or rectangle, or the shape of your choice) around the hole about ½ inch (1.3 cm) on all sides or until you attain the shape desired. Be sure to extend the shape at least about ½ inch (1.3 cm) from the edge of the hole to ensure you are stitching into the undamaged part of the garment.

3

4

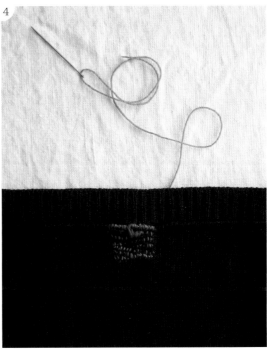

3 Insert the needle from the underside of the sweater and begin making vertical lines of running stitches (page 41) along the first marked line. When you get to the end of the first row, simply turn and repeat in the opposite direction. Maintain that 2 to 3 inches (5 to 7.5 cm) of thread tail at the needle end as you work. If you run out of thread before the darning is complete, pull the thread tail to the underside of the sweater, rethread the needle, and reinsert it into the mending, leaving a new tail.

4 When your stitches reach the hole, try to keep them close together to cover the hole completely—jump from one edge of the hole to the other, landing a scant ¼ inch (6 mm) from the hole to stitch into the undamaged fiber. In weaving terminology, these are the vertical (warp) stitches that will be woven with horizontal (weft) stitches in the next step. See next photo for details. Continue making warp stitches, as in Step 3, until you've filled in the outlined shape.

5

6

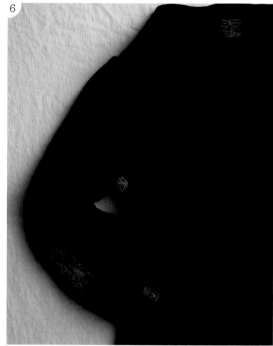

5 With your vertical (warp) stitches in place, begin a row of horizontal (weft) running stitches. When you get to the hole, weave the weft stitches through the warp stitches—a very simple under/over pattern—then continue to the edge of the shape. Reverse direction and continue making weft stitches, again weaving across the hole, until you've filled the outlined shape. If your weaving is uneven, it's okay. Just do your best to get the stitches close together so that there is no gap or hole remaining.

6 When you've finished weaving the weft stitches, take the thread to the inside of the sweater, turn the sweater inside out, and weave the ends of the yarns into the underside of the repair. With a bit of wear, perhaps a gentle handwashing or blocking, the darning will settle into place. Be forewarned: People will take notice! I have a friend who has been flagged down from across the street for her gorgeous darning.

For further reading on weaving patterns that can be applied to darning, try *On Weaving,* the seminal work of the late textile artist Anni Albers.

"I find similarities to drawing and mending, the mending is not just a means to fix a hole—it's also meant to be visually appealing, about composition, and about the linear elements of the threads and shapes of the patches. Sometimes the damage will dictate the shape and composition of the end product, at which point it's really about the history of the piece through its use. But in other instances, I use other aspects to determine the shape, such as if I want to bring an image to the piece or use the structure of the garment to inform the shape of the mend. I like working with a variety of mediums and I think when they are combined together it builds up layers that make it visually interesting. I really enjoy embroidery; it has a slow, meditative quality that makes you aware of your movements and gestures."

AROUNNA KHOUNNORAJ
Bookhou

DARN: **gloves**

These elbow-length cashmere gloves were a gift years ago, and I have treasured wearing them under three-quarter-sleeve sweaters ever since. They bring back fond memories of an overcast, drizzly day in San Francisco when I convinced a couple of friends to be my models for a photography project. One of them wore these gloves and twirled and frolicked through various parks as I photographed until we were so cold that we sought out steaming cups of hot chocolate.

Years later and three thousand miles away, I came across these gloves stashed beneath some winter sweaters. I'd worn the gloves so much I'd torn a hole in the thumb. In order to get them in shape to face Hudson Valley winters, some darning was needed. So, complete with plant-dyed yarns and some basic mending methods, I've put these beloved gloves back in my wardrobe. At some point I'll reinforce many of the fingertips to keep them strong and steady, just as they were back in San Francisco. (Note: Model Denise Bayron wears her own hand-knit sweater, Indoorsy, and hand-knit accessory, Droplet Capelet, of her own design.)

MATERIALS
Garment to be mended
Yarn
Tape measure or ruler
Fabric or embroidery scissors
Yarn/darning needles
Darning tool, such as a glove
    darner, darning egg or
    mushroom, or wooden spoon
Washable pen/pencil, such as
    tailor's chalk or a quilter's pen
Rubber band or ribbon (optional)
Thimble (optional)

1 Lay the glove flat on your work surface. Choose contrasting or matching yarn for the repair, matching the weight and fiber to the glove, if possible. Cut approximately 18 inches (46 cm) of yarn from the skein. Thread your yarn needle. There's no need to knot the end of the yarn, as it will be woven in at the end. Leave 2- to 3-inch (5- to 7.5-cm) tail on your yarn for easy weaving later.

2 Insert a glove darner, wooden spoon handle, or darning tool into the glove. If desired, cinch the tool in place with a rubber band or ribbon. Use a fabric pencil to draw a square around the hole about ½ inch (1.3 cm) on all sides or until you attain the shape you desire. Be sure to extend the shape about ½ inch (1.3 cm) from the edge of the hole to ensure that you are stitching into the undamaged part of the garment.

3 Insert the threaded needle from inside the glove and begin making vertical lines of running stitches (page 41), starting at the marked outline. When you get to the end of the first row, simply turn and repeat in the opposite direction. Keep your stitches directly adjacent and parallel to the previous row—this is the warp of your simple weaving that will darn the hole.

4 When your stitches reach the hole, try to keep them close together to cover the hole completely—jump from one edge of the hole to the other, landing ¼ inch (6 mm) from the hole's edge in the undamaged fiber. In weaving terminology, these are the vertical (warp) stitches that will be woven with horizontal (weft) stitches in the next step. (See next photo for details.) Continue making warp stitches, as in Step 3, until you've filled in the outlined shape.

5

6

5 With your vertical (warp) stitches in place, begin a row of horizontal (weft) running stitches. When you get to the hole, weave the weft stitches through the warp stitches—a very simple under/over pattern—then continue to the edge of the shape. Reverse direction and continue making weft stitches, again weaving across the hole, until you've filled the outlined shape. If your weaving is uneven, it's okay. Just do your best to get the stitches close together so that there is no gap or hole remaining. If you like, the weft stitches can be a contrasting color to the warp stitches, creating a lovely pattern.

6 When you've finished weaving the weft stitches, turn the glove inside out and weave the ends of the yarns into the underside of the repair. With a bit of wear, perhaps a gentle handwashing or blocking, the darning will settle into place. Your gloves are now ready to tackle the elements.

"Mending begins as love. We mend a beat-up garment because we love it. And the more we mend it, the more our love for it grows. So, we keep mending. And wearing. And mending and wearing again.

And then one day we discover something a little bit startling. Something new emerges in the garment. It transforms into something not just lovable, but beautiful. A nobility emerges. It becomes an old soul.

It's strange that a humble, mundane act, repeated enough times, can lead to something as lofty as transcendence. To be honest, I don't know how it works. As often as I've seen the transformation, each new mend still begins with uncertainty, fueled by love for the garment and led by hope for its transformation. And it's precisely this mystery that keeps me coming back to mending as a practice. Every mend is a new chance to exercise love and embrace hope."

MATT RHO
denim mender

DARN: **socks**

There's something so lovely about a repaired wool sock. It feels extravagant and subversively beautiful all at once. While I don't darn every cotton sock for my family of four, I do treasure my mended wool socks. Surprisingly, as beloved knee socks wear and tear, I am oddly eager to mend them. If you knit your socks, you can surely relate. I have several darning tools—vintage wooden eggs and darning mushrooms—but tennis balls, potatoes, plastic Easter eggs, and various firm household objects will do. For this project, I chose bright pink yarn from my stash and plant-dyed yellow yarn to create a simple contrasting pattern.

Project 22

MATERIALS
Garment to be mended
Yarn
Yarn/darning needles
Fabric or embroidery scissors for
    cutting yarn
Tape measure or ruler
Washable fabric pen/pencil, such
    as tailor's chalk or a quilter's pen
Darning tool, such as a darning egg
    or mushroom (optional)
Thimble (optional)

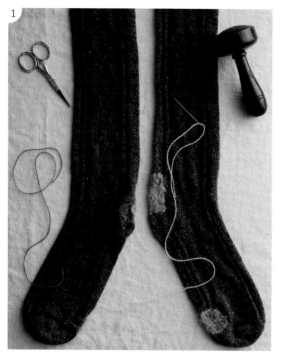

1 Lay the sock flat on your work surface. Choose contrasting or matching yarn, matching the weight and fiber of the sock, if possible. Cut approximately 18 inches (46 cm) of yarn from the skein. Thread your yarn needle. There's no need to knot the end of the yarn, as it will be woven in at the end. Leave 2- to 3-inch (5- to 7.5-cm) tail on your yarn for easy weaving later.

2 Insert a darning egg or darning tool into the sock. If desired, cinch the tool in place with a rubber band or ribbon. Use a fabric pencil to draw a square around the hole about ½ inch (1.3 cm) on all sides or until you attain the shape you desire. Be sure to extend the shape at least ½ inch (1.3 cm) from the edge of the hole to ensure that you are stitching into the undamaged part of the garment.

3 Insert the threaded needle from the underside of the sock and begin making vertical lines of running stitches (page 41), starting at the marked outline. When you get to the end of the first row, simply turn and repeat in the opposite direction. Keep your stitches directly adjacent and parallel to the previous row—this is the warp of your simple weaving that will darn the hole.

4 When your stitches reach the hole, try to keep them close together to cover the hole completely—jump from one edge of hole to the other, landing about ¼ inch (6 mm) from the hole's edge in the undamaged fiber. In weaving terminology, these are the vertical (warp) stitches that will be woven with horizontal (weft) stitches in the next step. (See next photo for details.) Continue making warp stitches, as in Step 3, until you've filled in the outlined shape.

5 With your vertical (warp) stitches in place, begin a row of horizontal (weft) running stitches from one corner. When you get to the hole, weave weft stitches through the warp stitches—a very simple under/over pattern—then continue to the edge of the shape. Reverse direction and continue making weft stitches, again weaving across the hole, until you've filled the outlined shape. If your weaving is uneven, it's okay. Just do your best to get the stitches close together so that there is no gap or hole remaining.

6 When you've finished weaving the weft stitches, turn the sock inside out and weave the ends of the yarns into the underside of the repair. With a bit of wear, perhaps a gentle handwashing or blocking, the darning will settle into place and might even felt with walking. Wear with a pair of backless clogs to show off your darning!

208

Mending as Healing:
Individual and Collective Action

The metaphors related to mending and repairing are endless. The work of mending our clothing quickly transfers to the work of healing our relationship to our bodies and our planet. Through textiles we can analyze the history of capitalism, colonialism, economics, export, import, agriculture, labor, religion, art, costume, culture, and nearly everything we've touched as humans. We've been wearing and repairing our clothing since the beginning of recorded history.

Yet this moment in fashion and life on this planet is unlike any before. This moment is begging us to consider our habits. It's showing not-so-subtle symptoms of being overworked, overharvested, and underappreciated. We can point fingers in every direction—and some need pointing at the legislators who can affect policy to make colossal shifts—yet we can also point that finger at ourselves. As consumers, we can use our resources (time, money, and skill) to influence industry and politics. We don't have to look much further than the eruption of organic food options to remember that consumption is a two-way relationship between supply and demand or industry and consumer. Just a few decades back, organic food was not nearly so readily available. Individuals and collectives of individuals forced that shift.

We can look at our individual and collective behaviors and see an opportunity for seismic change. I believe in top-down (policy-led) and bottom-up (citizen-led) social change, and that sustained social shifts take both. All too often our politicians are a few months, or even years, behind activists' messages and the pulse of community interest. In the United States, we send our messages by voting for politicians that represent our values. Or that's the hope. But even amid the fiercest pessimism we can see the changes in the environmental movement in the last fifty years and know that more change is possible, probable, and essential.

The seventies paved the way toward contemporary sustainable fashion with secondhand clothing and leather sandals and now we are witnessing a huge shift in mainstream fashion—gigantic fashion brands, mainstream publications, and iconic fashion leaders are proclaiming their dedication to reducing environmental impact. This is reason to celebrate. Yet the rate at which we consume and discard goods still needs to shift. We can buy all the organic cotton T-shirts on the planet and still need to confront what we'll do with those shirts when they need to be washed, dried, repaired, recycled, or ultimately discarded. We cannot buy our way to a sustainable future.

We will need to shift consumer habits and start discerning what we bring into our homes—or what our industries produce—from the onset. We will need to claim responsibility for those goods from the moment we purchase or design them until we discard them or use them as recycled materials to make something else. If we do, we'll hopefully see a proliferation of buy-back, take-back, and recycling programs from fashion brands around the world.

We're still living in a linear economy trying to create circular systems—like mending our blue jeans instead of tossing them into a landfill while denim companies continue to use raw materials to make new jeans. Amid all of this conversation of circularity, mindful shopping, and sustainable fashion, there's still an incredible opportunity in repair. Through mending we slow down consumption, extend the life of our garments, and increase resilience and technical skill.

Just as importantly, though harder to assess, when we repair our clothing, we repair a bit of ourselves. We take the time to stitch, patch, darn, and mend, and this metaphor seeps into our relationship with our bodies, our behaviors, and our mindset. It creates a shift. It disrupts a pattern. It mandates a pause. And in this interruption, we can make the time and space for healing.

If we let mending conjure up all the images of healing—broken bones, heartfelt conversations, vulnerable decisions, splints, casts, and patches—then we can see the act of mending as an act of repair. We can go deep into the tissues of the heart as we study the weave of our fabrics. Repairing, restoring, repatterning as we go. Synonyms for mending are numerous: fixing, restoring, repairing, healing, relieving, rebuilding, recovering, reforming, correcting, altering, strengthening, reconciling, amending, and improving. We mend torn clothes, broken bones, fraught relationships, a leaky roof, and ingrained behavioral patterns. We mend people. We mend places. We mend things. We also mend interpersonal dynamics, painful emotions, and haunting memories. All of these repairs are linked in some subtle or not-so-subtle ways.

As I mend my torn blue jeans I recognize that I'm also mending my relationship to my body—the body that broke the clothing—and accepting my body as it is. Instead of masking the repairs, I embellish, celebrate, and honor them. I accept that as long as I keep wearing clothing, and moving, playing, working in that clothing, my clothes will fray and rip. But through my repairs I can honor the body and the experience that distressed the fibers. What better way to rip a pair of jeans than by dancing? The body swaying and spinning with delight. Or what better way to age a favorite cardigan than by pressing elbows into studio desks and kitchen countertops and resting on armchairs while knitting? The points of the arm relaxing against the table surface while the hands toiled away at making art, food, or warm garments.

Yet mending has a larger global metaphor. As we mend our textiles we work on an individual scale to mend overconsumption, fast fashion, and the unethical treatment of people and the planet. I'm not suggesting that mending a garment corrects the ills of underpaid employment—it doesn't. Nor am I suggesting that repairing a sweater is an act equal to repairing the exploitation of unrenewable resources. It isn't. But it's an important start for individual lifestyles. And maybe one person mending their jeans doesn't reverse climate change or save the planet, but thousands of menders will have an impact. Through this action we can start to shift behaviors and mindsets that led to overconsumption. And maybe we can also inspire our neighbors, colleagues, and families to mend their jeans and more.

Instead of tossing that torn garment and buying another, we mend the one we own, keep it from the landfill, and honor the resources of labor and materials that created it. We keep the garment in rotation. We learn the technical skill of mending. We extend the garment's usefulness and we honor the handwork required to mend. We also resist the economic model of fast fashion that says it would probably be "cheaper" to toss that garment and buy new. But the cost of overconsuming and discarding textiles goes much deeper than our wallets. Cost analysis needs to include the cost of the raw materials, labor, transportation, laundering, recycling, discarding, and more. Ultimately, this cost would include its carbon footprint and that of buying new.

Marketing convinces us daily that we will feel better if we buy better. But we all know this isn't true. That quick elation is soon replaced by feelings of want. And if we don't unearth the cause of the want, then we can't redirect the habit.

Some of these healing opportunities are literal—we can wear plant medicine as natural dyes in our garments—but most of these experiences are metaphorical. It's difficult to explain the way it feels to wear a pair of jeans I've mended more than twenty-one times, but I can tell you that it feels like commitment. Like creative expression. Like the manifestation of skill-building—the visible record of my mending skills progressing with each patch. And it also feels like an act of love. For my pants. For my body. For my creativity. And for the plants and people who made my clothing.

If we use our impact in our personal industries (work, schools, offices, homes, studios, etc.) we can create and sustain environmental action. Then we can use this momentum to pressure policy shifts and engage local, regional, national, and international politicians and businesses to enforce or implement change. And this can all grow and deepen. But it takes all of us doing what we can. Together. It starts with one action and the ongoing commitment to that action: Today I will mend my jeans as they continue to break down, and tomorrow I will keep mending.

resources

CONTRIBUTORS

quoted artists

Aidan Owen, www.
    groundinginthespirit.wordpress.com
Arounna Khounnoraj,
    www.bookhou.com
Celia Pym, www.celiapym.com
Christi Johnson,
    www.mixedcolor.net
Hikaru Noguchi,
    www.hikarunoguchi.com
India Flint, www.indiaflint.com
Jen Hewett, www.jenhewett.com
Kathy Hattori,
    www.botanicalcolors.com
Kenya Miles,
    www.travelingmilesstudio.com
Kristine Vejar,
    www.averbforkeepingwarm.com
Matt Rho,
    www.instagram.com/rhomatt
Meg McElwee, www.sewliberated.com
Nina & Sonya Montenegro,
    www.thefarwoods.com
Sasha Duerr,
    www.sashaduerr.com
Sonya Philip,
    www.100actsofsewing.com

sewing pattern designers

100 Acts of Sewing by Sonya Philip,
    www.100actsofsewing.com
Klum House by Ellie Lum,
    www.klumhouse.com
Made by Rae, by Rae Hoekstra,
    www.made-by-rae.com
Sew Liberated by Meg McElwee,
    www.sewliberated.com
Wiksten by Jenny Gordy,
    www.shopwiksten.com

models

Denise Bayron,
    www.bayronhandmade.com
David Szlasa, www.davidszlasa.com
Katharine Daugherty,
    www.dropforgeandtool.com
Yuko Yamamoto,
    www.instagram.com/yukoyp

further reading

The Act of Sewing, Sonya Philip

A Field Guide to Color, Lisa Solomon

Alabama Studio Sewing + Design,
    Natalie Chanin

All We Can Save, Ayana Elizabeth
    Johnson and Katharine K. Wilkinson

Boro, Yukiko Koide and Kyoichi Tsuzuki

Braiding Sweetgrass,
    Robin Wall Kimmerer

The Common Thread,
    Vanessa von Gliszczynski

The Conscious Closet, Elizabeth Cline

Craft, Tanya Harrod

Craft of Use, Kate Fletcher

The Curated Closet, Anuschka Rees

Darning, Hikaru Noguchi

Eco Colour, India Flint

Eco Fashion, Sass Brown

Fashion and Sustainability,
    Kate Fletcher and Lynda Grose

Fibershed, Rebecca Burgess

Fray, Julia Bryan-Wilson

The Geometry of Hand-Sewing,
    Natalie Chanin

Harvesting Color, Rebecca Burgess

How to Do Nothing, Jenny Odell

How to Not Always Be Working,
    Marlee Grace

Journeys in Natural Dyeing, Kristine
    Vejar and Adrienne Rodriguez

Lo-TEK, Julia Watson

Loved Clothes Last, Fashion
    Revolution

Make Ink, Jason Logan

Make + Mend, Jessica Marquez

Mend & Patch, Kerstin Neumüller

Mending Life, Nina and Sonya
    Montenegro

Mending Matters, Katrina Rodabaugh

The Modern Natural Dyer,
    Kristine Vejar

More Than Enough, Elaine Welteroth

Mystical Stitches, Christi Johnson

Naked Fashion, Safia Minney

The Nani Iro Sewing Studio, Naomi Ito

Natural Color, Sasha Duerr

Natural Palettes, Sasha Duerr

On Weaving, Anni Albers

Overdressed, Elizabeth Cline

Print, Pattern, Sew, Jen Hewett

Punch Needle, Arounna Khounnoraj

ReFashioned, Sass Brown

Rise & Resist, Clare Press

Second Skin, India Flint

Sewing Happiness, Sanae Ishida

Slow Fashion, Safia Minney

Slow Stitch, Claire Wellesley-Smith

Sustainable Fashion and Textiles,
    Kate Fletcher

This Long Thread, Jen Hewett

Tie-Dye, Shabd Simon-Alexander

Visible Mending, Arounna Khounnoraj

Vitamin T, Jenelle Porter

Wardrobe Crisis, Clare Press

Wild Color, Jenny Dean

Woven & Worn, Canopy Press

select organizations and
educational resources

Alabama Chanin, School of Making
Blue Light Junction
Blue: The Tatter Textile Library
Center for Craft
Centre for Sustainable Fashion
Clean Clothes Campaign
Craft of Use
Eileen Fisher Renew
Ellen MacArthur Foundation
Fabric Workshop and Museum
Fashion Revolution
Fibershed
Intersectional Environmentalist
Maiwa School of Textiles
Patagonia Worn Wear
Repair Café
RiverBlue (documentary)
Slow Factory Foundation
Textile Arts Center
The Textile Museum at George
    Washington University
The True Cost (documentary)

you can often find supplies at
your local fabric shops or major
craft chains, but here are some
of my favorite supply shops for
mending, dyeing, and sewing:

A Verb for Keeping Warm
Botanical Colors
Brooklyn General Store
Dharma Trading Company
Echoview Fiber Mill
Fancy Tiger Crafts
Gather Here
Loop London
Maiwa
Merchant & Mills
Organic Cotton Plus
Purl Soho
Shibori Dragon
Sri Threads
Stonemountain & Daughter

acknowledgments

Thank you to my colleagues, students, and creative community who make my work possible. Your support means everything. Thank you for encouraging me to carve this unknowable journey towards Slow Fashion and sustainable living.

A huge thanks to my photographer, Karen Pearson, for making my photography dreams come true. Endless thanks to my editor, Shawna Mullen, and my agent, Judy Linden, for continued mentorship, wisdom, and enthusiasm. Thank you to the entire team at Abrams Books, especially Deb Wood for another beautiful book and Nanette Maxim for thoughtful edits.

To my incredible models and friends—Denise Bayron of Bayron Handmade, Katharine Daugherty of Drop Forge & Tool, and Yuko Yamamoto. Thank you for collaborating with me and wearing my clothes. A big thank you to Toni Brogan for styling some of the most beautiful images. Thank you to Jamie Lyn Kara, for ongoing support, wit, and invaluable insights.

Thank you to all the artists, designers, and makers who shared their work in these pages. Thank you to the plants, animals, and ecosystems that supported all the fibers and dye materials in this book. And to all the humans who worked in the factories, farms, and spaces of the fashion industry to make these clothes, fabrics, and fibers—thank you.

To my mother and grandmothers, Carol, Mary, and Leona, for this lineage of stitches and love of textiles. Thank you for making the time to make beautiful things with all you were tending. Thank you to my husband, David, for being the best chef, model, cheerleader, collaborator, co-parent, and life partner I could imagine, while writing a book and otherwise. I love you and this wild journey. To my sons, Maxwell and Jude: You are everything! You can be anything! You are all the things. This book is for you. All the books I ever write are for you. Forever.

about the author

Katrina Rodabaugh is an award-winning artist and writer working across disciplines to explore environmental and social issues through craft techniques. Put simply, she works at the intersection of fiber, fashion, and sustainability. She has gained international attention from artists, designers, and editors for her work ranging from visible mending to plant dyes to handmade objects and multimedia art installations. Straddling fine art and contemporary craft, her artwork, writing, and designs have been featured in venues across the United States and abroad, including various books, magazines, blogs, galleries, theaters, libraries, craft fairs, and a portable tiny house built by her husband.

Since launching her fast-fashion fast Make Thrift Mend in 2013, she has been leading sold-out textile workshops across the United States and teaching her unique mending and sustainable fashion techniques to thousands of students. In addition, Katrina writes, advocates, and organizes special events like fiber-arts retreats in her converted barn studio and across the United States. Her bestselling book, *Mending Matters: Stitch, Patch, and Repair Your Favorite Denim & More,* was published by Abrams Books in 2018. She earned a B.A. in Environmental Studies and an M.F.A. in Creative Writing. Katrina currently lives with her husband and young sons in a two-hundred-year-old farmhouse in the Hudson Valley of New York, where she grows dye plants, forages herbs, and tends chickens and honeybees. Visit www.katrinarodabaugh.com or Instagram @katrinarodabaugh.

Editor: Shawna Mullen
Designer: Deb Wood
Production Manager: Kathleen Gaffney

Library of Congress Control Number: 2020944099

ISBN: 978-1-4197-4399-3
eISBN: 978-1-68335-900-5

Printed and bound in China
10 9 8 7 6 5 4 3 2 1

Note: The activities and materials discussed in this book may be potentially toxic, hazardous
or dangerous. Please take all safety precautions and follow all instructions. Handle dyes,
mordants, and foraged plants with the utmost care. The author has made every effort to provide
well researched, sufficient and up-to-date information; however, we also urge caution in the
use of this information. The author and publisher do not accept liability for any accidents,
injuries, loss, legal consequences, or incidental or consequential damage incurred by any reader
for the mishandling or misuse of these materials or in reliance on the information or advice
provided in this book. Readers should seek health and safety advice from physicians and safety
and medical professionals.

Abrams books are available at special discounts when purchased in quantity for premiums
and promotions as well as fundraising or educational use. Special editions can also be created
to specification. For details, contact specialsales@abramsbooks.com or the address below.

Abrams® is a registered trademark of Harry N. Abrams, Inc.

ABRAMS The Art of Books
195 Broadway, New York, NY 10007
abramsbooks.com

MIX
Paper from
responsible sources
FSC™ C144853

COLLINS GUIDE TO

Animal Tracks and Signs

*The tracks and signs of
British and European mammals
and birds*

Text
PREBEN BANG

Illustrations
PREBEN DAHLSTROM

Translated and adapted by
GWYNNE VEVERS

Collins

St James's Place, London

How to use this book

In order to make this a useful field handbook the contents have been arranged according to the type of track or sign that the reader may find in the wild, rather than in a systematic zoological order.

For instance, if you find a broken hazelnut shell, turn to the table dealing with nuts (see Contents). By comparing the nut with the specimens illustrated you should be able to determine the animal that has handled it. The table will also refer you to the text section which gives a more detailed account of the characteristic way in which the animal concerned actually handles nuts, and gives information on its feeding places. By reading this section and comparing the nut with the illustrations you can check on the accuracy of your first identification.

The same method can be used for all other signs and tracks, such as footprints, gnawings, handled cones, droppings and pellets. In the case of dead prey, lairs, shelters and other signs, that cannot be satisfactorily shown in a table, you should refer to the relevant subject in the contents list.

ISBN 0 00 216106 0

DYRESPOR was first published in Denmark by G.E.C. Gads Forlag in 1972

© G.E.C. Gads Forlag 1972

© in the English Translation Wm. Collins Sons and Co. Ltd., 1974

Colour Plates printed in Denmark by F. E. Bording

Text printed in Great Britain by Collins Clear-Type Press, London and Glasgow

Foreword

In producing this book it has been our intention to provide a practical field handbook describing the tracks (footprints) and signs (feeding signs, droppings, pellets, homes etc.) left by European mammals and birds. Because of the scope of the book we have not attempted to include birds' nests, but this we feel is justified as these are fully described in most of the larger handbooks on birds. The book ends with a section on making plaster casts of footprints and on the preservation of material handled by animals.

The drawings, general arrangement and lay-out have been the responsibility of Preben Dahlstrøm, while the text has been written by Preben Bang of the Government Pest Infestation Laboratory. The tables were drawn from collected material, and of the other drawings those that are not original are based on material published in specialist journals. Most of the photographs were taken by the author.

During the preparation of this book we have received a great deal of assistance, and we should like to extend our cordial thanks to all those individuals who have helped us in so many ways. For the loan of material handled by animals and for much other help we are grateful to the Zoological Museum, the Zoological Laboratory of the Royal Danish Veterinary and Agricultural College and the National Museum—all in Copenhagen—and to the Natural History Museum in Aarhus, the Game Biology Station at Kalø and the Hunting and Forestry Museum at Hørsholm.

For much assistance and hospitality we would like to thank Professor Lauri Siivonen and his colleagues of Oulanka Biological Station in northern Finland, where the author in the winters of 1968 and 1972 and the artist in the winter of 1971 had an opportunity to study the tracks and signs of northern Scandinavian animals.

Finally, and by no means least, we are most grateful to Mr Mogens Lund of the Danish Pest Investigation Laboratory for much good advice and for his critical reading of the manuscript and to Mrs Inger Hansen for so carefully typing a manuscript that was not always easy to decipher.

Preben Dahlstrøm

Preben Bang

Contents

Tables

Fossil footprint of a cave bear, about 20,000 years old. Ariège, France.

Introduction

For those who make a living by hunting it is, of course, a matter of life and death to know about animal tracks and signs. The hunter must be completely familiar with the marks that animals leave in the wild, so that he can accurately judge which tracks it will pay him to follow and where he should set his traps. Without an exact knowledge of the habits of animals the hunter would simply be unable to survive.

In modern society a knowledge of the activities of wild animals does not play such an important role. For the farmer, forester and gardener, how-ever, it is still of great importance to be able to sort out from the various tracks left by animals exactly which species has been damaging his trees or eating his crops. He can then take effective and sensible measures to pro-tect his economic interests, without injuring innocent animals.

In the busy times in which we live more and more people are seeking rest and recreation in the open air. This has brought with it a great interest in animals and plants and an increas-ing understanding of the need for nature conservation, if we ourselves are to survive. While it is easy to observe and admire plants which have to remain where they have taken root, it is much more difficult to observe mammals, especially the larger ones. First, the majority of these are nocturnal or crepuscular, and secondly they are very shy and tend to vanish at the slightest disturbance. They do, however, betray their presence in several different ways, such as by their tracks, droppings, feeding signs and so on. Once one has acquired an eye for these things and has tried to interpret them, they can provide much information on the mode of life of wild animals, and this can greatly enhance the enjoyment of a trip in the country.

Most tracks and signs only last for quite a short time, and they usually become indistinct and then disappear quite quickly. However, as the pictures on this and the preceding page show, they may, under favourable conditions, be preserved for years and sometimes for thousands of years. In southern France, for instance, fossil footprints of the long extinct cave bear have been found which are 15,000 to 20,000 years old. Pieces of timber have been dug up from Danish bogs bearing distinct tooth marks of the beaver, a mammal which disappeared from Denmark in prehistoric times. Such bogs have also yielded bones and antlers which still show clear signs of having been gnawed thousands of years ago.

Elk antler with tooth marks, probably made by a squirrel. Found in a Danish bog. The elk disappeared from Denmark 5000 to 6000 years ago.

Timber gnawed by a beaver in prehistoric times. Found in a bog in Rude Forest, Denmark.

TRACKS

Animal tracks are best observed when the ground is covered with snow. The ideal is a layer of fine snow about one inch thick and not too wet, lying on a hard level substrate, such as a road or a flat area of ice or firm snow. Here the footprints will stand out clear and sharp and the characteristics of the different tracks will be distinctly marked and easy to distinguish. In loose snow the edges of the tracks will usually fall in and blur the track itself, and if the snow is too thick the tracks will appear as deep holes which are difficult to identify.

It is important to emphasize that a track in loose snow will nearly always be considerably larger than if the track had been made on a firmer substrate. Similarly, during a thaw—particularly if the sun is shining at the same time—a track will quickly become enlarged as its edges will thaw very rapidly, and one may easily be led to believe that a track was produced by a much larger animal than was actually the case.

When there is no snow it is much more difficult to find and identify animal tracks. It requires a trained eye to observe that an animal has run across a forest floor covered with dry leaves or traversed a grassy meadow, and in most cases this is only possible if the animal involved is large and heavy.

In those parts of the year when there is no snow one must therefore look for animal tracks in places without vegetation and preferably after a period of rain, when the ground is soft. The best imprints will usually be found on damp, slightly muddy earth, but good tracks can also be found in wet sand on the beach at low tide, or even on sand dunes in the morning when the sand is still damp from the dew. Later in the day, when the sand dries, the grains slide together and the tracks are obliterated. Woodland paths and newly dried out ditches in forests are good places to look for animal tracks, and some of the very best tracks, especially of small animals, can be found in puddles that have just dried out leaving a thin layer of mud over a firm substrate.

The best way to learn how to recognize a track is to prepare a sketch showing its exact dimensions (see pages 11, 13 and 19). This compels one to note all the details of the track and thus to remember them better. A quicker, although scarcely such a good method, is to take a photograph. If this is done it is essential to include a scale in the photograph—something which many people omit to do. If it is thought to spoil the picture, then take two photographs, one with and one without the scale.

A very attractive way to learn how to recognize the different tracks is to prepare a collection of casts in plaster of Paris or paraffin. The method used is described on page 232.

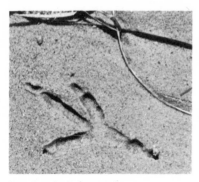

Crow footprint in damp sand.

Footprint of roe deer. A scale should always be included when photographing tracks.

Footprints

A mammal's track shows the form of the sole of the foot as a concave impression and so, to identify a track, one has to know a little about the structure and appearance of the feet of different species.

The original or primitive mammals had five clawed toes on each of the four feet and they were plantigrade, that is, they trod on the whole sole of the foot. This primitive type of foot is found almost unaltered in most of the insectivores, of which the hedgehog can be taken as a typical example, but it is also found in other mammals, such as the badger and the bears.

In animals with five well-developed toes these are of different length. The toes are numbered from 1–5 beginning with the inner toe (this corresponds with the thumb on our own hand) and ending with the outer toe (little finger). The longest toe is no. 3, followed in order by nos. 4, 2, 5 and 1. The shortest toe is, therefore, the inner toe, so if a footprint shows all five toes and the shortest toe is on the left side of the foot, then the track must have been made by the right foot. In many cases the inner toe only makes a weak impression—sometimes none at all—and the footprint will then show four toes of unequal length, and the shortest will now be the outer toe.

Plantigrade animals have relatively short limbs, which normally move at a steady pace, for the construction of their feet is not well adapted for jumping or for running any distance. An

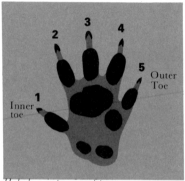

Hedgehog, impression of paw.

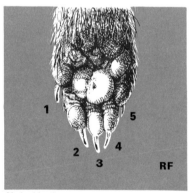

Underside of paw.

animal that runs fast and over long distances must have long limbs and the area of foot touching the ground must be as small as possible. We know this from our own movements. When walking the whole sole of each foot comes into contact with the ground, but when running only the front part, that is, the toes and the ball of the foot.

During the course of geological time the plantigrade type of foot has evolved into a series of other types adapted to various methods of movement and different speeds, such as running and jumping. Those animals which move mainly by running, do so on the toes or on the tips of the toes, and by the elongation of the limb bones they have evolved long slender legs. At the same time there has been a reduction in the number of the toes, and those which remain—or some of them—usually become very powerfully developed. The most common reduction involves the first toe which may disappear completely, so that the animals become 4-toed. Often there is also a reduction of the 2nd and 5th toes, as for example in deer where these toes are represented as small dew claws. In horses all the toes have disappeared except the 3rd and the animal treads only on the outermost toe joint which is enclosed in a hoof.

The undersides of the foot are protected by pads which are thick, elastic masses of connective tissue covered by a strong but flexible horny layer. These pads have sweat glands, the secretion from which is transferred to the footprint, giving it a scent. The pads themselves are naked but in most animals the skin between them is covered in hair, and in some cases such as the pine marten and squirrel the hair covering becomes so dense in winter as to cover the whole pad. Hares lack pads which are replaced by a tight, springy layer of strong stiff hairs. It goes without saying that a dense growth of hair on the sole of the

Development of the foot in dog, deer and horse. Pig is essentially the same as deer.

Paw of hare.

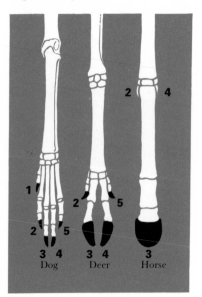

Dog	Deer	Horse

foot will tend to mask many of the characteristics of the footprint.

Basically there is a pad beneath the tip of each toe and behind these there is a further row of pads, sometimes called intermediate pads. In many animals these latter pads are more or less fused. Thus, in the dog, fox, badger and cat they form one large pad. In addition, some animals have one or sometimes two so-called proximal pads which lie further back on the front foot.

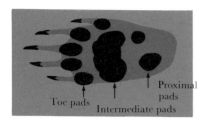

Toe pads   Intermediate pads   Proximal pads

Types of footprint

Animal footprints can be divided into two main groups according to the structure of the foot, namely tracks made by animals with paws and claws, and those made by animals with cloven or non-cloven hoofs.

When examining a track made by a paw, particular attention should be paid to the number of toes, the shape and size of the claws and pads and their relative positions.

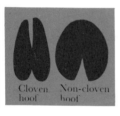

Paw   Cloven hoof   Non-cloven hoof

Whether the claws produce marks in the track depends very much on their size and the siting of the toes, as well as on the nature of the ground. Thus, the long digging claws on the fore-feet of the badger will always leave a clear track, but one never sees claw marks in the footprint of a cat or lynx, because the claws are always retracted during walking, so that they do not touch the ground.

In almost all animals except the rodents the prints of the fore-feet are broader and deeper and more distinct than those of the hind-feet. Furthermore, even when moving slowly the toes on the fore-feet are somewhat more splayed than those of the hind-feet, and this can be checked by measuring the distance between the claws of the central toes of each foot. This condition is even more marked when the animal is moving fast.

Each individual footprint shows the direction in which the animal has moved and in the vast majority of cases this is not difficult to determine. In deep snow where the track is a more or less deep hole the hindmost edge of each footprint slopes down towards the bottom of the track, whereas the fore-edge is more vertical,

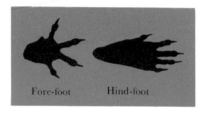

Fore-foot   Hind-foot

Tracks of Rodents.

and the foot will nearly always have cast up a little snow in front of it.

In measuring a footprint one nearly always takes its length from the front edge of the longest toe's pad mark to the hindmost edge of the most central intermediate pad. The claws are not, therefore, reckoned in the measurement. If the whole footprint can be seen, one also takes a measurement to its hindmost border. The breadth is measured at the broadest part of the footprint. To obtain measurements that are as accurate as possible it is best to take these from tracks made when the animal is moving slowly. In rapid locomotion the feet tend to slip a little and the tracks thus become a little too large.

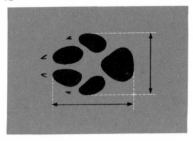

Measuring a paw track.

Animals with cloven hoofs have a very characteristic foot which leaves an easily recognizable track. These animals have four toes (the first toe is lacking), but they only tread on the tips of the third and fourth, the central toes, which are well developed and almost completely symmetrical. The second and fifth toes, known as dew claws, are much smaller and have moved round to the rear of the foot. In most cases they are positioned so high up on the leg that they do not touch the ground during normal walking. It is only when the animal treads on soft ground or in snow, or when the foot joints give way during running or jumping that the dew claws leave a mark in the track. There are exceptions, as for example in the wild boar and reindeer, in which the dew claws

are positioned so low that they touch the ground even during ordinary walking.

The cloven hoof, which is really a modified claw, consists of the wall and the sole. The wall forms the smooth, curved upperside of the hoof, the sole is on the underside of the hoof. The wall usually extends a short distance beyond the sole and forms a hard sharp edge which is shown clearly in the track. In tracks on very hard substrates only this edge will appear in the footprint. The sole is followed behind by the toe pad (or 'frog' in a horse), which takes in a varying proportion

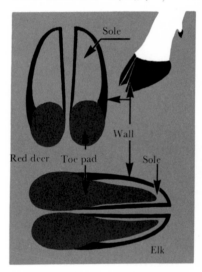

Cloven hoof.

of the underside of the hoof. In very distinct tracks of, for example, red deer, fallow deer or reindeer, the toe pads appear as rounded depressions. In roe deer and elk the sole has almost disappeared, and the toe pad extends right out to the tip of the hoof.

When trying to identify the track of a cloven-hoofed animal the first thing to do is to determine the shape and

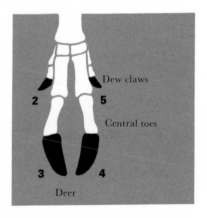

size of the hoof. If the impression of the track is very clear the size of the toe pad may also be important. The imprint left by the two halves of the hoof are almost flat underneath, but the outer edges are more or less curved, and the impressions are almost mirror images of each other. Sometimes, however, the two hoofs on a foot are not the same size, and then the inner hoof is nearly always the shorter.

The track made by a fore-foot is larger than that of a hind-foot, for in the former case the two hoofs be-

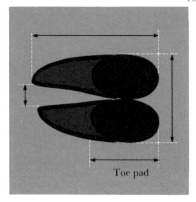

Measuring a cloven hoof track.

Track of cloven hoof.

come somewhat splayed, even during a slow walk, whereas the hoofs of a hind-foot tend to approach each other. If the animal is moving fast this difference is even more marked, for the front hoofs will then splay to form a V. The same applies to the dew claws, the tracks of which are always larger and more distinct in the fore-foot track.

When measuring the track left by a

cloven hoof one must find one that has been made by an animal that has been walking slowly, and in addition to the length and breadth it is advisable also to measure the distance between the tips of each half of the hoof and—if possible—the length of the toe pads.

In Europe there are no wild animals with hoofs having only one toe, but the tracks of horses are common and so they must be briefly described. A horse has only one toe—the third—on each leg and it only treads on the outermost toe joint which has a very well-developed hoof, in which the wall curves round the toe pad (or 'frog'). The track is almost circular.

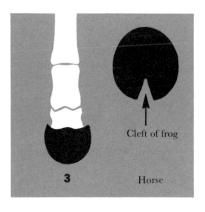

Gaits

When identifying a track it is often a considerable help, in addition to noting the characteristics of each individual footprint, to look at their positions in relation to each other. This, of course, presupposes that one has a series of tracks, which always happens when the ground is covered with snow, but is not always the case in summer. The positioning of many animal tracks is so characteristic that one can identify the animal that made them at a distance and without a detailed examination of the individual footprints. Therefore, in cases where the latter are indistinct and show no details, identification may depend entirely upon the relative positions of the footprints.

The positioning of the tracks reflects the animal's method of moving, and once one knows the relative positions that correspond to the different gaits one can read from the tracks whether the animal has been walking, trotting, jumping or galloping. It becomes more interesting to follow the tracks of an animal once one is conversant with these points, for one gets a more realistic idea of what the animal has been doing. For instance, one can deduce when it has been walking slowly, when it has been stealthily creeping up towards its prey or when it has moved off in full flight.

In order to learn how to recognize the different gaits it is a good idea to watch domesticated animals and see the tracks they leave when moving in different ways. When they are moving slowly it is easy to see how they place the feet in relation to one another, but when they are going fast it is impossible to follow the movements in detail. Television transmissions of horses galloping and trotting often show the animals passing the winning post in slow motion, and this provides an opportunity to observe how they move their legs when moving fast.

The main types of gait are: walking, trotting, galloping and jumping.

Trotting. Note that the front horse is not touching the ground.

Walking

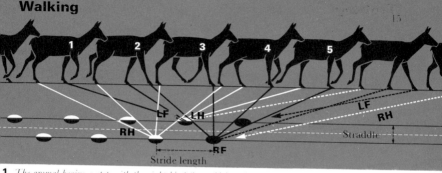

Stride length · Straddle · LF · LH · RH · RF

1 *The animal begins a step with the right hind-foot which registers in the track of the right fore-foot. The right fore-foot has just left the ground. The left fore-foot is on the ground, and the animal is therefore resting diagonally on two legs, the right hind-leg and the left fore-leg.*

2 *The right fore-foot is placed on the ground, and the animal is now supported on three legs, the right hind-leg, the right fore-leg and the left fore-leg.*

3 *The left hind-leg moves forwards and before it reaches the ground to register in the track of the left fore-foot, the latter is raised. The animal is now supported on two legs of the same side.*

4 *The left hind-foot is placed on the ground. The left fore-foot is moved forwards and the animal is again supported on three legs, the left hind-leg, the right hind-leg and the right fore-leg.*

5 *The right hind-foot is lifted, and the animal is once more resting on two legs, the left hind-leg and the right fore-leg. The position is as in No. 1, but with the opposite diagonal. The next foot to be placed on the ground will be the left fore-foot, followed by the right hind-foot which will register in the right fore-foot's track, and so on.*

Walking

The characteristic of walking is that each of the four feet is lifted and set down on the ground at a different time, each limb moving separately. So when a horse is walking along a hard road one hears the individual clops of each hoof quite separate from one another. The legs are moved in a quite definite order and it appears the whole time as though the animal is trying to tread on its own heels. For example, if it starts with the right hind-leg, this is followed by the others in the following order: right fore-leg, left hind-leg, left fore-leg, then the right hind-leg again, and so on.

The hind-foot is always placed close to the point made by the fore-foot, so that its track comes to be just in front of, a little behind or right over the track of the fore-foot. In the latter case, where the track of the fore-foot becomes more or less covered the tracks are said to register. This happens regularly with deer, and in many other animals, particularly in deep snow where it is obviously easier for the animal to place the hind-foot in the hole already made by the fore-foot.

When an animal is walking the footprints form two distinct and separate, parallel rows. The length of the stride is the distance between two successive tracks from the same foot, and the straddle is the distance between the left and right tracks, so the trail of a walking animal is characterized by a short stride and a considerable straddle.

There is a special type of walking, known as pacing in which the fore-leg and the hind-leg of the same side move at the same time. This gait, which is used by camels, can be observed rather exceptionally in, for example, horses, dogs and cats.

Trotting

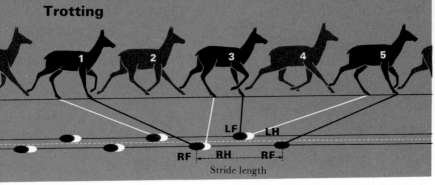

Stride length

1 *The animal starts off diagonally with the right fore-foot and the left hind-foot. The left hind-foot registers in the track of the left fore-foot. The fore-foot takes off a fraction before the hind-foot.*

2 *While the animal is airborne, the left fore-leg and the right hind-leg are moved forwards.*

3 *The left fore-foot and the right hind-foot touch the ground simultaneously. The right hind-foot is placed approximately in the track of the right fore-foot.*

4 *The animal is again airborne and the right fore-leg and the left hind-leg now move forwards.*

5 *The right fore-foot and the left hind-foot again touch the ground. The left hind-foot registers approximately in the track of the left fore-foot.*

Trotting

Trotting is a considerably faster mode of locomotion which is characterised by the fact that the fore-leg of one side moves synchronously with the hind-leg of the other side. For example, the right fore-foot is lifted and set down again at the same time as the left hind-foot. When a horse is trotting on a hard road, one hears a series of clops at equal intervals, but each audible clop actually consists of two simultaneous clops.

A trotting animal appears almost to be gliding along. The animal's centre of gravity moves along in a more or less straight horizontal line, and little or no energy is expended in lifting the body at each 'take-off'. Relative to the speed, which may be considerable, trotting is the least energy-consuming and least tiring gait.

The trail is very similar to that produced by a walking animal, but the stride is greater and the straddle less, and the faster the animal trots the more is this condition accentuated,

so that in a very fast trot the tracks of the right and left side almost lie on a single line. On firm ground the hind-foot usually strikes the ground in front of the track made by the fore-foot, and the further in front it is the faster the speed. The hind-foot may register in the track of the fore-foot, and in snow this is nearly always the case

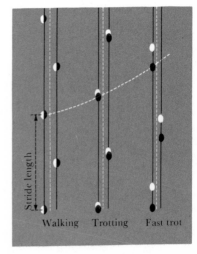

Stride length

Walking   Trotting   Fast trot

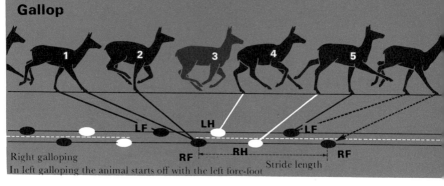

Gallop

1 *The animal is supported on the left and right fore-feet, but is just shifting its weight from the left fore-leg to the right. Both hind-legs are moving forwards.*

2 *The right fore-foot alone bears the whole weight of the animal in the take-off.*

3 *The animal is momentarily airborne while the hind-legs move forwards.*

4 *The left hind-foot touches the ground, while the right hind-foot and left fore-foot move forwards.*

5 *The right hind-foot and left fore-foot now carry the animal's weight, but immediately after the right fore-foot has reached the ground, the hind-legs will again be in the air as in No. 1.*

Galloping

The gallop is a faster gait than the jump, and in contrast to the latter all four limbs take part in moving the animal forward. In a typical gallop,

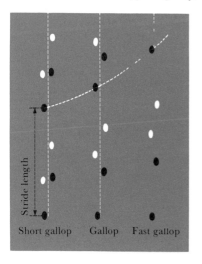

Short gallop   Gallop   Fast gallop

as in the jump, there is a phase in which the animal is airborne, but in contrast to the jump the animal takes off from the fore-limbs. It lands on the hind-limbs, first on one, then on the other, and then in turn on each fore-limb, without losing contact with the ground. Thus, the four legs work in quick succession one after the other.

In a typical gallop the positions of the individual tracks are very equally separated and lie almost on a straight line.

As the speed increases during a gallop the gait becomes more like a jump. In fact the bound is a fast gait intermediate between a gallop and a jump. In this the take-off by the hind-limbs is so powerful that the animal is lifted from the ground and is propelled into the air. In fact, there are many possible transitions between a jump and a gallop, and it is not possible to define any sharp boundary between these two gaits.

Jump

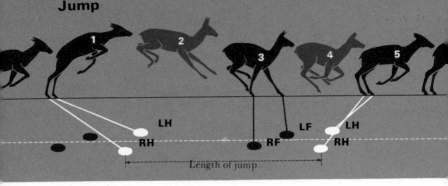

1 *The animal moves off with a powerful thrust of the hind-legs.*
2 *The animal is airborne. The fore-legs are stretched out first, before landing.*
3 *The right fore-foot reaches the ground a fraction before the left fore-foot, which then takes off.*
4 *The animal is airborne with all four legs tucked up under it.*
5 *The hind-legs reach the ground and immediately start a new jump.*

Jump or Hop

In jumping or hopping the animal is momentarily airborne, as in the gallop. In a jump or hop the animal takes off with both the hind-legs, so that it is projected forwards in an arc, to land on the fore-legs, which usually hit the ground one a little in front of the other. The fore-legs carry the animal a short distance forwards, and then leave the ground again. Then the hind-legs land a little in front of the fore-foot tracks and as a rule more laterally than these. The animal then takes off again with a powerful thrust from the hind-legs. In a jump, therefore, the animal takes off mainly with the hind-limbs and lands on the fore-limbs.

A typical track from a jump consists of groups of four footprints. Looking at the trail in the direction of the animal's movement the two fore-foot tracks will lie close to each other, with one a little behind the other, and in front of them the hind-foot tracks will lie more or less side by side. In marten-like animals, where the footprints in a group of tracks are always placed close alongside one another, one or both of the hind-feet may register in the tracks of the fore-feet.

For large, heavy animals jumping is a very strenuous and exhausting method of locomotion and it is therefore almost only used in deep snow and to overcome obstacles such as ditches, small streams and fences. On the other hand, jumping or hopping is the commonest gait of many small animals with long, supple backs and powerful, strongly angled hind-legs, as for example the martens and the small rodents.

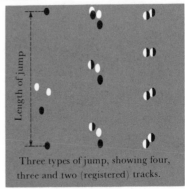

Three types of jump, showing four, three and two (registered) tracks.

Measuring track groups

When measuring a group of tracks it is a great help to stretch a piece of string between two small sticks so that it runs through the centre of the group, and to use this as a base line. The distance from this line to the middle of the front edge of each footprint should then be measured and recorded on a sketch. Additional measurements should include the length of a single group of tracks (this is the distance from the front edge of the foremost track to the rear edge of the rearmost track) and also the stride length (the distance from the front edge of the foremost footprint in a group to the front edge of the corresponding footprint in the following group).

In addition to these measurements the sketch should also show which are fore-foot tracks and which are hind-foot tracks, and if some of the tracks are turned outwards, the angle made by their midlines with the base line should be measured and recorded as accurately as possible. It is practical to use paper marked in millimetre squares, and so far as possible always to use the same scale, so that direct comparisons can be made between different sketches.

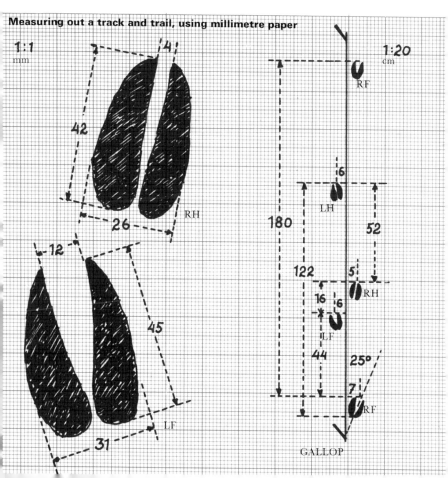

Measuring out a track and trail, using millimetre paper

Paths

Most animals do not move at random round their home area, but have a network of paths or runs, which they follow most of the time and which they know well so that they can take flight along them when disturbed. These paths are often very well marked, and even those made by small, light animals may be incredibly hard packed. The paths are to a large extent used at night, so the animals are guided not so much by sight as by the scent which their previous passage has left behind. According to the local conditions these paths will always take the route that is easiest for the animals, and so they will often be full of bends, and will skirt round tree-stumps, rocks and other obstacles. They may also

follow various lengths of path or road made by man. Sometimes several animal species use the same path or at any rate a part of it. For example, the tracks of hare and deer may appear on the same path, and a camera set up alongside a mouse run, so that it takes a picture automatically when an animal passes by, will often show that several different species of mouse have used the same route.

Paths made by the larger vegetarian animals can be seen particularly clearly on the outskirts of woodland, from the shelter of which the animals move out to forage in fields and meadows. In general, animal paths will always be most distinct in the vicinity of good feeding places. Thus, if one follows a

A fox's run. The animal has scraped earth away in order to get under the fence.

Turnip field with a path much used by hares and roe deer. ▶

Field vole runs. The grass which covered the runs has been removed.

hare path from a turnip clamp, the first part will be very clearly marked, but further on it will become branched and increasingly indistinct.

Many small rodents make very conspicuous runs, which connect their underground tunnels with feeding places or merely lead from hole to hole.

Black rat runs are marked with a dark, fatty deposit.

The runs of the field vole, which lives in dense grassy vegetation, are particularly striking. They are often hidden at the foot of the vegetation and are only seen when the grass is turned aside. In winter they make comparable runs under the snow and these are often lined with pieces of bitten-off grass, which remain in the form of small tunnels when the snow melts in the spring. Water vole runs can be seen along river banks and in swamps, and at refuse dumps one can almost always find very distinct brown rat runs which lead from the rats' home in the immediate vicinity into the refuse where the animals forage. The black rat, which is a much better climber than the brown rat, lives mainly in lofts and the upper storeys of buildings where its runs along the roof timbers are marked by a characteristic dark, fatty deposit.

In moving through fences and hedges game birds may use paths previously made by other animals, but

Paths made by partridges in the snow.

when the ground is covered in snow there will often be paths actually made by pheasants or partridges.

Beavers build a very special type of

A beaver's channel.

'path' in the form of the small channels that lead from a lake into low-lying swampy areas. Lengths of timber are floated along these channels to the beaver's lodge, and stored nearby as a food supply.

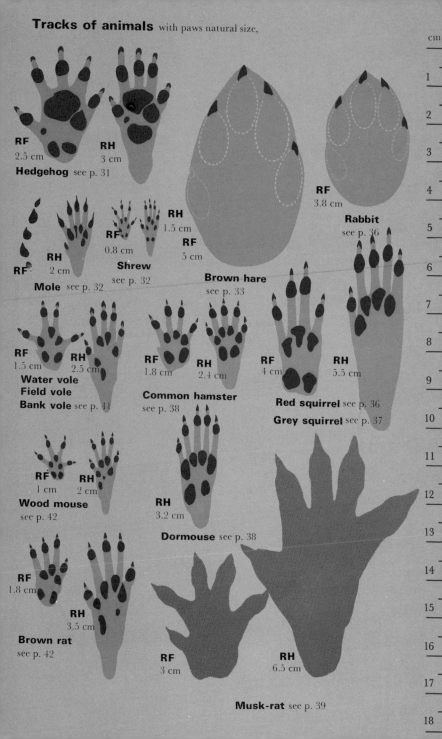

Tracks of animals with paws natural size,

cm

RF 2.5 cm **RH** 3 cm
Hedgehog see p. 31

RF **RH** 2 cm
Mole see p. 32

RF 0.8 cm **RH** 1.5 cm
Shrew see p. 32
RF 5 cm
Brown hare see p. 33

RF 3.8 cm
Rabbit see p. 36

RF 1.5 cm **RH** 2.5 cm
Water vole
Field vole
Bank vole see p. 41

RF 1.8 cm **RH** 2.4 cm
Common hamster see p. 38

RF 4 cm **RH** 5.5 cm
Red squirrel see p. 36
Grey squirrel see p. 37

RF 1 cm **RH** 2 cm
Wood mouse see p. 42

RH 3.2 cm
Dormouse see p. 38

RF 1.8 cm **RH** 3.5 cm
Brown rat see p. 42

RF 3 cm **RH** 6.5 cm
Musk-rat see p. 39

natural size

Beaver see p. 38

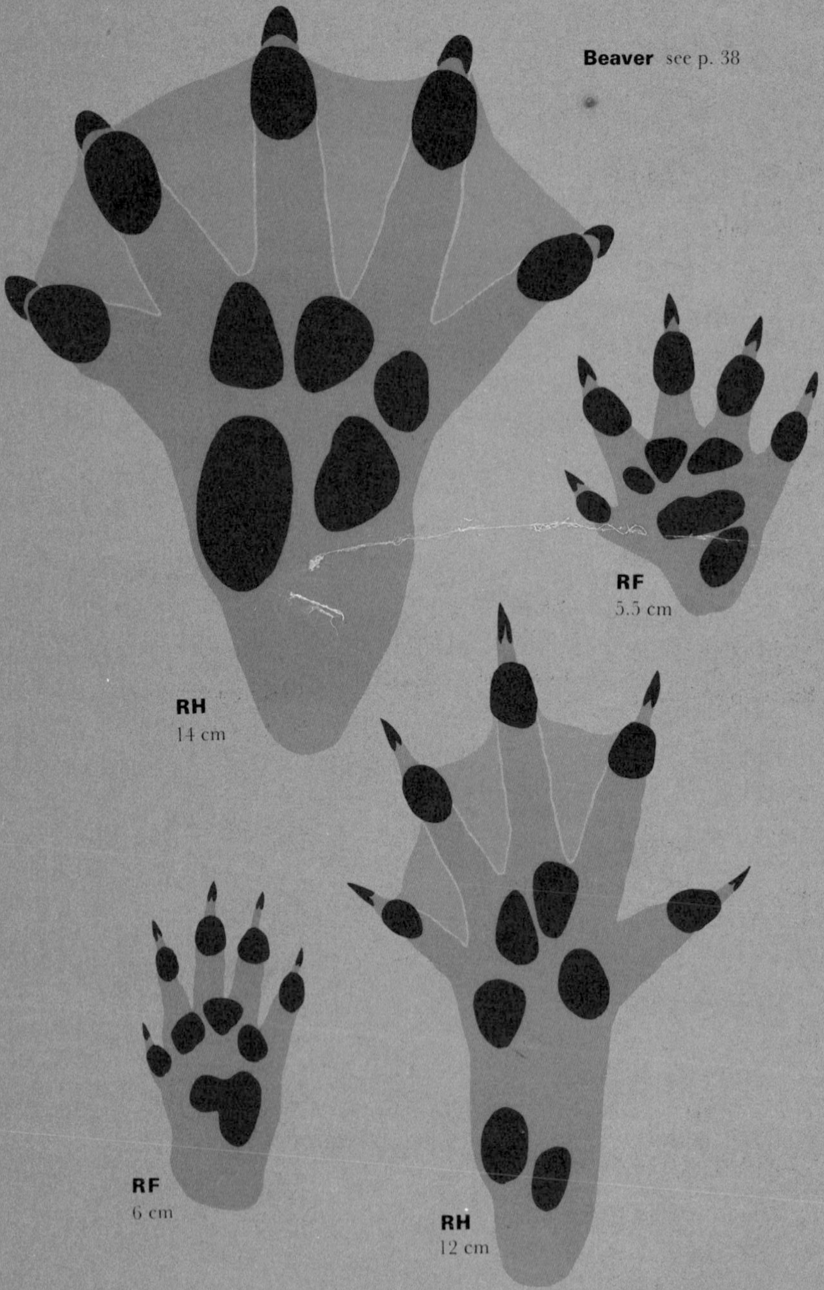

RF
5.5 cm

RH
14 cm

RF
6 cm

RH
12 cm

Coypu see p. 39

Tracks of animals with paws ⅔ natural size

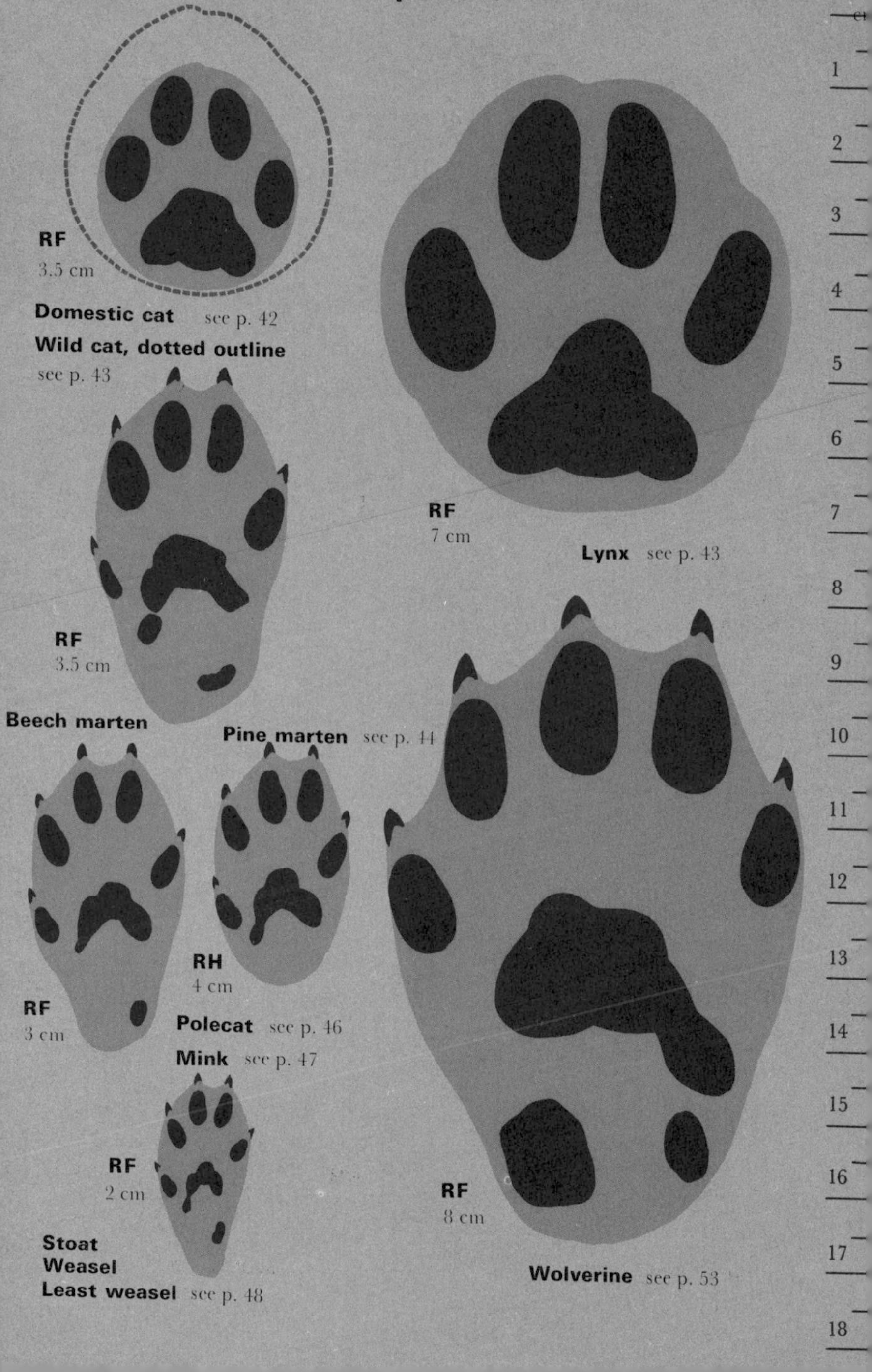
RF
3.5 cm
Domestic cat see p. 42
Wild cat, dotted outline
see p. 43
RF
7 cm
Lynx see p. 43
RF
3.5 cm
Beech marten
Pine marten see p. 44
RF
3 cm
RH
4 cm
Polecat see p. 46
Mink see p. 47
RF
2 cm
Stoat
Weasel
Least weasel see p. 48
RF
8 cm
Wolverine see p. 53
cm
1
2
3
4
5
6
7
8
9
10
11
12
13
14
15
16
17
18

Natural size

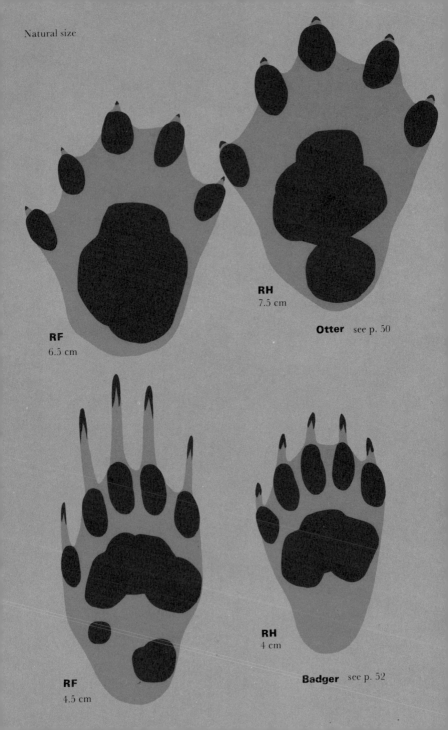

RF
6.5 cm

RH
7.5 cm

Otter see p. 50

RF
4.5 cm

RH
4 cm

Badger see p. 52

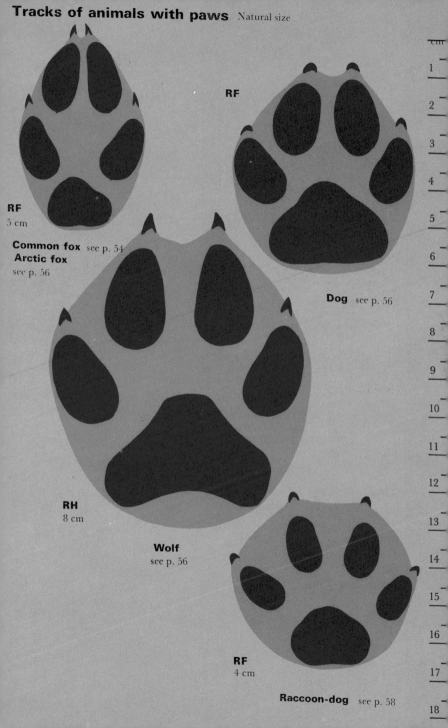

Tracks of animals with paws Natural size

RF

RF
5 cm

Common fox see p. 54
Arctic fox see p. 56

Dog see p. 56

RH
8 cm

Wolf see p. 56

RF
4 cm

Raccoon-dog see p. 58

cm
1
2
3
4
5
6
7
8
9
10
11
12
13
14
15
16
17
18

RF
28 cm

RH
30 cm

Brown bear c. ¼ natural size
see p. 58

RF
7 cm

RH
9 cm

Seal
1/30 natural size

see p. 60

Raccoon ⅔ natural size

see p. 60

Tracks of animals with paws

Hedgehog

Tracks:

Plantigrade. Five toes with relatively long claws, particularly on the hind-feet. Toes and claws clearly separated from the inner toe (thumb), which even in clear tracks often only produces a very faint impression. As a rule the foot-print appears to have four toes. The toes on the fore-foot are thick and much splayed, those on the hind-feet somewhat more slender and more bunched together; the pads usually leave very clear impressions. The tracks of the fore- and hind-foot are about the same size, c. 2·5 cm long and 2·8 cm broad.

Trail:

Hedgehogs nearly always move by walking, but when going fast they may almost break into a trot. The track of the hind-foot is usually found behind that of the fore-foot, but in fast movement the hind-foot may register in the track made by the fore-foot or even be in front of it. The stride is short, about 10 cm, but the straddle is large, c. 6 cm.

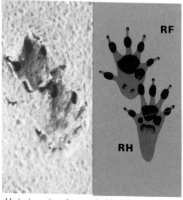

Hedgehog, fore-foot track, hind-foot below.

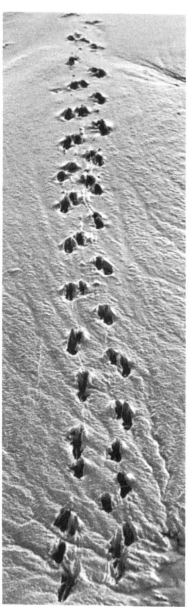

Hedgehog. Walking tracks on muddy ground.

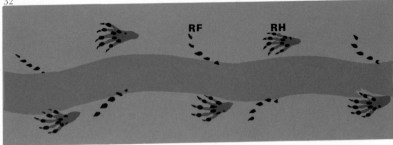

Mole, trail

Mole

As moles live mainly underground their tracks are very seldom seen.

Tracks:
The fore-legs, which are much modified, cannot be used in the normal walking position. The foot is turned so that its inner edge turns downwards and the sole, which has no pads, faces backwards. Thus, the animal treads on the front edge of the foot and in the track the five long, broad claws leave a slightly curved row of 5 depressions in the track.

The hind-foot, which is considerably smaller than the fore-foot, is normally developed with five toes, all with long, narrow claws, which form distinct marks in the track, and small pads. The animal treads on the whole of the sole. The track is c. 1·5 cm long and 1·1 cm broad.

Trail:
When walking the stride length is 3–4 cm and very straddled, particularly between the tracks of the hind-feet.

On soft ground the animal's belly may leave a drag mark. When walking fast a mole is said to place the fore-feet twice on the ground for each step taken by the hind-feet.

Shrew

Plantigrade, with five clawed toes on both fore- and hind-feet. Shrews are very small and light animals, and their tracks are usually very faint and indistinct, and in practice it is impossible to distinguish the tracks of the different species from one another.

Tracks:
The tracks are very similar to those of mice, but they can be distinguished by the fact that mice have only four toes on each fore-foot. Shrew tracks can be seen in fine mud along the banks of rivers and lakes and in similar places, but they are most frequently seen in snow, in which the animals often build runs, which open out into a

Shrew, tracks and trail in fine mud.

Walking

Tracks made in snow by a shrew which moved in jumps.

Brown hare

Hares have five toes on each fore-foot, but the inner toe (thumb) is short, and its impression is very rarely seen in a track. The hind-foot is long and narrow with four toes. All the toes have straight, narrow claws which form distinct marks in the track, and are seen particularly in snow, usually inside the outer border of the track. On firm ground only the claws will leave a mark.

The soles of the feet are covered with a thick layer of strong, springy, forward-directed hairs, which replace the pads. This hair is especially well developed under the toes and in clear tracks it may give an impression similar to that of a pad.

The individual footprint has a characteristic pointed form. The print of the fore-foot on earth is c. 5 cm long and c. 3 cm broad, that of the hind-foot c. 6 cm long and 3·5 cm broad. In snow the hind-foot track may be considerably longer, and the breadth of both fore- and hind-foot tracks will usually increase, because the animal spreads its toes in order to provide the largest possible treading surface. When moving on firm ground the hind-feet tread only with the toes, and the track is then not much larger than that of the fore-feet.

small, circular hole on the surface of the snow. From this hole the tracks usually go out like a narrow furrow in the snow, at the bottom of which one can see the footprints and a sinuous mark made by the tail.

Trail:
In snow the individual footprints vary from $\frac{1}{2}$ to 1 cm in length. Shrews usually move by running or in short hops. Depending upon the species the stride length varies from c. 3 cm to 5–6 cm, and the length of a hop is normally only about 2–4 times the straddle.

Hare

Leaping

Hare, trail.   *Track left by sitting hare.*

The characteristic group of tracks left by a hare. Above, the hind-foot tracks lying side by side, below the two fore-foot tracks, one a fraction behind the other. Note the impressions made by the furry toe pads.

Trail:

The trail of a hare can be recognized primarily by the relative position of the tracks, which is typical of those animals which move by jumping and galloping. In the hare the trails are very regular and always the same, regardless of whether the animal is moving slowly or in full flight. In addition, the track of the hind-foot in snow will be longer than that of the fore-foot. Each of the regular track groups consists of four separate footprints, of which the two rearmost are the two short fore-foot tracks, placed one a little behind the other and almost in a line, while the two foremost are the two hind-foot tracks, usually somewhat longer, and positioned more or less alongside one another. The distance between each group of tracks and also that between individual footprints in a group will increase with the speed of the animal, and is therefore very variable. At normal speed a hare moves in a gallop, and only at greater speeds does the gait change to something more like a jump.

In snow one can often find the track left by a hare that has been sitting on the ground. Here the tracks of the long hind-feet are placed side by side and straight in front of them are those of the smaller fore-feet.

In following a hare trail, one can observe that the animal sometimes

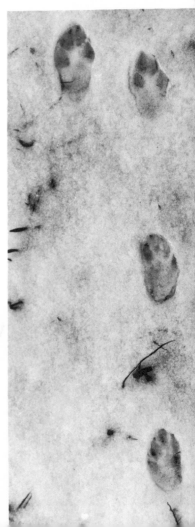

turns round and follows its own tracks back for a short distance, before making a big jump to the side and then continuing in a completely different direction. This remarkable manoeuvre must surely be intended to confuse and divert an enemy following the trail.

A hare's trail looking in the direction in which the animal has moved.

A mountain hare's trail. Note the very large hind-foot tracks.

Mountain hare

A mountain hare's trail is difficult to distinguish from that of a brown hare. The individual footprint is, however, somewhat broader as the animal spreads its toes more, particularly those on the hind-feet. This becomes particularly marked in deep, loose snow, where a large treading surface is an advantage, and here the tracks of the hind-feet are very large and almost pear-shaped.

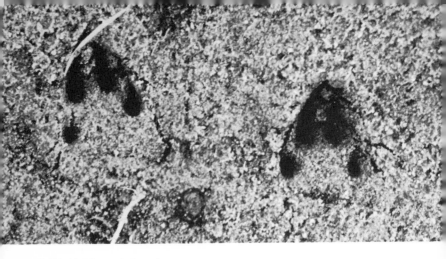

Rabbit, hind-foot tracks in sand.

Rabbit

Track and trail as in the hares. However, the individual footprints, the distance between each group of tracks and the distances between each footprint in a group are considerably smaller than in the hares. On firm ground the track of the hind-foot is c. 4 cm long and 2·5 cm broad. The tracks of hare and rabbit can be easily distinguished with the help of an ordinary matchbox. If the breadth of the hind-foot track is about the same as the breadth of the box, the track was made by a hare, but if it is only about two-thirds the box's breadth, then it is a rabbit track.

Red squirrel

Tracks:
The fore-foot has four long, slender toes with claws, which are clearly marked in the track; the toes are much splayed. The thumb is rudimentary and not seen in the track. The track is c. 4 cm long and c. 2 cm broad.

The hind-foot has five toes, of which the three centre ones are long and slender and about the same size. These are clearly marked in the track, where

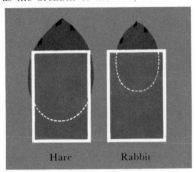

A matchbox covers a hare's track, but a rabbit's track is only ⅔ the width of the box.

Hare   Rabbit

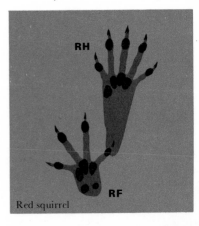

RH

RF

Red squirrel

they lie very close alongside one another. The outer toe and the inner toe (nos. 1 and 5) are much shorter and they leave a less distinct track, and are more or less directed outwards. All the toes have pointed claws which nearly always leave marks in the track. The hind-foot track is c. 5 cm long and 2·5–3·5 cm broad, depending upon the degree to which the toes are splayed.

Trail:
Red squirrels always move by hopping (or jumping) when on the ground. The tracks lie close together in very regular groups of four, which are reminiscent of those of hares, but naturally much smaller. The rearmost two footprints in the group are those of the fore-feet, and they usually lie side by side and very close together. The prints of the large hind-feet lie alongside one another a little in front of the fore-foot tracks, a little further apart and usually turned somewhat outwards. It is a characteristic of squirrel trails that they nearly always start and end at a tree.

Grey squirrel

The tracks and their relative positions are difficult to distinguish from those of a red squirrel. However, the heel of the hind-foot is more distinctly marked and in a jump the tracks lie closer together.

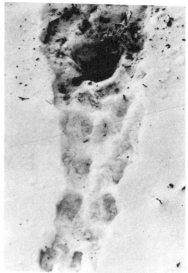

A squirrel has dug up a food cache.

Squirrel tracks in firm snow. Above, the hind-foot tracks with prints of 5 toes, and below the fore-foot tracks with only 4 toes.

Trail made when jumping.

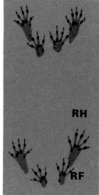

RH

RF

Russian flying squirrel

The trail is very different from that of other squirrels, for here the tracks of the hind-feet lie close together and behind those of the fore-feet, while the latter are alongside each other and relatively far apart. This animal can also move by hopping in an upright position and the track then consists only of the prints from the hind-feet, lying close together.

Track of Russian flying squirrel.

Dormouse and hamster

Dormice have five toes on each foot, but the first toe on the fore-foot is much reduced and leaves no mark in the track. The corresponding toe in the hind-foot is also considerably smaller than the other toes. The tracks are similar to those of a squirrel but are smaller, the fore-foot track being c. 2 cm long and c. 2·2 cm broad,

and the hind-foot track c. 3 cm long and c. 2·5 cm broad. The claws rarely leave any mark and the impressions

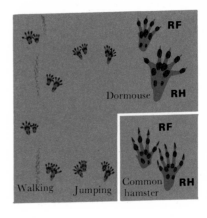

made by the toe pads of the fore-feet form a less marked curve than in the squirrel. On soft ground the bushy tail often leaves a mark.

The common hamster has five toes on each foot. The inner toe of the fore-foot is reduced and is not seen in the track. The toes are long, with claws which are clearly seen in the track. The fore-foot track is c. 1·5 cm long and c. 1 cm broad, that of the hind-foot 2·0–3·5 cm long and c. 1 cm broad.

Beaver

The fore-foot has five toes with pointed claws but no webs. The track often shows only the impressions of four widely spread toes with distinct claw marks. The track is c. 5·5 cm long and c. 4·5 cm broad.

The hind-foot has five toes with short claws and with webs between the toes. The toes and the broad claws nearly always show up in the track, and on soft ground the webs also leave clear marks. The hind-foot is considerably larger than the fore-foot, being c. 15 cm long and c. 10 cm broad. On soft ground and in snow the beaver's broad tail leaves a drag mark which often partially obliterates the footprints. On land the normal gait is walking.

Musk-rat

Five toes with long, pointed claws on both fore- and hind-feet. The inner toe on the fore-foot is, however, so small that the footprint often shows only four toes. The fore-foot track is c. 3·5 cm long and c. 3 cm broad. The hind-foot toes are united at their bases by a narrow web, and the toes are fringed with stiff hairs, which make the toe impressions appear broad. The hind-foot track is c. 7 cm and c. 5 cm broad. The long, compressed tail often leaves a sinuous drag track.

Coypu

The fore-foot has five free toes (small thumb) with long claws. The hind-foot also has five clawed toes which, except for the outer toe (No. 5), are joined by a web. Normally the toes, claws and pads are clearly marked in the track and the imprint of the web is also seen on soft ground. The track of the hind-foot is considerably larger than that of the fore-foot, but there is great variation in their size, depending upon the age and sex of the animals. As a guide, the relative sizes may be: fore-foot 6 cm long and 6 cm broad, hind-foot 12 cm long and 7 cm broad.

The normal gait is walking, but when moving fast a coypu may make short jumps. The long, cylindrical tail usually leaves a continuous wavy drag track.

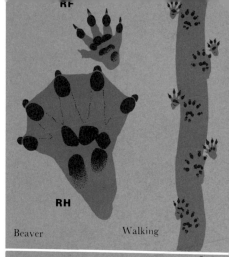

Beaver   Walking

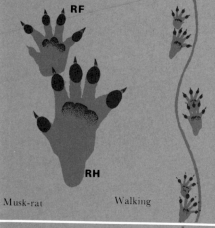

Musk-rat   Walking

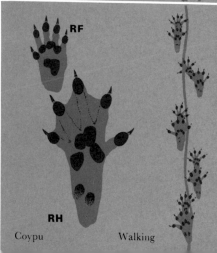

Coypu   Walking

Small rodents, rats and mice

These animals are characterised by having four well-developed, clawed toes on each fore-foot, and these appear widely splayed in the track. The hind-foot has five clawed toes, of which the two outer toes are short and placed far back on the foot, while the three central toes are long and slender. In the track the outer toes are much splayed but the central toes lie close together and directed forwards. As in other rodents the fore-feet are considerably smaller than the hind-feet.

These are mainly small, light animals and their footprints are usually faint and indistinct, and in practice it is nearly always impossible to distinguish the tracks of the many different species from one another. Any attempt at identification must, therefore, depend very largely on other signs, such as feeding signs and drop-pings; the habitat in which the track occurs may also provide a clue. Most of the small rodents live hidden among vegetation so one more or less never sees their tracks, except in snow. Those that live near water or on sand dunes may leave a visible track in mud or damp sand. The tracks of rats and mice can be seen in dust on the floors of mills, corn warehouses and similar places. The small rodents may be conveniently divided into two main groups, the voles and the true mice.

Voles

These have relatively short tails. They are more stoutly built than the true mice and in general move more slowly. The difference in size between the tracks of the fore-foot and hind-foot is usually quite distinct, but not so striking as in the true mice.

Tracks made by black rats on a dust-covered plank in a corn store. The fine meandering double lines are the trails left by beetles.

Water vole, tracks in mud.

Voles normally walk, although some species can jump well, but anything approaching a trot is rare. The size of the tracks varies according to the species; thus, the hind-foot track of a water vole is 20–25 mm long, of a field vole 17–18 mm and of a bank vole 16–17 mm.

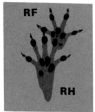

Water vole.

A bank vole has jumped down from a tree. On the right is the impression of its body, legs and tail, on the left two groups of tracks made as it jumped away.

Field vole, walking tracks in soft snow, showing▲ clear impressions of the paws and tail.

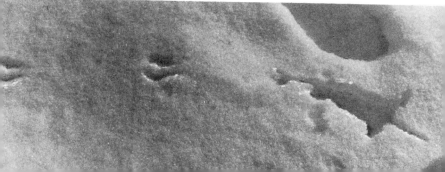

Wood mouse, groups of tracks made as the animal hopped around the hole leading to its burrow.

True mice

These are lighter in build and their tail and legs are long, particularly the hind-limbs which are well adapted for jumping. In fact, jumping is the commonest gait of the wood mouse and yellow-necked mouse, but rats and house mice just as frequently walk. In snow, where the tracks made in jumping are most frequently seen, the four footprints lie close together in groups, with a distinct size difference between the tracks of the fore-foot and hind-foot, and usually also a clear drag mark made by the long tail. The lengths of the hind-foot tracks are: brown rat 30–45 mm, house mouse 12–14 mm, striped mouse 16–18 mm, wood mouse 20–21 mm and yellow-necked mouse 22–24 mm.

Domestic cat

Cats are digitigrade (walking on the toes) with five toes on the fore-foot and four on the hind-foot. However, the inner toe of the fore-foot is positioned so high that it leaves no

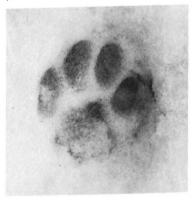

Domestic cat, track in soft snow.

Brown rat, tracks and trail.

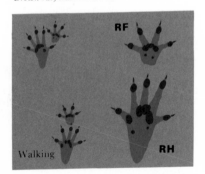

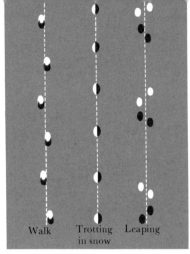

Domestic cat, trails.

Wild cat

Track and trail very similar to those of the domestic cat, but the individual footprints are larger and relatively longer (about 4 cm long and 3·5 cm broad).

European lynx

Tracks:
Like those of a cat but three times the size. The track of the fore-foot is

track. Four well-developed toe pads clearly separated from the large, three-lobed main or intermediate pad. Long, pointed claws which can be retracted so that they do not touch the ground during walking. The track is characterised by its almost circular shape, by the clearly marked pads and by the absence of claw marks. The footprint of a medium-sized cat is about 3–3·5 cm long and 3 cm broad.

Trail:
When walking on firm ground the hind-foot is normally placed in front of the track made by the fore-foot, but in snow it registers in the fore-foot track. The length of stride is about 30 cm and there is a distinct straddle.

When trotting the hind-foot and fore-foot tracks register and the stride is increased to 35–40 cm. The straddle is now so small that the tracks lie almost on a straight line. The track made by a trotting cat is thus similar to that of a trotting fox in snow, but it is smaller and the stride is much shorter.

In flight a cat makes jumps of varying lengths.

Lynx, tracks in soft ground.

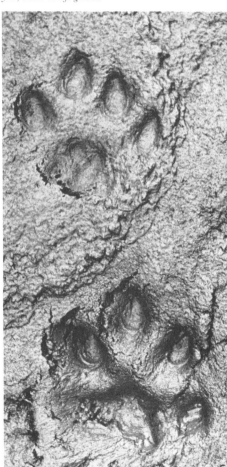

Lynx, walking tracks in hard snow.

c. 6·5 cm long and c. 5·5 cm broad, that of the hind-foot about 7·5 cm by 6 cm.

Trail:

The normal gait is a walk or a slow gallop. In both cases the hind-foot usually registers in the track of the fore-foot and there is little straddle, so the tracks lie almost on a straight line. When walking very slowly, however, the hind-foot is placed in front of the fore-foot track, and there is a marked straddle. In normal walking the length of stride is about 80 cm, which increases to about 135 cm when trotting. A lynx in flight usually breaks into a gallop, with a stride length of about 150 cm. When it jumps the length of stride may be up to 7 metres.

Beech marten and pine marten

Tracks:

Each foot has five clawed toes, all of which leave a mark in the clear footprint. In many cases, however, it may be difficult to see the track made by the inner toes. The claws nearly always give distinct impressions. The track shows a large, more or less semicircular main pad and five toe pads.

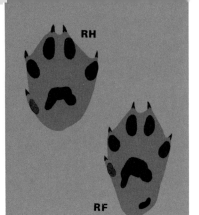

Marten.

Pine marten, walking tracks. The fur on the underside of the paws causes the contours of the tracks to become blurred.

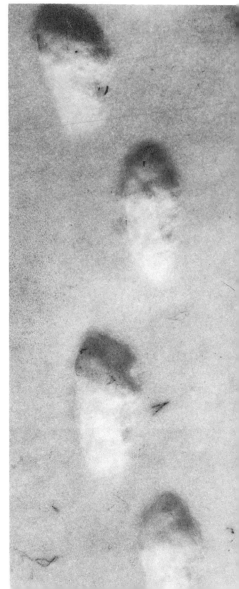

The fore-foot also has a small, round proximal pad on its outer edge behind the main pad. As these animals tread on the sole of the fore-foot, which is very short, the impression made by the proximal pad can usually be seen in clear tracks, and is thus a good recognition sign for a fore-foot track.

The footprints of the beech marten and pine marten are almost the same and very difficult to distinguish from one another. The track of a pine marten is, however, a little larger than that of a beech marten and the contours appear more blurred, because in the pine marten the growth of hair on the sole is so well developed, particularly in winter, that it completely covers the pads. On the other hand, the pads in a beech marten's track are nearly always very distinct. On fairly firm ground the fore-foot track of a beech marten is about 3·5 cm long and about 3·2 cm broad, that of the hind-foot about 4 cm by 3 cm.

The tracks of a pine marten are about 4–5 cm in length and the same in breadth. In loose snow the tracks may be surprisingly larger—often twice as large or even more.

Trail:

The length of stride is usually relatively short. Martens mainly move in jumps or leaps, but sometimes they walk or trot, and will then usually

Pine marten, a trail with the typical tracks in pairs.

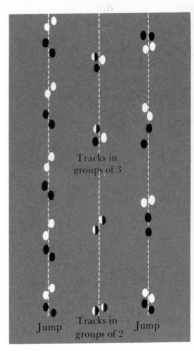

Tracks in groups of 3

Jump   Tracks in groups of 2   Jump

Marten, trails.

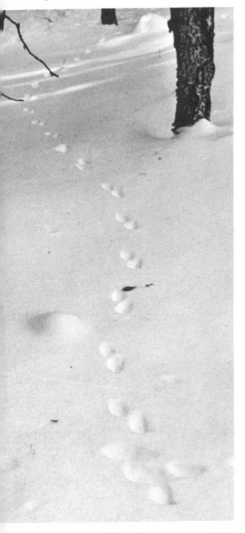

place the hind-feet behind the track made by the fore-feet.

The groups of tracks made when jumping are very characteristic of most members of the marten family. The individual footprints in a group are always very close together and as a rule one or both of the hind-feet will register in the tracks of the fore-feet, giving groups of three or two tracks. If one follows a series of tracks it will be seen that the track varies continuously in the same animal, and scarcely two groups of tracks are the same. Groups showing two tracks are commonest in snow, where the two lie close alongside, often at a slight angle from one another. The length of stride may vary from about 40 cm up to about one metre.

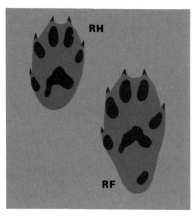

Polecat.

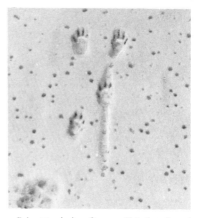

Polecat tracks in soft snow. Note the tail track.

European polecat

The individual footprint is very similar to that of a beech marten, but is smaller (size intermediate between that of beech marten and stoat). On fairly firm ground the fore-foot track is 3–3·5 cm long and 2·5–4 cm broad, depending upon the spread of the toes. On soft ground or in snow, where the animal treads on a larger area of sole, the hind-foot track may reach a length of 4–4·5 cm. The growth of hair between the pads is short and so the impressions made by the pads and claws are usually clearly marked.

The trail is the same as in the martens but when jumping it very often shows four separate footprints. The length of stride varies, being about 50–60 cm on firm ground, 35–50 cm in loose snow.

Mink tracks in snow.

48

Mink

In form and size the track is like that of the polecat, and it is practically impossible to distinguish the two tracks one from the other. The mink possibly has a tendency to spread the toes less than the polecat, and when jumping the distances between the groups of tracks seem more constant.

Stoat

The stoat has a typical small marten-like foot (see beech marten), but because of the animal's small size and light weight the tracks are often very indistinct, particularly in winter when the pads are covered with hair. It is only on very soft ground that the tracks show clear impressions of five splayed toes with claws and a curved but rather angular main pad.

The fore-foot track is about 2 cm long and 1·5 cm broad, the hind-foot's about 3·5 cm by 1·3 cm. Walking tracks are very rare as stoats move almost exclusively by jumping or hopping. On fairly hard ground such as firm snow, the tracks may be placed in groups of four, often like those of a

Stoat.

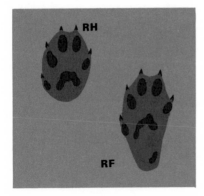

Stoat, jumping tracks in firm snow.

small hare. In loose snow they are most commonly in threes or in pairs. The distance between groups made when hopping may be very variable. Often the distance over long stretches may be very constant at about 40 cm, but there may also be a regular shift between long and short hops of, for example, 70 cm and 30 cm.

If one follows a stoat's tracks in the snow, one can often see that when hunting small rodents the animal suddenly burrows down into the snow and makes a tunnel which opens out again on the surface of the snow a little further on.

Weasel and least weasel

The tracks and trails of these two small carnivores are the same, and very similar to those of the stoat. The individual track is, however, smaller (about 1·4 cm long and 1 cm broad), and when hopping the distance between groups of tracks is rarely constant, but changes regularly between long and short hops.

Weasels do not move over the surface of snow so much as stoats, but make tunnels and holes in it. When a mouse has been caught a weasel will carry it back to its den by holding the body crossways in the mouth, so that in snow there will be an impression of the prey in front of each pair of tracks.

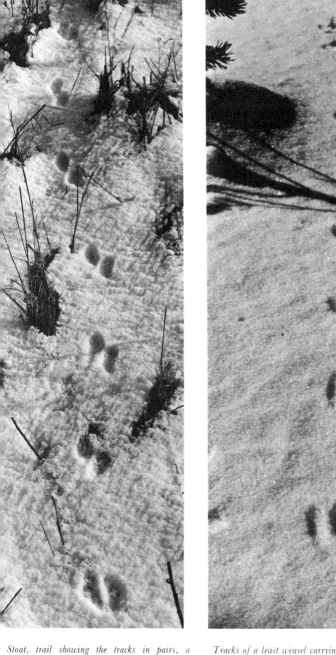

Stoat, trail showing the tracks in pairs, a characteristic feature of this group of animals, in which the hind-feet register in the fore-foot tracks.

Tracks of a least weasel carrying a mouse. The front and rear ends of the mouse have left marks in the snow on each side of the paired tracks made by the weasel.

Otter

Tracks:

The otter has five toes on each foot, and these are joined by a web. The tracks are very characteristic and easy to recognise.

The fore-foot track is almost circular (6·5–7 cm long, about 6 cm broad). Impressions of the inner toes only appear in very clear tracks and the web is only seen when the track is made in soft snow or mud. The claw marks are very small and only show as tiny points.

The track of the hind-foot is longer than that of the fore-foot and varies in length from about 6 to 9 cm, according to how much of the sole the animal treads on; the track may often show the complete sole. Impressions of the claws and web appear as in the fore-foot.

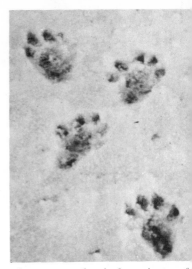

Otter, a group of tracks from a jump on firm ground. Above, the fore-foot tracks, below the hind-foot tracks.

Trail:

In walking, a gait that is seldom used, an otter places the hind-foot behind the track of the fore-foot, and there is considerable straddle. In a trot, which is also rare, the fore-foot track is more or less covered by the hind-foot and the length of stride is about 70–80 cm.

An otter normally moves in leaps

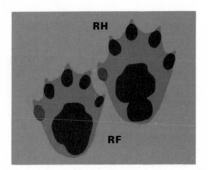

Otter, tracks and trail. ▶

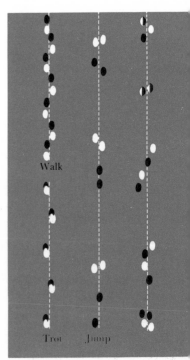

Walk

Trot   Jump

and there is great variation in the placing of the individual tracks in a group. A very peculiar trail is seen when all four footprints are on a diagonal or oblique line. In snow it is common for tracks to appear in pairs, and in deep, loose snow the body makes a furrow, because of the shortness of the legs, in the bottom of which the paired tracks can be seen at relatively short intervals. In snow the tail often makes a drag mark. In a normal jump an otter will cover a distance of about 40–45 cm.

An attractive and not uncommon track occurs in the form of long, broad furrows which are produced when an otter slides down a snowy slope on its belly. When playing they often use suitable slopes as real toboggan runs.

A snow slope showing a slide made by otters playing.

In deep snow an otter leaves pairs of tracks and its body makes a furrow which joins the groups of tracks.

52

Badger

Tracks:
Badgers are typical plantigrade animals with five toes with long claws on each foot. As they tread heavily the details of the tracks are usually distinct, and in fact a badger track is always easy to recognise as it has a characteristic form and is rather like the track of a small bear.

In a track the five toe pads lie close alongside one another and almost in a straight row. The impression of the inner toe is, however, usually faint, and is often completely absent. The

Badger, fore-foot track.

Badger, hind-foot track.

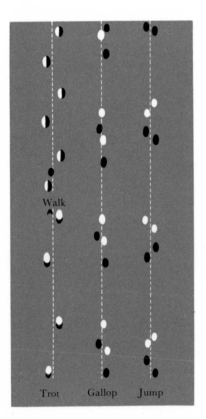

Walk

Trot   Gallop   Jump

Badger, trails.

large, main pad and the claws are always seen; the very long claws on the fore-foot make particularly clear impressions which may extend beyond the toe pads. The claws on the hind-foot are considerably shorter. Normally a badger treads only with the front part of the fore-foot and the track is then about 5 cm long and 4 cm broad; when the whole foot is used the length is about 7 cm. The hind-foot track often shows an impression of the whole foot, which has a breadth of

about 3·5 cm, and a length of about
4·5 cm to the rear edge of the main
pad, or about 6·5 cm to the heel.

Trail:

The normal gait is a walk, with the
hind-foot usually registering in the
track made by the fore-foot. The
length of stride is about 50 cm, and
there is a large amount of straddle.
When travelling over longer distances
badgers trot and on firm ground the
hind-foot then lands in front of the
fore-foot track and the stride is about
70–80 cm in length. When travelling
fast over open ground or when scared
a badger may use a galloping or
jumping gait.

Wolverine or Glutton

Tracks:

Wolverines are only partly plantigrade
and their tracks often only show impressions of the front part of the feet.
They have five toes with powerful
claws on each foot. The tracks usually
show clear impressions of the five toe
pads and the two proximal pads at the
rear of the fore-feet, but owing to the
dense hair on the sole the main pad
is less distinct, and similarly the claw
marks may be lacking. When the impression of the inner toe is indistinct
or completely lacking the track may be
confused with that of a wolf, particularly in snow. However, the wolverine's
track is more elongated and pointed
posteriorly and confusion is not possible when one looks at the trail. The
fore-foot track, which is about 8 cm
long and 7 cm broad will often be
more or less covered by the hind-foot
track, which is about 8 × 6·5 cm.

Trail:

The wolverine moves primarily in
leaps, like its close relatives the

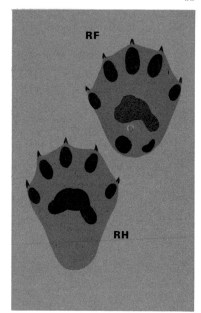

Wolverine.

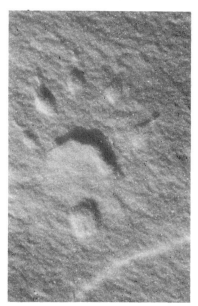

*Wolverine, hind-foot track showing clear im-
pression of heel.*

53

54

martens, and with the variations in trail pattern that are so characteristic of the latter. Thus, in snow the tracks most commonly occur in pairs. Wolverines also trot, but only exceptionally walk.

Wolverine, trail in firm snow.

Common red fox

Tracks:
The fox is digitigrade (walking on its toes) with five toes on each fore-foot and four on each hind-foot. However, the inner toe of the fore-foot is placed so high up that it leaves no mark in the track. Each footprint has four well-developed toe pads and a large main pad. The claws are long, narrow and pointed. The track shows the pads and claws clearly, and is so symmetrical that it is usually impossible to tell from a single print whether it comes from a left or a right foot. The track of the fore-foot is somewhat larger than that of the hind-foot, but is otherwise almost the same. The length is about 5 cm, the breadth 4–4·5 cm.

A fox's track can easily be confused with that of a dog of the same size. In a fox the pads are smaller and not so close together as in a dog. Furthermore, the two central toe pads lie further forwards in the fox, so that there is a relatively large space between the rear edges of these pads and the front edge of the main pad;

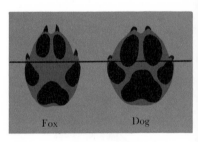

Fox   Dog

Comparison between fox and dog tracks.

also if one draws a line through the front edges of the outer toe pads it will touch or lie behind the rear edges of the two central toe pads. Compared with that of a dog, a fox's track is

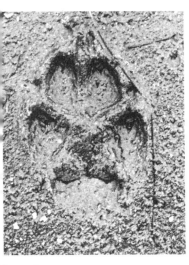

Fox, trails.

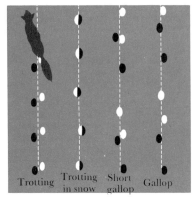

Trotting | Trotting in snow | Short gallop | Gallop

Fox, trotting tracks on firm and on soft ground.

more elongated and slender and the claw marks are slimmer and more pointed.

In winter—especially in northern regions—the hair between the naked pads grows so dense as to cover them. The track will then become larger and more rounded, with blurred contours.

Trail:
The fox may use all types of gait, but by far the commonest is a trot.

On firm ground the trail of a trotting fox differs somewhat from the more normal type produced by a dog or wolf. For a fox leaves a row of obliquely positioned pairs of footprints, each of which consists of a forefoot track with a hind-foot track placed obliquely forwards and to one side. All the hind-foot tracks lie on the same side. This remarkable trail is due to the fact that the animal trots with its body positioned at an angle to the direction of travel. Now and again it can be seen to shift the rear part of its body over to the other side. In snow or on

Fox, tracks on firm and soft ground.

soft ground, however, a fox always holds its body straight, facing the direction in which it is moving, and places each hind-foot exactly in the track made by the fore-foot of the same side. In a trot the stride length is about 70–80 cm.

When walking on firm ground the hind-foot is generally placed in front of the fore-foot, and the stride is 25–35 cm in length. When frightened or pursued a fox will jump or gallop, and the stride length is then very variable.

Arctic Fox

The track is similar to that of a common red fox but somewhat smaller, and in winter more rounded and less distinct, on account of the dense growth of hair on the sole of the foot. The trail is also similar but the length of stride is shorter in all gaits. An Arctic fox uses a trot less than a red fox, but does more galloping.

Dog

The track and trail are the same as those of a fox, and footprints of the same order of size may be confused. However, the track of a dog appears

Dog: left, fore-foot track and right, hind-foot track.

more compact, for the pads are large and closer together. Thus, the main pad extends forwards almost to the toe pads of the central toes, and if one draws a line through the front of the outer toe pads it will usually cut through the central toe pads (see p. 54). The claw marks are thick and blunt. The track of the fore-foot is considerably larger than that of the hind-foot and the rear edge of the main pad is concave, whereas in the hind-foot it is convex.

Wolf

The tracks and trail are like those of a large dog with which they can very easily be confused. In the wolf, however, the toe pads are more elongated and are not so close together, so that the spread between the two middle toes is somewhat greater than in a dog. The claw marks are also larger, longer and more pointed than those of a dog. In an adult wolf the fore-foot track is about 11 cm long and 10 cm broad, the hind-foot track about 8 cm by 7 cm.

When walking, which they do relatively seldom, the length of stride is 80–90 cm, when trotting (the commonest gait) the stride is about one metre, and when jumping or galloping it may be 1·5 m or more.

Wolf track.

Tracks of a wolf that has been foraging on the remains of a reindeer.

Raccoon-dog

The track is somewhat like that of a fox but it can be distinguished by the fact that the toes are very widely spread, so that the impressions of the toe pads are fanned out in front of the main pad, and not bunched together as in the fox. The toe pads and claws are usually clearly marked. The track of the fore-foot is 4–5 cm long and 5–6 cm broad, but that of the hind-foot is a little smaller. The tracks are never on a straight line—as is often seen in the fox—but follow an irregular rolling course.

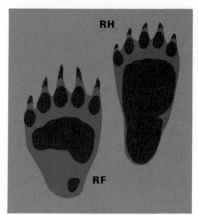

Brown bear, tracks and trail. ▶

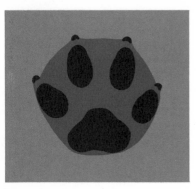

Raccoon-dog.

Brown bear

Tracks:

Plantigrade animals having five toes with long claws on each foot. The impressions of the large toe pads lie close alongside each other, and the claw marks are usually distinct. Between the impressions made by the toe pads and by the main pad there is a clearly marked ridge of compressed tissue. The track of the fore-foot is short and broad, for the animal mainly treads on the front part of this foot, and only in very clear tracks does one see the complete sole. The size of the track varies considerably according to age, but in a fully grown bear the length is about 28 cm, the breadth about 21 cm.

The track of the hind-foot, which often shows the whole sole, is not unlike that of a very large, naked human foot, but in the bear the first toe, corresponding to our big toe, is the smallest and shortest. In a fully grown bear the hind-foot track is about 30 cm long and 17 cm broad.

Trail:

The normal gait of a bear is walking, and the hind-foot is placed a good way in front of the fore-foot track. Usually the tracks are set more or less at an angle to the direction of movement. There is considerable straddle and the length of stride, which is very variable, may be about 150 cm for a fully grown specimen. When trotting the straddle decreases and the tracks are directed more in the direction of movement. The hind-foot is placed in or near the track of the fore-foot. Bears rarely jump and then only over short distances, but they usually do so in very deep snow.

Raccoon

A native of North America introduced into Germany for its fur, these are plantigrade animals having five long toes with large claws on each foot. The track is somewhat similar to that of a bear but is very much smaller. The fore-foot track is about 7 cm in length and about the same in breadth and has widely separated toes. The track of the hind-foot, in which the toes lie closer together, is about 9 cm long and 6 7 cm broad. The tracks are often placed in pairs with, for example, the left hind-foot alongside the right fore-foot (compare the fox p. 55).

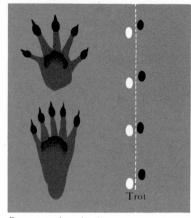

Trot

Raccoon, tracks and trail.

Seals

Seal tracks can be found on mud or sand banks or on snow-covered ice. They are very characteristic and cannot be confused with any other animal tracks. When moving the body is scarcely lifted, but is dragged along the surface with the help of the fore-limbs; in fast movement, as for example when the animal takes flight, the hind-limbs can also be used to move the body forwards. The track, therefore, consists of a broad drag mark made by the body and on each side—arranged in pairs—a row of fore-limb tracks in which the five claws are usually closely marked and positioned on a line parallel with the direction of movement.

Seal tracks on a sandbank. Between the tracks of the front flippers one can see the depressions made in the sand by the seal's body. The animal has not used the back flippers in moving.

Tracks of animals with cloven hoofs

Natural size

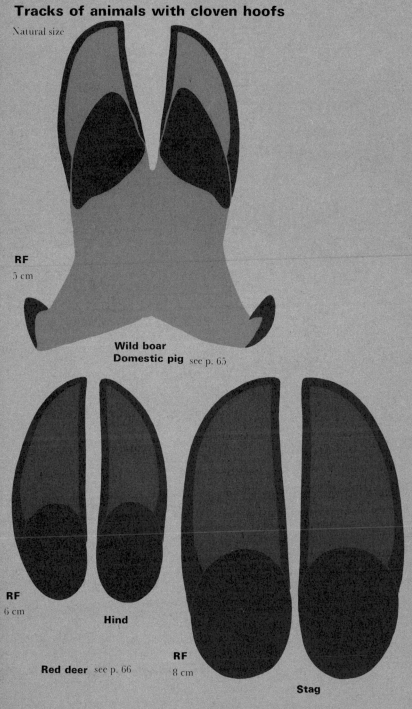

cm
1
2
3
4
5
6
7
8
9
10
11
12
13
14
15
16
17
18

RF
5 cm

Wild boar
Domestic pig see p. 65

RF
6 cm

Hind

Red deer see p. 66

RF
8 cm

Stag

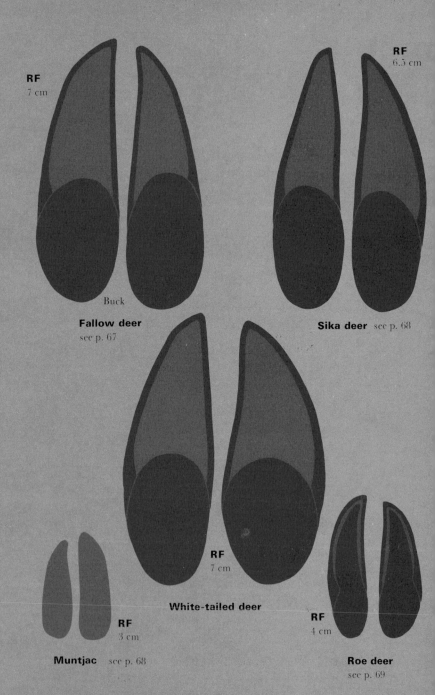

RF
7 cm

Buck

Fallow deer
see p. 67

RF
6.5 cm

Sika deer see p. 68

RF
7 cm

White-tailed deer

RF
3 cm

Muntjac see p. 68

RF
4 cm

Roe deer
see p. 69

Tracks of animals with cloven hoofs

Half natural size

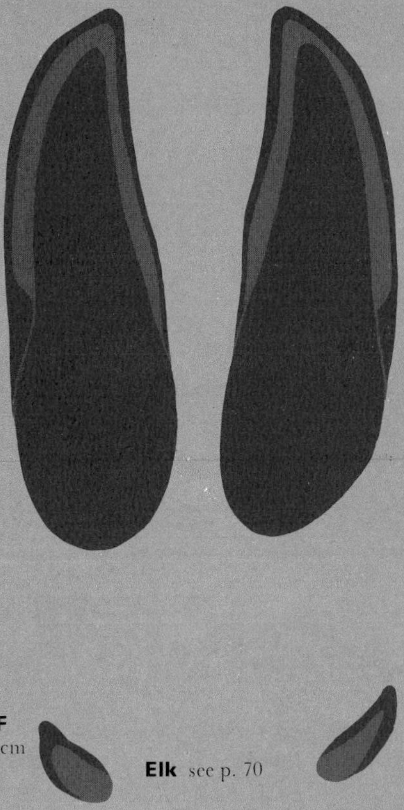

cm

1

2

3

4

5

6

7

8

9

RF
14 cm

Elk see p. 70

10

11

12

13

14

15

16

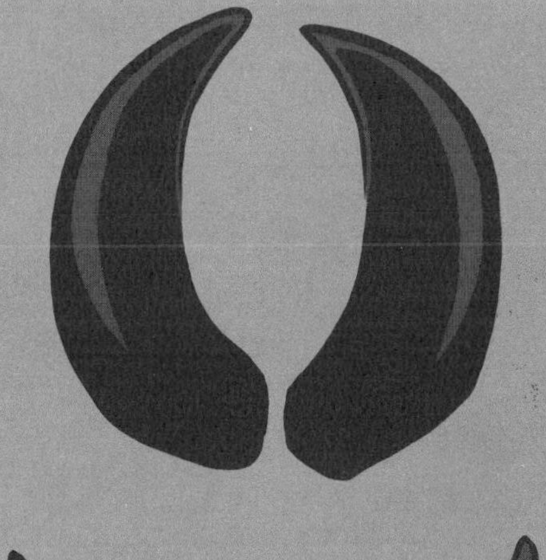

RF
9 cm

Reindeer see p. 72

17

18

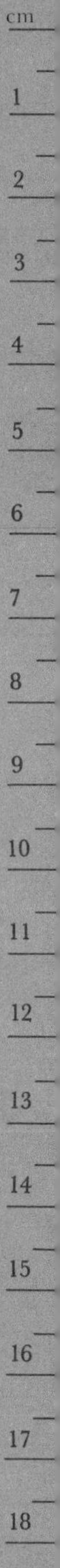

Natural size

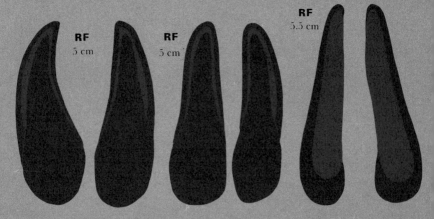

RF
5 cm

RF
5 cm

RF
5.5 cm

Mouflon see p. 72   **Domestic sheep** see p. 73   **Chamois** see p. 73

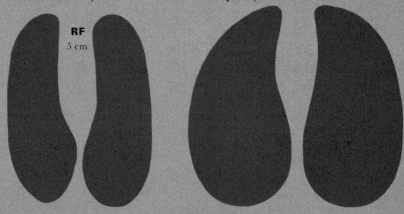

RF
5 cm

Domestic goat
see p. 74

Domestic cattle
about ⅔ natural size
see p. 74

Track of an animal with non-cloven hoofs

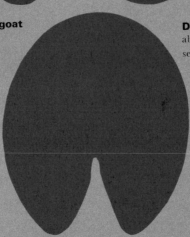

Horse
about half natural size.
see p. 74

Tracks of animals with cloven hoofs

Wild boar

Tracks:

The track of a wild boar, in contrast to most of those made by deer, is characterised by the fact that the dew claws nearly always leave clear impressions whatever gait the animal is using. In very young animals, however, the impressions may be weak or completely lacking. In deer the impression of the dew claws—when found—is straight behind that of the main hoofs, so that the whole track is rectangular, whereas in the wild boar the dew claws lie further out to the sides, so that the track becomes trapezoid. In snow, for example, where the track is often just a hole showing no detail, one can always tell a deer from a pig, because the track of the latter is broadest posteriorly.

The size of the track varies considerably according to age and sex. In an adult the breadth of the main hoofs is about 6–7 cm. In young animals the hoofs are pointed in front, but they are more rounded in adults.

Trail:

In walking and trotting the individual footprint is turned somewhat outwards, and the hind-foot usually registers exactly in the track of the fore-foot. Sometimes, however, the hind-foot track is slightly displaced in relation to the fore-foot, so that the trail may show two pairs of hoofs, one slightly behind the other. In adults the length of stride when walking is

Wild boar, track (above) and trail.

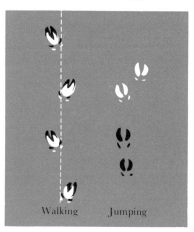

Walking   Jumping

about 40 cm. In a fast gallop or jump the tracks appear separately in groups of four, and the hoofs are widely splayed.

Domestic pig

In general the track is the same as in the wild boar. However, the shape and size varies somewhat depending upon the race and the degree to which the hoofs have become worn.

Red deer

Tracks:
The track of a red deer is relatively broad and the outer edges of each half of the hoof curve symmetrically towards the tip. The front hoofs are particularly curved and in a large animal may look rather like the heel of a boot seen in reverse. In a clear track the impression of the pads can be seen as rounded depressions at the back, accounting for about one-third of the track's length; in front of this there is a slight ridge corresponding to the arch made by the sole. In a fully grown stag the fore-foot track is 8–9 cm long and 6–7 cm broad, while the hind's track is somewhat smaller— 6–7 cm long by 4–5 cm broad.

Trail:
When walking or gently trotting, which are the commonest gaits when the animal is undisturbed, the hind-foot registers in the fore-foot track. Normally the dew claws do not leave

a mark, and the straddle is relatively small in the hind and fawn, but considerable in the stag. In an adult the length of stride varies between 80 and 150 cm. In a fast trot on firm ground the hind-foot is placed in front of the fore-foot track, the faster the speed the further in front. At the same time the straddle is reduced, the hoofs are much splayed and the dew claws

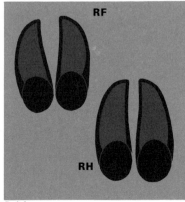

Red deer.

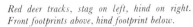

Red deer tracks, stag on left, hind on right. Front footprints above, hind footprint below.

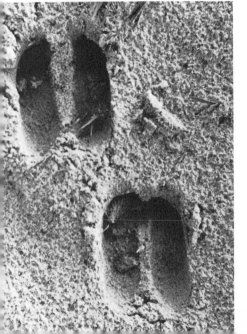

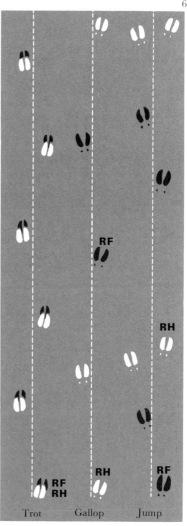

Red deer, trotting tracks in sand.

Red deer, trails.

usually leave marks. The stride length varies considerably according to the trotting speed and may be up to 350 cm. When in full flight deer frequently gallop or jump, and they will then leave tracks showing widely spread hoofs and clearly marked dew claws.

Fallow deer

The track of a fallow deer is narrower and more elongated than that of a red deer. The hoof impressions are often very pointed and the outer sides at the rear of the track are almost parallel. The impression made by the pad accounts for almost half the length of the track and is often quite distinct. The track made by a doe is 5–6 cm long and 3·5–4 cm broad, but that of the buck may reach a length of 8 cm and a breadth of 5 cm. The trails produced by the different gaits are similar to those in the red deer, but the stride lengths are somewhat shorter.

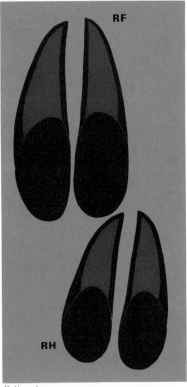

Fallow deer.

Sika deer

The track is very like that of a fallow deer but is relatively broader and the trail shows more straddle.

Muntjac

These are small Asiatic deer which have been introduced into England and France. The tracks are very small, usually less than 3 cm long, and there is a tendency for the inner half of the hoof to be less well developed than the outer half, although in many specimens the hoofs are symmetrical. The dew claws are small and will usually only leave a mark in very soft ground, or when the animal jumps.

A pair of muntjac tracks, the hind-foot placed in the fore-foot track. Note that the hoofs are asymmetrical.

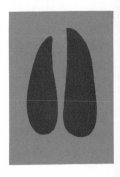

Muntjac.

White-tailed deer

A North American species which has been introduced into Finland. The track, which is about 7 cm long, is somewhat similar to that of a fallow deer.

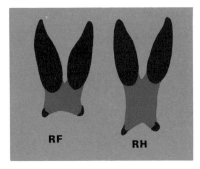

White-tailed deer, the distance between the hoofs and the dew claws is greater in the hind-foot track.

Roe deer

Tracks:

The track is characterised by its small size and the narrow, pointed shape of the hoofs, and also by the fact that the impression is flat, because the pads extend right out to the tip of the hoof. In old animals, however the hoof tips are blunt. The track is about 4·5 cm long and 3 cm broad, and there is no significant size difference between the sexes.

Trail:

Roe deer move mostly by walking, and the straddle is usually small although this may vary. The tracks are turned somewhat outwards and the dew claws make no mark. The length of stride is 60–90 cm and the hind-foot normally registers in the fore-foot track. The front hoofs are usually slightly splayed, but the hind hoofs are kept close together.

In a trot the tracks are almost in a line, with the individual footprints directed forwards. In a slow trot the hind-foot registers in the fore-foot track, but as the speed increases the hind-feet land further and further in front of the fore-foot tracks. The front hoofs are often much splayed in a trot and the stride length is usually 100–140 cm.

A roe deer in flight will gallop or jump and the dew claws will then make a mark, which in the fore-foot

Roe deer.

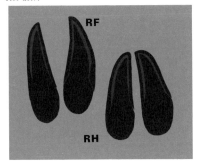

Roe deer, tracks from a jump, with fore-feet below, hind-feet above.

are almost at right angles but are more parallel in the hind-foot. In a jump the hoofs are always splayed, the front hoofs very markedly in the form of a V, the hind ones less so. The length of a jump is usually about two metres but is very variable and may be more than twice as much.

Elk

Tracks:

On account of its size the track of an elk could only be confused with that of domestic cattle. It is, however, easy to distinguish these two tracks for the elk has long, pointed hoofs which leave an almost rectangular track, while a cow's hoof is less pointed and much more rounded. Furthermore, an elk's track often shows the impression of the dew claws, particularly of the fore-feet, but this is rare in the case of cattle. As in the roe deer the pads extend right out to the tip of the hoof.

The size of the track varies considerably with age and sex and in old animals the tips of the hoofs are usually more rounded than in the young. In a fully grown bull elk the fore-foot track is 13–15 cm long and 11–13 cm broad, and the corresponding measurements for the hind-foot are 14–15·5 cm and 10·5–11 cm. The track

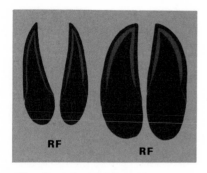

Elk, calf on left, adult bull on right.

Elk tracks, hind-foot above, fore-foot below.

Elk, walking tracks in snow.

of the cow is somewhat smaller than that of the bull.

Trail:
An elk normally walks or trots, and only rarely breaks into a gallop, and then only over short distances; usually it is only the young which use this gait. When walking there is a considerable amount of straddle.

Reindeer

Tracks:
The track of a reindeer is very characteristic and easy to recognise by the half moon-shaped hoofs which leave an almost circular impression with sharply marked edges. The dew claws are large and positioned low down, and they leave a mark even when the animal is walking slowly. In a fully grown bull the track of the fore-foot is about 8·5 cm long and 10 cm broad, that of the hind-foot about 8·5 cm by 9·5 cm. The track of the cow is generally a little smaller and rather more pointed than that of the bull.

Reindeer track, note dew claws.

Trail:
Reindeer normally move by walking or trotting, although exceptionally they may gallop and jump. When walking the amount of straddle is considerable, the tracks turn outwards and the stride length is 100–120 cm. In a trot the stride may be 130–150 cm.

Reindeer, trails.

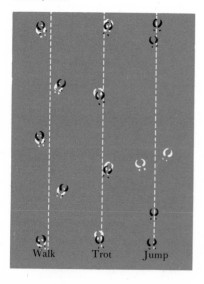

Walk   Trot   Jump

Mouflon

These wild sheep have long, slender hoofs, in which the two halves do not join completely, even when compressed. Apart from the elongated shape, the track is characterised by the fact that the hoof tips are almost always splayed, even in a slow walk, and the track is very angular posteriorly. The dew claws never leave a mark, even when the animal jumps. In a fully grown ram the track is about 5·5 cm long and 4·4 cm broad, but is a little shorter and narrower in the ewe.

The normal gait is a walk or trot, but when in flight mouflon gallop or jump. There is usually considerable straddle but the length of stride is relatively short.

Mouflon, fore-foot track.

Domestic sheep, tracks.

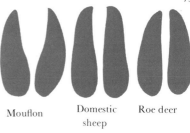

Mouflon   Domestic   Roe deer
               sheep

Domestic sheep

The track of a domestic sheep is some-what reminiscent of a roe deer's, but is broader and more rectangular and has distinctly rounded tips to the hoofs. The dew claws are positioned so high on the legs that they never leave a mark. The size of the individual track varies according to age and race, but in an adult it is usually about 5–6 cm long and 4–5 cm broad.

Chamois

Chamois live in mountain regions and the hoofs are adapted in various ways for moving about on rocks and steep slopes. Thus, the edge of the hoof, on which the animal treads, is well developed and consists of an elastic, rubber-like substance. In addition, there is a relatively great ability to move the two halves of the hoof, which are very mobile in relation to one another. As chamois live mainly in rocky terrain the tracks are not often seen, except in winter.

The individual track has a very characteristic shape. The impressions of the two halves of each hoof are angular, and there is always a large and distinct space between each half hoof. When walking the track is rect-angular and almost square, but as the speed increases it becomes more trape-zoid owing to the marked splay of the hoof tips. The dew claws are positioned

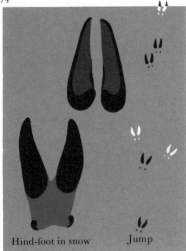

Hind-foot in snow   Jump

Chamois, tracks and trail.

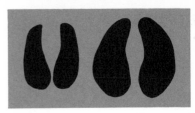

Domestic goat   *Domestic cattle*

Domestic cattle

The tracks vary considerably in shape and size according to the farmer's treatment of the cow's hoofs. The individual hoof is rounded and broad in relation to its length. The outer edge is convex, but the inner edge is concave in front, convex behind. The dew claws do not normally leave a mark. The size of each track varies considerably according to the race but may, for example, be 10–12 cm long and 9–10 cm broad.

high up and they only leave a mark in sufficiently deep snow or when the animal is in flight. In contrast to the normal track in snow, the track left by an animal in flight shows the dew claws far behind, about 10 cm behind the rear edge of the hoof. This is because, when jumping down, the legs 'give' to such an extent that the dew claws come to touch the surface. The track of a fully grown chamois is about 6 cm long and 3·5 cm broad.

Domestic goat

The track of a goat is characterised by the fact that the hoofs are rounded at the tips and narrower in front than behind. The tips are often very widely splayed and each half of the hoof has a convex outer margin and a concave inner margin. The dew claws leave no impression. The size of the individual track varies somewhat according to the race.

Tracks made by animal with non-cloven hoofs

Horse

The track of a horse can be found in two forms, namely, with or without a shoe. When shod one sees only the impression of the shoe and identification is easy. Without shoes a horse leaves large, almost circular tracks, each deeply indented at the back. The size of the track varies considerably, depending upon the race.

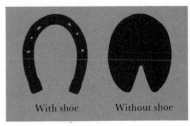

With shoe   Without shoe

Bird tracks

When moving on the ground a bird treads only on its toes, because the metatarsus which is the long piece of bone nearest to the foot never touches the ground when the bird is walking. The first joint after the foot therefore corresponds to the heel and not the knee, as one might think.

The foot of a bird never has more than four toes, of which three usually point forwards and the fourth is turned backwards. When compared with the foot of a mammal (see p. 9), it is the fifth toe which has disappeared and the first (or thumb) which is turned backwards. Of those that face forwards the middle or third toe is usually the longest. The first toe may be large, but it is often small and positioned so high up that it leaves no mark in the track. In some birds, such as the golden plover and kittiwake the first toe is completely absent.

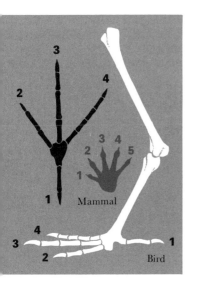

In certain birds, as for example grouse, the plumage extends right out on to the toes, but in most the upperside of the toes is clad with horny scales, while the treading surfaces are covered with horny papillae which give protection against the cold and prevent slipping. The outermost joint of each toe carries a claw which is large and powerful in, for example, the birds of prey, but only poorly developed in the ducks.

The shape of the foot, which is reflected in the footprint, shows great variation and provides a clue to the habits and habitat of the different species and sometimes also to their diet. Thus, in swimming birds the upper surface of each foot is enlarged by a web, a leathery fold of skin which joins the three forward-directed toes in ducks and gulls, and all four toes in the cormorants. In the coot and the grebes each individual toe has a series of lobate webs. Wading birds have long, slender toes which are widely spread and thus well adapted for walking on a soft substrate without sinking in. The feet of pheasants, partridges and domestic fowls are short and powerful, and well adapted for running, while those of the perching birds (passerines) have a long first toe which is opposable to the front toes, so that the foot can firmly grip a branch.

On the ground a bird may move by hopping, walking or running. In a hop the tracks occur in pairs, but walking produces tracks in a zigzag, or sometimes in a straight line. When running the length of stride is greater than when walking, but the straddle is less.

The tracks of birds are seen almost

The wings leave marks as the bird takes off.

Two blackbirds have landed in the snow, no wing marks.

exclusively on very soft substrates, such as the muddy banks of lakes, in snow or wet sand. In snow one often also sees the impression of the wing feathers in places where a bird has flown off. When it lands it may leave a mark where the body has touched the ground, and in snow a pheasant often leaves a track of its long tail feathers.

On account of the great number of possibilities the identification of bird tracks is often a very difficult task which requires experience and a considerable knowledge of ornithology. The first point to observe is the size of the track, and particularly the length of the central toe and the length and shape of the first toe. Similarly, a note should be made of the size of the angle between the two outer toes (2nd and 4th), and whether the toes are long and slender or short and thick. The presence of a web is also an important clue to identification.

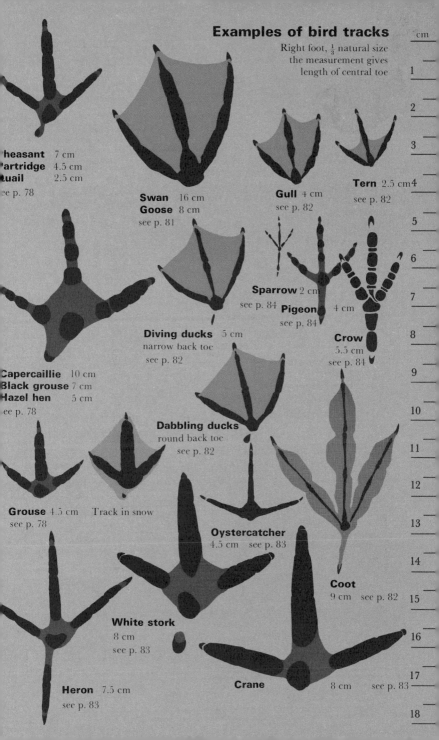

Examples of bird tracks

Right foot, ⅓ natural size
the measurement gives
length of central toe

cm

heasant 7 cm
artridge 4.5 cm
uail 2.5 cm
ee p. 78

Swan 16 cm
Goose 8 cm
see p. 81

Gull 4 cm
see p. 82

Tern 2.5 cm
see p. 82

Sparrow 2 cm
see p. 84

Pigeon 4 cm
see p. 84

Crow
5.5 cm
see p. 84

Capercaillie 10 cm
Black grouse 7 cm
Hazel hen 5 cm
ee p. 78

Diving ducks 5 cm
narrow back toe
see p. 82

Dabbling ducks
round back toe
see p. 82

Grouse 4.5 cm
see p. 78

Track in snow

Oystercatcher
4.5 cm   see p. 83

Coot
9 cm   see p. 82

White stork
8 cm
see p. 83

Heron 7.5 cm
see p. 83

Crane   8 cm   see p. 83

Game birds

These birds are closely associated with the ground, where they nest and where they also search for most of their food. Their tracks will therefore be found on soft ground in fields or on woodland paths, and in snow during the winter.

The legs are powerful with feet adapted for walking and running. The three forward-directed toes are thick and have strong, blunt claws which are well adapted for scratching food from the ground. The claws will usually leave distinct marks in the track. The toes are widely spread, with an angle of 90 degrees between the outer toes. The first toe is quite short and directed slightly inwards, and only its claw leaves a mark in the track.

On the ground, game birds move by walking or running, and the tracks form either a zigzag or an almost straight line.

Pheasants have very slender toes compared with related members of the group. The track is usually very large, 6–8 cm long, and with distinct claw marks, including that made by that of the inturned first toe. Pheasants live mainly in open woodland and on agricultural land where their tracks can be seen along the hedges and on paths, after rain has softened the ground. They often follow the same routes, and form paths which are best seen in the snow, where the long tail also leaves a mark.

The tracks of the *common partridge*, *rock partridge* and *red-legged partridge* are similar to those of a pheasant but smaller—only 4–5 cm long. These birds live in open country, and often in dry areas where there is little chance of finding their tracks in summer. On the other hand, in winter, when the birds gather into small flocks, the tracks are very striking and are seen as interweaving, often parallel rows of tracks in the snow. The individual footprints are nearly always on a straight line.

The *quail* which is only half the size of a partridge leaves a track that is 2–2·5 cm long.

The track of a *capercaillie* is easy to recognise, if only on account of its size; it is 10–11 cm long and 8–9 cm broad in the male, and somewhat smaller in the female. These birds live in well established conifer forests, where in winter their trails on the snow-covered ground wind in and out among the trees. At their courtship grounds or leks, one can see how the males have dragged their wings, forming furrows in the snow (see p. 228).

The track of a *black grouse* is similar to that of the capercaillie but is smaller—7–8 cm long and 6–7 cm broad. These birds live in more open country than capercaillie and their tracks are found, in particular, along the edges of woods, on moorland, heaths and similar places. As with the capercaillie the leks show furrows in the snow formed by the dragging wings of the courting males (see p. 228).

The track of a *hazel hen* is similar in form to that of a capercaillie or a black grouse but smaller, being only 5–5·5 cm long and 4·5–5 cm broad. This species lives in hilly country with mixed woodland and scrub, especially in areas with damp valleys where there is a growth of birch and aspen.

Grouse (willow grouse, ptarmigan and red grouse) have feather-clad toes and so their tracks, mainly seen in snow, become blurred and ill-defined and the impressions of the toes appear very broad. The length of the track is 4–5 cm. These tracks are most often found winding in and out among small bushes in heathland or moorland.

Pheasant tracks.   *Track from a covey of partridges.*   *Capercaillie tracks in soft snow.* ▼

Willow grouse, tracks from a pack feeding on buds from the bushes.

Grouse tracks in snow.

Swimming birds

In birds that can swim the feet nearly always have characteristic webs which increase the effective surface of the feet. In swimming the toes are held apart so that the foot presents a large surface area when pushed backwards through the water. The toes are then folded together as the foot moves forwards, so that it presents a minimum surface area and little resistance. The web varies in form in the different groups of swimming birds and is therefore an important aid to the identification of bird tracks.

The tracks made by swimming birds are naturally seen mainly along the banks of lakes and rivers, and on the seashore, but in some cases they may also be found far from water. Thus, it is well-known that black-headed gulls and common gulls gather in large flocks to pick up insect larvae and worms turned up by the plough. In most cases, however, the tracks left in such places will be very indistinct and difficult to recognise. In fact, a really clear footprint will usually only be found on a very soft substrate, such as mud, wet sand or snow.

The tracks of *swans* are easy to recognise on account of their size; the centre toe is about 16 cm long in the mute swan, in the whooper swan about 14·5 cm, and in Bewick's swan about 11·5 cm. The web, which unites the three forward-directed toes, extends right out to the blunt claws, and has an almost straight front edge. The outer toes are somewhat curved; the first toe is short and turned inwards, and usually only its claw leaves an impression in the track. On account of the bird's great weight the tracks of the webs and claws are usually very distinct. On land, swans move by walking with the feet turned in and the stride is 30–40 cm long.

Goose tracks have the same shape and appearance as those of swans, but they can be distinguished by their smaller size. Thus, in the greylag, one of the largest geese, the middle toe is about 8·5–9 cm long, usually a little less, and the middle toe of a brent goose is only 5–5·5 cm long. As geese are large birds with a heavy tread their feet, which are stout and broad, will often leave clear impressions of the claws, web and toes. As ducks' toes are more slender than those of geese the breadth of the toe prints is a good distinguishing character. Goose tracks can be seen on the seashore and along the banks of lakes and also in soft ground in meadows where the birds have been feeding.

Mute swan, walking tracks in snow. As with geese and ducks, the feet turn inwards as they walk.

The feet and tracks of *ducks* are, in general, similar to those of swans and geese but they are smaller. For instance, the middle toe of a mallard is about 5 cm long. The web, which has an almost straight front edge, extends out to the claws, and the outer toes are slightly curved. In the diving ducks, the short first toe has a small web lobe which in clear tracks leaves a narrow, oblong mark. In the dabbling ducks the impression of the first toe is shorter and more rounded.

In comparison with goose tracks, those made by ducks appear less robust, the toes being more slender and the claws more pointed. It is not possible to distinguish the tracks of the many duck species from one another.

On land ducks move in a waddling gait with inturned toes. In the mallard the length of stride is about 15 cm.

Gulls have a web joining the three forward-directed toes; this extends out to the claws and has an almost straight or slightly concave front edge; the outer toes are almost straight. The first toe is small and positioned so high that it only leaves a mark on very soft ground. The claws are pointed. The length of the middle toe is c. 3 cm in the black-headed gull, 3–4 cm in the common gull, 6–7 cm in the herring gull and greater black-backed gull and 5–5·5 cm in the lesser black-backed gull.

Gull tracks occur mainly on the coast, although black-headed gull and common gull tracks are also seen far inland. The pointed claws usually leave a mark, but an impression of the web is only seen on a soft substrate. Gulls usually use a walking gait, but will occasionally run.

In *terns* the web does not extend right out to the claws and its front edge is very concave. The first toe is small and the claws are pointed. The tracks are small and in most species the middle toe is 2–3 cm long. With the exception of the black tern which lives mainly in the vicinity of marshes, swamps and lakes, the terns are almost exclusively coastal birds.

The foot of a *coot*, which leaves a most characteristic track, is intermediate between that of a swimming bird and a wader. The foot is very large with long front toes which have lateral lobes of web, with a deep

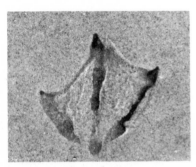

Herring gull track. In gulls the outer toes are almost equal and the claws are pointed.

Coot track; with lobed web. ▶

indentation at each toe joint. The middle toe is 8–9·5 cm long. The first toe which has a very broad web fringe is a little over 3 cm in length. The tracks can be seen near lakes, in marshland and sometimes on the sea-shore.

Waders

The wading birds, usually known collectively as waders, have characteristic feet with a long, naked metatarsus and long slender front toes with small claws. The first toe is usually small, but may be large as in the herons, or completely lacking as in the oystercatcher, golden plover and ringed plover. The toes are so widely spread that the angle between the outer toes (2nd and 4th) is almost 180°. In many waders there is an incomplete web at the base of the toes, but this can seldom be seen in the track.

Heron tracks differ somewhat from the normal wader tracks. In addition to the long, slender front toes they also have a long first toe, and each toe has a large, pointed claw. The long first toe must surely be associated with the arboreal habits of herons, for it enables them to grip a branch. The track is easy to recognise on account of its size, the length of the first toe and the distinct claw marks. In the common heron the middle toe is 7–8 cm long. The tracks can be seen along the banks of lakes and on the coast.

The tracks of a *white stork* differ from those of herons in having somewhat shorter and much broader toes, and the first toe, which is short and positioned high up, leaves only a small round impression.

The track of a *crane* is the same size as that of a heron but rather more robust. The first toe is small and it

Heron track.

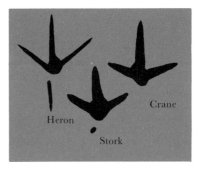

Crane track.

usually leaves no mark in the track. During the breeding season the tracks can be seen in places without vegetation, in swamps and moorland, and

84

also in meadows and along the banks of rivers.

When walking along the seashore at low tide or along a river, a keen observer will nearly always find numerous tracks on sand and mud banks that have been made by various small and medium-sized waders. There are so many different species involved that it is extremely difficult or virtually impossible to identify the species concerned.

Crow track.

Passerines and pigeons

The passerines, which live mainly in trees and bushes, have feet adapted for perching, with long, pointed claws and a relatively long first toe which can be bent forward towards the front toes, so that the foot can grip a branch. These birds often search for food on the ground, and in winter their tracks are commonly seen in the snow, more rarely in summer. Passerines are mostly small, light birds and their tracks are usually not very clear, but in fine soft snow they leave distinct and characteristic impressions, with long, usually slender front toes (the angle between the outer toes being acute), a large first toe and long claw marks.

The smallest passerines, such as tits and sparrows, normally move by hopping, so that the tracks occur in pairs, but the medium-sized species, such as thrushes, and the larger passerines, such as crows, walk as well as hop. On account of the rough underside of the feet the tracks made by crows show a characteristic segmented appearance.

Pigeons and *doves* have perching feet with large toes as in the passerines. Their tracks occur in meadows and

woodland and are also common in towns. In the wood pigeon the middle toe is about 3 cm long. It moves by walking with the toes turned in and the stride is about 7–8 cm long.

House sparrow, hopping tracks.

Pigeon, walking tracks.

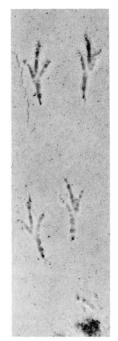

Tracks of a fox hunting for mice.

FEEDING SIGNS

In following a trail one will sooner or later come to a place where the animal has stopped to feed. These feeding places may be quite close to one another, particularly in animals that are purely vegetarian. The track of a roe deer may show where it stopped to graze briefly and then quite soon afterwards it will have stopped again to nibble a few twigs from a tree. On the other hand, one can follow the trail of a carnivore for long distances before finding evidence that it has made a kill.

In snow the trail will often show where a fox has stopped to investigate a tuft of grass or a tree stump in the hope of surprising a mouse or finding something else edible.

The number of feeding places is therefore dependent upon the type of food and the feeding habits of the different species. If the food is very nutritious the animal will only need to eat a relatively small amount in order to satisfy itself, and so there will be few feeding places. If, on the other hand, the food has a low nutritional value the animal has to feed often and take large amounts, and the number of feeding sites increases. The wood mouse and field vole provide excellent samples of this. The wood mouse feeds largely on seeds which are very nutritious and so it needs only a relatively small amount. This also allows it to have its main period of activity during darkness which on grounds of safety is an advantage for a mouse. The field vole, however, feeds mainly on grass, a less concentrated food, so that it has to feed several times a day. This species therefore has to be active both by day and by night in order to survive.

Most animals prefer to remain more or less hidden when feeding. Thus, small rodents will usually bring their food to a special feeding place under a tuft of grass, a pile of brushwood or similar site where they can be fairly safe while feeding.

On the other hand, some animals have feeding places out in the open which are very conspicuous. This applies, for example, to the larger carnivores, most of which have nothing to fear, and to animals such as squirrels and birds of prey which mainly orientate themselves by vision and can therefore detect an approaching enemy at a distance.

Some feeding signs, such as the barking of trees by deer and the bark gnawed by bank voles up in trees, are very striking and can even be identified after some years, but more usually

animal feeding places are obliterated or disappear relatively quickly. This applies particularly to the feeding places of carnivores, and here of course several species may be involved. For instance, it is quite common for small carnivores to utilise the remains of prey left by larger carnivorous animals.

Detailed examination of an animal's feeding place will always yield much interesting information on the animal concerned. Thus, the feeding place not only tells one about the animal's choice of food and the way it feeds, but from its site and appearance it is often possible to deduce much more about the habits of the animal.

The remains left over from an animal's meal often provide evidence in the form of marks left by the teeth or beak. The marks themselves are usually known as feeding signs and those left by carnivores are usually the remains of its prey.

In addition to observations made at feeding places on choice of food, feeding signs, methods of handling the food and so on, one can nearly always deduce which type of animal, and with a little practice even which species, has used the feeding place concerned.

As an aid to this fascinating job of detection the following section describes the most commonly occurring feeding places, arranged according to where the feeding signs occur: on woody plants (trees and bushes), fruits herbaceous plants and so on.

Feeding signs on woody plants

Bark, twigs and buds, especially of young trees and bushes, form an important part of the diet of many animals during winter. This is true of several species of deer and of goats, hares, numerous small rodents and squirrels. In most cases the marks made by the animal's teeth will be clearly shown in the bark and the size and shape of the individual tooth marks will provide a good clue to the identification of the animal concerned.

The feeding signs of birds, which can be seen particularly on old trees, are of a more indirect character. These are usually the peck marks made in bark and wood by insectivorous birds, such as woodpeckers, in their search for food.

There is seldom any difficulty in deciding whether a feeding sign was left by an animal with teeth or by a bird. Tooth marks occur either as large or small half-moon figures, lying two or more alongside one another, or as deep parallel grooves. Beaks make quite distinct peck marks.

In addition to the size and shape of feeding signs, their position on the tree, as shown in the diagram, may also be important as an aid to identification.

When examining the damage inflicted on trees by deer, care must be taken to differentiate between bark-stripping (see p. 90) and fraying (see p. 222). In the former case the animal eats the bark, leaving tooth marks, whereas in fraying the animal rubs its antlers on the bark, to remove the velvet, and leaves abrasions in the bark and wood.

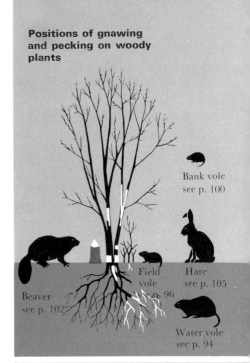

Positions of gnawing and pecking on woody plants

Bank vole see p. 100

Hare see p. 105

Field vole see p. 96

Water vole see p. 94

Beaver see p. 102

Woodpecker see p. 109

Squirrel see p. 104

Sheep, goat see p. 92

Deer see p. 88

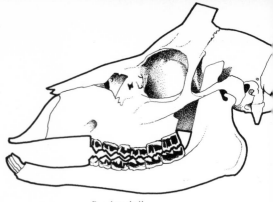

Roe deer skull.

Deer

During the winter the different species of deer feed on the buds and shoots of trees and bushes and on bark.

As deer are relatively large animals it is not surprising that they leave very striking and often extremely characteristic feeding signs. First, however, one must understand a little about their dentition.

Deer are ruminants, in which the upper jaw incisors are absent and replaced by a horny area against which the lower jaw incisors work. Because of this peculiar structure, the

Shoots bitten off.

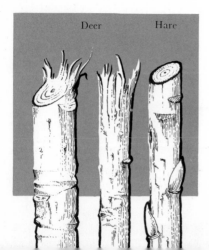

shoots and twigs bitten off by deer look more as though broken or torn off rather than bitten off. The surface of the break appears uneven and frayed and not smooth as it would be if it had been bitten by a hare (see p. 106). It is particularly on thicker twigs that one side of the break is sharply bitten through by the lower jaw incisors but the opposite side is uneven and frayed. When deer use their cheek teeth for biting off twigs the surfaces are always much frayed at the point of fracture.

Deer are particularly prone to bite off the top shoots of small trees, an action which is particularly damaging to the trees. Young trees which have been repeatedly cropped in this way soon come to resemble part of a well clipped hedge. If, however, such a tree manages to send up a shoot high enough so that it can no longer be reached by deer it will develop normally and produce a good tree, but with a frill of small branches around the base.

In areas with a large stock of deer, these will also leave their mark on large trees. This is particularly noticeable in deer parks, where the crowns of the free-standing trees and those along the edges of wooded areas are sharply cut off at a certain height, the deer having bitten off all the branches they could reach.

Examination of trees barked by deer will show two different types of damage, that produced by summer barking being quite different from that due to winter barking.

In fact, these terms refer not so much to the seasons as to the condition of the bark. When the sap is rising and the tree is growing the bark is 'loose' and the animal's feeding activities result in summer barking. On the other hand, when the tree is not growing the bark is more firmly attached and the deer's feeding results

Spruce tree with basal 'frill' of branches.

Woodland edge clipped by deer.

Summer barking of elm by fallow deer.

Winter barking of cypress by fallow deer.

in winter barking. Much of the so-called summer barking actually takes place early in the spring.

When the bark is loose, the animal presses its teeth through the bark and down to the wood. It then bites on the bark thus freed and pulls it off in long shreds so that the underlying woods is completely exposed.

In winter, when the bark is firmly attached, barking acts more like a plane and the marks left by the lower jaw incisors will be seen as distinct grooves on the surface of the bole, with the lower layer of bark remaining behind as narrow bands between the marks left by the individual teeth.

Normally a tree is barked on one side only and it does not die, but closes the wound by growing tissue over it. Barking does, however, delay the growth of a tree, and the exposed area is often attacked by various rotting fungi. This, together with the area of healing, usually makes the lowest and normally most valuable part of the trunk useless as commercial timber.

Both deciduous and coniferous trees are barked by deer, and even though there are differences in the width of the tooth marks and the height to which various kinds of deer can reach, the signs left from barking are, in general, all the same. The frequency, however, with which different deer feed on woody plants varies considerably not only from species to species, but also from place to place.

In winter the *elk* feeds almost exclusively on the shoots, leaves and bark of different trees and bushes. Owing to its enormous size it leaves striking evidence of its feeding, including branches that have been broken off. To reach high shoots it may even bend trees over and tread on them to break them down.

Red deer, *fallow deer* and *sika deer* also bite off shoots and bark but not to such an extent as the elk, and it may be difficult to distinguish the feeding signs left by these three species from one another.

During winter *roe deer* feed quite extensively on the shoots and buds of various woody plants, but signs of barking by them are rare.

Reindeer will feed on the leaves and shoots of different bushes during the summer, but bark does not form part of their diet.

Muntjac, introduced from Asia into England and France, nibble shoots and to a limited extent also take the bark off branches and small trees.

The *white-tailed deer*, introduced from America into Finland, also barks trees and feeds on shoots.

Cross section of a 40 year-old Norway spruce barked by red deer. The barking on the left has affected more than two-thirds of the tree's circumference (yellow area). About 5 years later the tree has been barked again. Such barking results in decay and overgrowth, rendering the trunk valueless as timber.

Young oak trees barked by mouflon.

Branch barked by mouflon. ▶

Sheep and goats

Like deer, sheep and goats are also ruminants in which the upper jaw incisors are replaced by a horny area (see also p. 88). As they often eat shoots and bark their feeding signs may be confused with those left by deer. When sheep and goats bark trees the marks left by the lower jaw incisors are usually placed obliquely in relation to the long axis of the tree, whereas most of the tooth marks left by deer run vertically.

In places where domestic sheep and goats are kept in outside enclosures it is quite common to see barked trees, particularly in winter. The same happens in areas of woodland, as for example in Denmark where mouflon have been introduced for sporting purposes.

Rodents and hares

These animals live almost entirely on plant food and in winter they obtain some of this by gnawing trees and shrubs.

In order to recognise the signs these animals leave behind after feeding it is necessary to know something about the 'tools' and techniques they use when gnawing. The 'tools' are the large, curved incisor teeth, of which the rodents have two in the upper jaw and two in the lower jaw. The hares and rabbits have four incisors in the upper jaw,

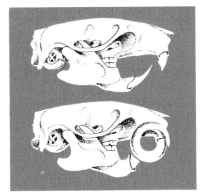

Rat skull, normal dentition above, abnormal below.

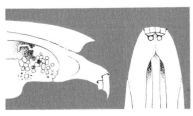

From the side   *From below*

Front part of a hare's upper jaw.

as they have a pair of small teeth just behind the two large incisors, but the former leave no mark when the animal gnaws.

The incisors are positioned very far forwards in the mouth and are separated from the cheek teeth by a large, toothless gap. They grow continuously, so that their growth can keep pace with the hard wear which gnawing entails. In a rat the incisors grow at the rate of 2·7 mm. a week, and a corresponding length is lost in wear. If for any reason an incisor grows obliquely so that it is not properly worn down, it will eventually reach such a length that the animal

can no longer feed and finally dies of starvation.

The fronts and part of the sides of these incisors are covered with enamel, while the rear either has no enamel or only a very thin layer, as for example in hares. This uneven distribution of the hard enamel results in the tooth being worn at an angle, so that it acquires a sharp, shearing edge which is being continually sharpened by gnawing.

In most rodents the upper lip has a slit, the so-called hare lip, which allows the incisors to work freely, and in the gap between the incisors and cheek teeth there are thickenings on the inner side of the lips which close off the rear part of the mouth cavity, thus preventing splinters of wood from entering the mouth during gnawing.

The actual gnawing is done primarily by the incisors of the lower jaw, while those of the upper jaw have the task of fixing the head in position during gnawing. The upper incisors therefore only leave quite short, often curved marks, whereas the lower incisors leave long furrows. It is

Rat's head seen from below. Note thickening of inner side of lips which prevents gnawed chips from entering the mouth.

important to be quite clear about this because the shape and general appearance of the tooth marks is often used in identifying the species of animal which has made them.

According to the type of plant gnawed one can speak of root gnawing, bark gnawing or bud gnawing.

Root gnawing

During summer the *water vole* feeds above ground on the green parts of plants, and in autumn it collects a winter store of juicy roots, tubers, bulbs, seeds and so on which it deposits in large stores communicating with its system of subterranean tunnels. During the winter half of the year it lives mainly below ground where it feeds on these stores and on the roots of trees and bushes.

Root gnawing may be very serious, and often the whole of the central part of a plant's root system is gnawed away so that the tree may become quite loose and can then be easily knocked over.

The water vole is a relatively large animal—about the size of a rat—and so the marks made by its teeth when gnawing are large and distinct. The total breadth of the mark made by the two upper jaw incisors is 3·5–4 mm.

In contrast to the field vole, the water vole seldom attacks very young trees, but it may completely gnaw away the root of a tree with a trunk diameter of 20–30 cm.

The water vole prefers deciduous trees, but also gnaws conifers, and generally speaking it may attack any native woody plant. Among the apple trees it prefers a Cox's Orange Pippin.

Normally winter gnawing takes place underground, but sometimes gnawing of a tree's roots may be continued above ground as bark gnawing. This happens in places where the trees are surrounded by tall, dense, grassy vegetation, and it always starts at the end of winter or in the very early spring.

On account of its activities as a gnawer of roots the water vole is a very serious pest which every year causes considerable economic loss to fruit growing, horticulture and forestry.

The *field vole*, which is particularly noted for its gnawing of bark above ground, will often also feed during winter on the underground parts of woody plants, for it regularly attacks the roots of young trees just a short distance below the surface. In particular, it will attack small saplings of oak and beech in which the stem is up to 2–3 cm in diameter. It gnaws away part of the root, so that the little tree becomes top heavy and falls over. On digging it out one finds that apart from the gnawed area the root is quite undamaged (compare water vole).

The piece that has been gnawed is usually about 5–10 cm long. Often the root will not have been completely

Winter gnawing of an apple tree's roots by water vole. The animal eats not only the bark, but the whole root, so that the tree will topple in a gale.

gnawed through and the two parts of the tree will be joined by a length of varying thickness consisting of a strip of bark and a little wood.

The gnawed surfaces may run straight across, but they are often oblique. The tooth marks can be seen clearly on the gnawed surfaces and it is not difficult to distinguish the small marks of a field vole from the much larger tooth marks left by a water vole. In the field vole the total breadth of the mark left by the two upper jaw incisors is about 2·5 mm.

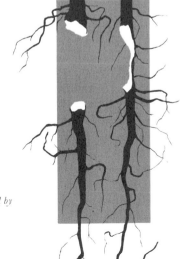

Roots gnawed by field voles.

Bark gnawing

Bark plays quite an important part in the diet of many rodents and of the hares and rabbit, but apart from the beaver, for which bark is the staple diet the whole year round, animals only use bark, which is not very nutritious, during periods of unfavourable weather and food scarcity.

Thus, most bark gnawing takes place in the winter, although in addition to that done by beavers there may be some gnawing during the summer by field voles, bank voles, water voles and squirrels.

In most cases one can see the individual tooth marks in the bark, and if one correlates these with the way the gnawing has been done and its position on the tree, it is usually not difficult to determine the species concerned.

Bark gnawing is, of course, very striking and compared with most other feeding signs it is far more permanent and can even be identified several months, or even years later.

The *field vole* is associated with areas of dense grassy vegetation, and in winter one can almost always be certain of seeing young trees gnawed by this rodent in woodland that is overgrown with grass. The attacks are often so widespread that the field vole is sometimes known as the forest's 'enemy No. 1'. It is also a great menace in orchards.

In captivity it has been shown that a field vole is capable of climbing a tree, but in nature it probably never does so. When gnawing bark it normally keeps to those parts which it can reach from the ground, and as a result

When a field vole rings a tree, the conducting vessels (between root and crown) are severed and the tree withers. Such damage is usually patchy, producing gaps in the plantation.

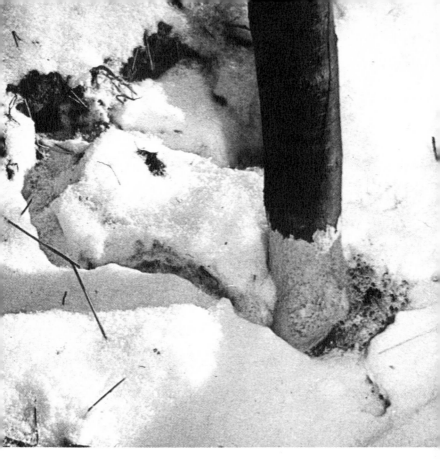

An apple tree ringed by a field vole. Note the run between the tree and the vole's burrow.

the gnawing becomes very concentrated, penetrating so far that the tree may be completely ringed and subsequently die.

The field vole will usually only gnaw bark from the lowest 10–15 cm of the stem. If there are branches on the ground on which the vole can sit the gnawing will extend further up, and snow cover also allows these rodents to reach even further up the tree.

The bark is usually gnawed off right in to the wood, on the surface of

which the tooth marks can clearly be seen. The marks made by the upper jaw incisors can best be seen on the edges of the remaining bark, where they form two slightly half-moon figures with a total breadth of about 2·5 mm. The two pointed incisors in the lower jaw form fine streaks which can be clearly seen on the surface of the wood. Field voles prefer the bark of deciduous trees, but conifers—especially species with soft bark—are also often attacked, and in fact any native tree may be gnawed by them. In orchards they always appear to prefer Cox's Orange Pippins.

Normally field voles gnaw bark in the winter, but sometimes also in July-August. This summer gnawing differs in many respects from winter gnawing. For in winter the voles eat most of the bark that they gnaw off, but in summer they scarcely eat any. The bark is relatively loose at this time

Summer gnawing by field voles. The bark is bitten off but not eaten.

of year, when the tree is actively growing, and it is bitten off in small pieces which can be found at the foot of the tree. When the bark has been bitten off some of the growing layer remains on the stem, and this is what the vole is seeking. Thus, on the exposed surfaces one can see that the voles have carefully rasped off this layer with the incisors, and the numerous fine tooth marks make the exposed surface of the wood quite rough.

A special type of bark gnawing can be seen along or in the immediate vicinity of the field vole's runs where one can sometimes find little piles of small sticks from which the bark has been removed. The pieces vary in length from a few centimetres up to about 20 cm, and the thickness may be up to 1 cm at the most. The ends show clear signs of having been gnawed off, and the sides have a mass of fine tooth marks.

In general, these pieces resemble miniature editions of beaver sticks (see p. 102) and are indeed produced by the field vole in a completely comparable way. In order to get at the bark the field vole, which does not climb, fells a shoot by gnawing it through at the bottom in the same way as a beaver. The vole then gnaws off a suitable piece and drags it to a special feeding place, where there may be quite a collection of gnawed bark and also piles of these little sticks. These gnawed sticks can often be observed in raspberry and blackberry plantations, and it also occurs when the snow has weighed down the branches of a young conifer so that the voles can reach and bite off the shoots. In addition to the gnawed bark and these sticks such a feeding place will also have the conifer needles which the animals do not eat.

Like the field vole, the *bank vole* also

Raspberry canes bitten into pieces and barked by field voles. To the right of the pile there is a gnawed stump.

Conifer twigs (from a tree weighed down by snow) gnawed by field voles. The bark has been eaten, but the needles are untouched. Note the numerous droppings. ▼

gnaws bark very actively, and as it is also a skilful climber it leaves signs of its activities up in the trees.

In spring it is very common to see elder bushes with the bark completely removed from large parts of the main stem and larger branches, so that they appear white. This is the work of the bank vole during the winter. Even large trees with a diameter of 20–30 cm are attacked, and the gnawing may extend several metres up into the tree.

On the ground below the gnawed tree, particularly in towards the trunk, there is often a thick layer of small, gnawed pieces of bark. This is the thick outer, corky layer of bark, which is of no interest to the voles and is therefore rejected, while they eat the inner, living part of the bark.

In addition to many deciduous trees bank voles also attack conifers, of which they prefer those with softer bark.

Gnawing usually starts in the angles of the branch, where the vole can sit comfortably while it gnaws. From there the gnawing spreads up the stem and also out onto the branches, and in the worst cases the trees may be completely stripped of bark from crown to root.

In comparison with gnawing by field voles, that of the bank vole is usually not so deep and this is surely correlated with the fact that the bank vole is smaller and weaker than the field vole. Thus, the gnawed surfaces are more or less covered with the remains of the bark, which lie as a thin brown layer that is delicately furrowed by the vole's teeth. In the bank vole the marks left by the two upper jaw incisors have a total breadth of 1·5–2 mm.

Bark gnawing by bank voles is usually distributed up in the trees and so it may not be so catastrophic for

the trees as that performed by field voles. Normally bank voles gnaw bark in the winter when food is scarce, but they may also do so in July-August for reasons which do not appear to be related to ordinary hunger.

Summer gnawing by bank voles is in general similar to that done by field voles (see p. 98), but it occurs up in the trees, and is much deeper and more destructive than winter gnawing.

The characteristic barked sticks described under the field vole (see p. 98) may also be produced by the bank vole, and it is difficult to distinguish one from the other. The sticks gnawed by bank voles can be seen, for example, under piles of new brush wood.

The *water vole*, known mainly as a gnawer of roots, may also gnaw bark during the summer. The gnawing which is very characteristic, is in general very like that done by field and bank voles, but has evidently only been observed on ash.

As a water vole cannot climb it has to be content with gnawing the trunks of ash trees as high as it can reach from the ground, which is about 20 cm. This nearly always results in the complete ringing of the tree. The bark is not eaten, but bitten off in very characteristic strips, $\frac{1}{2}$–1 cm across, which nearly all have a distinct curve at one end; these strips are left lying on the ground. The tooth marks can be clearly seen on the edges of the bark strips and on the bark left on the tree.

The characteristic shape of these strips is due to the fact that the animal finishes biting off the strips by gnawing along the stem, whereas the rest of the gnawing takes place traversely.

After biting off the bark the water vole rasps off and eats that part of the growth layer which remains on the

The bank vole, which can climb, gnaws bark up in the trees. It starts in the angles of the branches and continues up the trunk and out on to the branches.

Bark strips gnawed by a water vole

Summer gnawing of ash by a water vole. Note the bitten strips of bark, and the tooth marks on the surface of the wood. ▶

stem. This results in the surface of the wood having a characteristic rough appearance, with innumerable tooth marks.

It is characteristic that the attacks of water voles on ash trees only last a very short time, but they take place very quickly, and these animals can destroy several hundred trees in very few days.

The *beaver*, which is Europe's largest rodent, has very characteristic feeding places which cannot be confused with those of any other animal.

Its food consists primarily of bark, shoots and leaves, and the feeding places are large and striking because the animal has to eat a lot of food, partly on account of its size and partly because the food itself is relatively poor in nutritional value.

It prefers to gnaw deciduous trees, particularly aspen, but also feeds on alder, willow and birch. On the other hand, beavers very seldom feed on the bark of conifers.

In order to get at the bark a beaver will fell even quite large trees, and this gives beaver sites a quite characteristic appearance. In felling a tree the beaver gnaws right round the trunk at a height of about half a metre, so that it takes on the shape of an hourglass, and finally the gnawed area

becomes so thin that the tree topple Thin trees can be felled by gnawin on one side only, and small branche are bitten through, leaving a smoot cut.

The bite of a beaver is very powe ful and when felling a tree the spli ters bitten off may be up to 10–12 c long and 3–4 cm broad. The toot marks, which are about 8 mm acros can be clearly seen on both the tre and on the splinters.

In the autumn a beaver bites th thinner branches into suitable lengt and transports them to its lodg where they are stored for winter fee ing. Branches with a diameter up 10 cm, sometimes even more, a gnawed into pieces about one met long and dragged to the feeding pla which is at the edge of the wate Here the bark is taken off and th timber is then used for construction work on the beaver's lodge and dam

The lengths of gnawed branc (beaver sticks) can be found in pe diggings, sometimes in places fro which the beaver disappeared thou sands of years ago.

The *red squirrel* occasionally gnaw bark and this usually, but not alway occurs in the summer when the tre are growing. At this time the bark fairly loose and the gnawing produc

Section of branch barked by a beaver (see also p. 6).

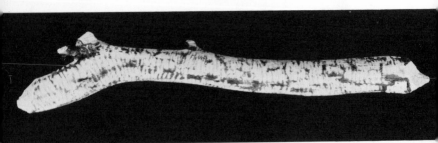

A tree felled by a beaver. Note the large splinters gnawed off and the tooth marks on the trunk (to the left)

A gnawed splinter, showing tooth marks.

signs that are more characteristic of stripping rather than that of true bark gnawing.

This takes place up in the trees, where the bark is flayed off in strips of varying length, leaving sharp edges without tooth marks on the remaining bark.

The bark is not eaten but can be seen on the ground under the stripped tree. The squirrel does, however, ea that part of the growth layer which remains on the trunk after the bark has been pulled off. Even this rasping of the growing layer leaves only fain

Beech barked by a squirrel. The bark torn off will be found on the ground below the tree.

Larch barked by a squirrel. The animal has rasped off some of the growth layer, leaving distinct tooth marks.

Silver fir from which the branches have been bitten off by a hare, for no apparent reason.

signs of teeth on the surface of the wood, and it is possible that the animals are searching for plant sap, which they may lick off.

Bark stripping may occur on both deciduous trees and conifers and it is characteristically only the trunk that is attacked.

On old conifers it is particularly the thin bark at the tops of the trees that is attacked, and the loss of the bark often means that the top dies and subsequently breaks off.

The feeding signs left on woody plants by *brown hares*, *mountain hares* and *rabbits* are very characteristic and easy to distinguish from those of other animals, but they are extremely difficult to distinguish from one another. Hares and rabbits bite off and eat the shoots of young trees, particularly during the winter, but to some extent also in the summer. Thus, one quite frequently sees young trees in exposed positions develop into bushy shrubs, because the shoots have been persistently bitten off, thus preventing the tree from growing straight up. Both deciduous trees and conifers may be attacked.

However, these animals do not always eat the shoots they have bitten off. The shoots are often seen lying on the ground around the tree and the attack then assumes the character of a pastime. In winter, the mountain hare often leaves the buds from these shoots at its feeding place, and this is remarkable because the buds probably have a particularly high nutritional value.

The bitten surfaces are very characteristic, because the sharp teeth of

Shoot bitten by a hare. The smooth oblique cut of a hare's bite is characteristic (see also p. 88).

these animals produce a smooth, oblique cut surface, as though sliced by a sharp knife. The bite is, therefore, easy to distinguish from the frayed bite of a deer (see p. 88).

In winter, hares and rabbits often gnaw bark and may then cause a certain amount of damage in woods and orchards.

The gnawing is very marked and can easily be recognised by the tooth marks, which look as though the gnawing had been done by an animal with four narrow teeth in the upper jaw and two broad teeth in the lower jaw. This is because the two upper jaw incisors each have a deep longitudinal furrow, and this leaves behind a narrow strip of bark in the tooth mark.

Tooth marks on an elder barked by a hare. The longitudinal furrows in the upper incisors are quite distinct (see also p. 93).

Young oak tree gnawed by a hare. The bite is deep and powerful.

Bud gnawing

Vegetative buds on the terminal shoot of a silver fir gnawed by a bank vole. Continued destruction of buds may turn the young tree into a bush.

In winter the nutritious buds of woody plants are eaten by squirrels and by those species of mouse or vole which can climb.

These include the bank vole, in particular, and also the wood mouse and the yellow-necked mouse. The gnawing done by the different species is so similar in appearance that one cannot distinguish between them.

In these attacks on buds it is characteristic that the mouse or vole gnaws a hole in the side of the bud and then scrapes out the contents with the long, pointed incisors of the lower jaw, leaving the outside behind like an empty husk. However, the bud may be gnawed so that only the lowest bud scales remain, forming a little saucer.

In young trees it is often the vegetative buds that are attacked, and repeated bud gnawing may result in the trees taking on a bushy form.

Bud gnawing appears to occur particularly on conifers, especially silver fir and larch, but is also seen on deciduous trees. Thus, if one examines an elder with bark gnawed by a bank vole one sees that a large number of the buds have also been gnawed, and there is much evidence to show that this has happened before the actual bark gnawing began.

In years when there is a poor set of seeds, one can often see during the winter a mass of small green shoots lying like a carpet beneath certain trees. It is now known that these shoots have been bitten off by squirrels, but at one time it was thought that the trees themselves had for some reason or another cast off the shoots.

These shoots are usually 5–10 cm long and one can see from the smooth breakage plane that they have been bitten off. They can therefore be easily distinguished from shoots that have been torn off in a storm, which would be ragged at the point of fracture.

Spruce twigs bitten off by squirrels which have eaten the male flower buds.

Closer examination of the bitten shoots shows that they are all one year-old shoots, which have been bitten off just below the circle of buds destined to produce the male flowers which are

Male flowers of Norway spruce gnawed by squirrels.

situated at the base of the shoot. These flower buds are particularly nutritious, and each one has been excavated and emptied by the squirrel, leaving only a cup-like husk. One often wonders how such a large animal as a squirrel can empty a bud without doing more damage to its outer covering. In many cases only a single bud scale has been torn off. The explanation is that the animal inserts one of the long, pointed upper incisors down into the bud and fishes out the contents. Sometimes squirrels empty vegetative buds further out on the shoot, but the end bud itself is almost never damaged.

Bud gnawing by red squirrels is particularly common on Norway spruce, but it may occur on Sitka spruce, silver fir, larch and other conifers, and has also been observed on beech. In a 60 year-old spruce plantation in Denmark, it has been calculated that in a winter with few cones but numerous flower buds, squirrels had bitten off an average of 1,200 shoots per tree.

Sometimes a squirrel's feeding signs may be of a somewhat different character. Thus, the animal may have gnawed the shoot further up in order to get at the large thick buds on the top shoot of a silver fir. The outflow of resin will then have quickly obliterated the tooth marks and the surface comes to look very like that left by the bite of a deer. Usually the height at which this occurs will preclude the possibility of a deer bite, and if the resin is removed the damage will be seen to have been caused by gnawing rather than by a straight bite.

Bark hacked off by a woodpecker searching for insects. The bill marks can be clearly seen on the trunk.

Birds, feeding signs on woody plants

The commonest feeding signs left by birds on woody plants are those produced by woodpeckers. In their search for insects, larvae and pupae that lie hidden in crevices in the bark they will hack away with their powerful beak so that the bark becomes frayed or falls off in strips. The tip of the beak which is shaped rather like a small chisel leaves long, narrow marks on the trunk. This type of feeding sign is most striking in areas where the three-toed woodpecker is common. There, one can see from quite a distance how the outermost, dark layer of bark has been completely removed from a Scots pine, so that the trunk has an unnatural colour.

Woodpeckers reach larvae and adult insects that live in the wood by hacking holes into the trunk and extracting

the prey with the help of the very long, sticky tongue which is provided

The long tongue of a woodpecker, which can be extended 10 cm beyond the bill, is anchored near the right nostril.

with barbs. The beak marks can usually be seen clearly on the sides of the hole and on the shavings.

This type of feeding sign is most

striking in places where the black woodpecker has been hunting for Hercules ants (*Campanotus herculeanus*). These large insects which are much sought after by black woodpeckers often have their home in living conifers, where their tunnels may extend several metres up the trunk, the ants gnawing away the soft wood in the annual rings. The tunnels frequently lie deep within the trunk, surrounded by a thick layer of young wood, so that the woodpecker has to expend a considerable amount of energy to reach the ants. The holes hacked out are very large, up to half a metre long and 10–15 cm across, and splinters 10–15 cm long and several centimetres across can be found on the ground. Although a black woodpecker is only about the size of a crow, one is always astonished, when standing below such a tree, at the bird's phenomenal power. Tree stumps and old windfallen trees may also be completely split apart by black woodpeckers.

It is also quite common for woodpeckers, particularly the greater spotted woodpecker, to hack holes in tree trunks or thick branches, into which they wedge cones or nuts while they are splitting them (see p. 121). These so-called woodpecker workshops can always be recognized by the remains of the food, which either remains in the hole or lies on the ground below.

Sometimes woodpeckers hack short or long grooves or a series of holes round the tree trunks. This can be seen particularly on young trees, and it is thought that the birds suck up the plant sap that flows out.

Some birds eat buds, which they nip off with the beak, without leaving any particularly characteristic sign. Flower buds are especially sought after, and considerable damage may be done to fruit trees by finches, especially bullfinches. In winter the buds and catkins of woody plants form an important part of the diet of game birds, such as black grouse, hazel hen and red grouse, and the fresh shoots and needles of the Scots pine are the principal food of the capercaillie. Often the capercaillie prefers to feed in certain individual trees which may be almost completely stripped of needles.

A tree trunk hacked into pieces by a black woodpecker.

Larch hacked by a black woodpecker searching for Hercules ants. The large hole is c. 30 cm high and 9–11 cm deep. Note how the woodpecker has torn off the bark using horizontal blows.

Feeding signs on seeds and fruits

Fruits, particularly seeds, contain a high concentration of stored products in the form of oils, starch and protein. These substances are intended for the first growth stages of the new plant but they are also much sought after by various animals on account of their high food value. During unfavourable parts of the year many rodents and birds survive by feeding almost exclusively on fruits. Squirrels and crossbills can breed while it is still winter and this may well be due to the fact that the spruce cones are then full of ripe seeds, so that the animals have no trouble in finding nutritious food for their young.

Although in many plants the majority of the seeds end up in a finely divided form in an animal's stomach, it is nevertheless a great biological advantage for these plants to have fruits or seeds which can be distributed by animals. Thus, a woodpecker may drop a spruce cone on the way to its workshop, a yellow-necked mouse may be seized by an owl before it has been able to consume all its winter store of beechmast, or the squirrel forgets where it has buried the nuts it has collected. All this means that with the help of animals a plant's seeds have become distributed to new growing sites.

Some small seeds are swallowed whole and pass undamaged through the animal which they eventually leave either in the faeces or in a pellet, perhaps several miles from where they were eaten. Such seeds show no marks that might provide a clue to the identity of the animal concerned, and here the other constituents of the faeces or pellet may help.

When an animal eats fruits, some parts usually remain at the feeding place, and in many cases tooth or beak marks left on these remains may enable one to identify the animal that has eaten the fruit.

Most fruits may be eaten by more than one species of animal. With such a wide range of possibilities it may be useful to discuss some of the commoner examples which can be found in the garden or during a walk in the country.

Conifer seeds form an important part of the diet of many rodents and birds, and feeding places with cones handled by animals are therefore very common and can be found almost everywhere in old conifer forests.

A cone, for example a Norway spruce cone, consists of a central axis and a large number of spirally arranged overlapping double scales, consisting of an outer and an inner scale; the latter lies closest to the axis and carries two ovules on its inner face. Each ripe seed has a membranous wing. In the Douglas fir the outer scales are longer than the inner ones and are seen to protrude.

The seeds ripen in the autumn, but as long as the weather is humid, the

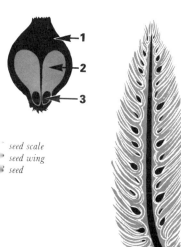

1 seed scale
2 seed wing
3 seed

Longitudinal section through a cone.

seed scales remain pressed firmly against the cone axis, so that the seeds are well protected and cannot fall out.

It is only in spring when the sun and wind dry the cone that the scales bend back so that the seeds can be shed. Fir cones do not ripen until their second year, or later.

As the cones ripen the outer scales become woody and are eventually so hard that the animals frequently have to expend considerable energy in reaching the seeds. This work leaves distinct signs, differing from one animal species to another, and it is normally quite easy to decide which animal has handled a cone.

Yew cones have a completely different structure, for they consist of a relatively large, thick-shelled seed surrounded by a fleshy covering or aril,

Yew twig with berries.

which is at first green, but later a beautiful red. Yew leaves are known to contain a poison, to which many animals, and particularly horses, are very susceptible, but the fruits are non-poisonous and much sought after by birds.

Rodents

Cones form a very important part of the diet of red squirrels, in particular, but a considerable number have to be

Cones handled by animals

1. Ripe spruce cone stripped by a squirrel. The base has a frayed tip. The cone has a more or less frayed appearance, depending upon how close the scales have been gnawed from the shaft. Cones of Sitka spruce and Douglas fir are treated in a similar way. Cones stripped by squirrels are always found out in the open (see p. 117).

2. Seed scale bitten off by a squirrel. The scale is removed whole.

3. Unripe spruce stripped by squirrel.

4. Spruce cone stripped by a mouse. The base is rounded and without a point. The close gnawing of the scales give the shaft a fairly smooth surface. Mice always strip loose cones in sheltered feeding-places (see p. 118).

5. Spruce cone handled by a crossbill. The seed scales are split longitudinally. Found under the trees (see p. 122).

6. Spruce cone handled by a woodpecker. Dishevelled appearance. Found at a 'woodpecker's workshop' wedged in a crevice or lying underneath, often in a large pile (see p. 121).

7. Ripe pine cone stripped by squirrel. The cone becomes more or less frayed, depending upon how close the scales have been gnawed. Closely gnawed cones may be confused with those stripped by mice, but squirrels' cones are always lying out in the open (see p. 117).

8. Unripe pine cone stripped by squirrel. As the cone is soft, the scales are torn off and the cone splits apart (see p. 117).

9. Pine cone stripped by a mouse. The scales are tidily gnawed off. Found in sheltered feeding places (see p. 118).

10. Pine cone stripped by a wood mouse while the cone was still attached to the tree, so the gnawing is lopsided (see p. 120).

11. Pine cone handled by parrot crossbill. The scales are pressed out from the shaft. Found under the tree (see p. 122).

12. Pine cone handled by woodpecker. The scales are split longitudinally. Found at 'woodpecker workshops' (compare No. 6).

13. Arolla pine cone stripped by squirrel. The scales are gnawed off regularly (see p. 117).

14. Larch cone stripped by squirrel. May vary somewhat depending upon whether the scales are torn or gnawed off. Found under the trees (see p. 117).

15. Larch cone stripped by a mouse. Feeding place in a sheltered position (see p. 118).

16. Left, a larch seed with wing; seed scales torn off by a mouse.

17. White spruce cone stripped by squirrel. The scales are torn off (see p. 117).

18. Yew seed split longitudinally by a hawfinch. Found on the ground under the tree (see p. 123).

19. Yew seeds opened by a marsh tit. The seed is removed through a fairly regularly hacked hole. Found beneath the feeding place (see p. 123).

20. Yew seeds emptied by a nuthatch. Found in bark crevices (see p. 123).

Norway spruce

1	2	3	4	5	6
Handled by:	**Squirrel**		**Mouse**	**Crossbill**	**Woodpecker**

PINE

7	8	9	10	11	12
Squirrel		**Mouse**		**Crossbill**	**Woodpecker**

AROLLA PINE **LARCH** **WHITE SPRUCE** **YEW**

Hawfinch 18

Marsh tit 19

Nuthatch 20

13	14	15	16	17
Squirrel	**Squirrel**		**Mouse**	**Squirrel**

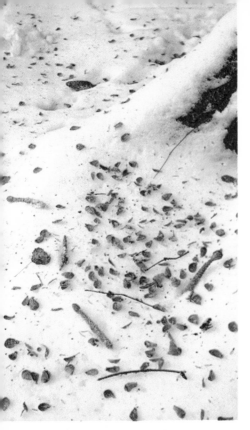

used to get enough food because the individual seeds are very small.

Squirrels feed mainly up in the trees and the axes of the stripped cones and the gnawed cone scales are found on the ground under the feeding place. Quite often a squirrel may have a particular favourite feeding place, and beneath this there may be hundreds of stripped cones. Those that have fallen naturally are usually gnawed on the ground. In such cases squirrels will usually sit on a small mound or on a tree stump so that they can see all around and have prior warning of danger. At these places the stripped cone axes and scales collect in a small heap. Norway spruce cones stripped by squirrels may vary in appearance, but as in almost all their cones the base is frayed.

The animal starts to gnaw from the base, holding the cone in its fore-feet at an angle with the top end pointing towards the ground. The basal scales are very small, often without seeds and are so loosely attached that the squirrel can easily tear them off with its teeth.

Spruce cones stripped by squirrels up in the tree. The remains are scattered on the ground below.

Pine cones stripped by a squirrel on the ground. The remains lie close together.

Some of the cone shaft is torn off at the same time, and this results in the characteristic frayed base (see plate on p. 115).

When the squirrel can tear off no more scales, it places the cone down on the substrate, and holds it firmly with one fore-foot on the base and the other on the scale-bearing part. It then starts to gnaw the hard scales one by one and to eat the seeds. As the scales are arranged spirally round the cone shaft, the squirrel has to keep turning the cone as it moves from scale to scale.

Normally a squirrel does not gnaw off all the scales, but leaves the uppermost ones, which form a little tuft at the top of the shaft. Clearly, it would be difficult for the animal to gnaw off the last scales, for it is just here that it is holding the cone with one paw. In addition, there are very few seeds at the top of the cone.

According to how close to the shaft the scales are gnawed, the stripped shaft may be thick and frayed or thin with a smoother surface.

In gnawing off the hard scales the animal leaves an oblique gnawed surface, one side of the remaining part of the scale being shorter than the other. The shorter or lower edge is always on the side on which the lower jaw teeth have gone in. The longer side of the gnawed scale base usually runs out into a little point. Depending upon whether the squirrel has held the cone's top end to the left or to the right while gnawing, this point will be on the right or left side of the gnawed surface when the cone is held base downwards.

Since the same squirrel always holds the cone in the same way, one can divide squirrels into right and left operators, a 'right-squirrel' being one which holds the cone with the top end

Squirrel holding cone with tip to the right.

to the right while gnawing, while a 'left-squirrel' does the reverse.

Young squirrels have to learn by experience how to gnaw cones. They start quite helpless, gnawing more or less at random, and it is only after some time that they learn the correct technique.

With slender cones having relatively thin scales, such as those of white spruce and larch, the squirrel usually tears off all the scales up to near the little tuft at the tip, the cone being held in the fore-paws (see plate on p. 115).

Many fir cones are stripped in the same way but, with the possible exception of the elongated cones of the Weymouth pine, it is only unripe fir cones that the squirrel can tear apart. The ripe, massive woody cones have to be gnawed apart. With the characteristic cones of the Arolla pine (*Pinus cembra*) the animal gnaws its way into each of the large, wingless seeds (see plate on page 115).

It is not uncommon, particularly in years with a good set of seeds, to find cones on the ground that have only been partially gnawed by squirrels. These may be cones which have been rejected as containing too

'Woodpecker workshop' with Norway spruce cones. Many of the cones have been previously strippe incompletely by squirrels.

few seeds, but they are usually those which the animals have dropped while gnawing them up in the trees. Such cones may then be finished off by other animals, often mice, but also birds.

Cones stripped by mice and voles— primarily wood mouse, yellow-necked mouse and bank vole—are easy to distinguish from those stripped by squirrels, for the cone shaft always lacks the characteristic basal point of the squirrel's cone. This is because the mice do not have the strength to tear off the basal scales but have to gnaw through them. The base of a cone stripped by voles or mice, therefore, has a smooth, rounded shape (see plate on p. 115).

Mice and voles normally gnaw cones on the ground, placing one fore-foot on the gnawed shaft and the other on the scaly part. The individual scales are usually gnawed off completely but when it has gnawed so far

the mouse may tear off the scales an throw them aside with a quick jerk c the head. However, the thick scale of fir cones are gnawed off in on piece (see plate on p. 115). When scale has been removed the mous turns the cone a little with its fore feet, so that it can get at the nex scale in the row. The exposed seeds ar picked out with the incisor teeth, an the animal then releases the cone an holds the seed in its fore-paws whil eating it.

The scale is nearly always gnawe off at the place where the seed lies, an the resulting gnawed surface is no oblique, as in the squirrel's work, bu roughly straight, so that a con gnawed by a mouse is more regula and uniform than one stripped by squirrel.

Generally speaking, mice leav fewer top scales than squirrels, presum ably because they do not need such long piece of shaft to hold on to, an frequently a mouse-gnawed cone is found in which all the top scales have been removed.

As in the case of the red squirrel, there are some mice which hold the top end of the cone to the right and others which hold it to the left when gnawing.

Cones stripped by mice or voles are not so commonly found in the wild as those stripped by squirrels. For unlike squirrels, mice and voles do not sit out in the open to gnaw cones, but seek shelter under piles of brushwood or tufts of grass, or they may drag the cones into their underground runs, where they can sit and feed in peace. They often use the same feeding place several times, so quite a number of stripped cones may accumulate.

As a rule mice and voles rely on the cones which can be found on the forest floor, those blown down by the wind or from fallen trees and those dropped by squirrels. Occasionally, however, a pine cone may be found which has been gnawed by mice on one side, but is still attached to the tree (see plate on p. 115).

White spruce cones stripped by a wood mouse. The grass covering the feeding place has been removed.

Mountain pine cones gnawed up in the tree by a wood mouse.

Birds

Cones stripped by birds differ considerably in appearance from those gnawed by rodents and are usually easy to distinguish, particularly when they are spruce or fir cones stripped by woodpeckers, crossbills or nutcrackers. Identification becomes much more difficult when it is a question of the fleshy fruits of yew, for these are taken by several different small birds.

During the winter the greater spotted woodpecker consumes a considerable number of conifer seeds. This bird hacks the cone free from the tree, flies away with it in its beak and wedges it firmly in a crevice, always with the tip upwards. It then attacks

A greater spotted woodpecker has used the deep dark crevices of an old oak tree to wedge Norway spruce cones. The bird has chosen a new crevice each time.

the cone with the chisel-shaped beak, hacking and twisting off the scales to get at the seeds. When it has finished with one side it loosens the cone and turns it round. A cone stripped by a woodpecker therefore acquires a very characteristic, tousled appearance with cone scales sticking out on all sides. Usually only the lower part of the cone is more or less untouched. The seeds, which are swallowed whole, are probably picked out with the very long, sticky tongue. It takes a woodpecker about four minutes to get all the seeds out of a cone and during this period it will have struck the cone about 800 times (see plate on p. 115).

The woodpecker often chooses a naturally occurring crevice to wedge the cone in. The deep furrows in the bark of an old oak tree are particularly suitable for this purpose, and where there are enough furrows each one is used only once. In the course of the winter such a tree may become completely embroidered with cones. Furthermore, as the cones are very firmly wedged they may remain there for years.

In many cases the woodpecker chips out its own crevice with its beak, and these are usually used several times so that the stripped cones accumulate in a heap underneath. When the woodpecker has finished with a cone it nearly always leaves it in the crevice and only removes it when bringing a fresh one. It might be thought that it would be difficult for the bird to manoeuvre with two cones at the same time, but it manages very cleverly by jamming the new cone in between its breast and the tree trunk while flicking the old one out of the crevice with its beak.

Crossbills which are essentially birds of the conifer forests are largely dependent upon the crop of conifer seeds. These birds have a very charac-

Pine cones handled by a greater spotted wood-pecker. Note the hole high up on the trunk which the bird has made for wedging the cones.

teristic breeding season, for they nest in the period December-April, and thus in the middle of winter. They are doubtless able to do this because of the available supply of nutritious conifer seeds, which they have become adapted to feeding on. The young are fed exclusively on these seeds which have a fat content of 35 per cent. The breeding season coincides exactly with the period when the cones are ripe and full of seeds.

The bill of a crossbill is a particularly well adapted tool for opening cones. It is compressed and very powerful, and the tips of both the upper and lower mandibles are much elongated and curved in such a way that they cross each other, hence the bird's popular name. In some individuals the lower mandible crosses to the left of the

Crossbill

upper mandible ('left-directed'), in others to the right ('right-directed').

It is also characteristic of the crossbill that the two lower jaw articulations are differently developed. One is a ball joint, while the other allows a considerable amount of lateral displacement of the lower jaw. For example, in a right-directed bird the lower jaw can only be displaced to the left until the two mandible tips are vertically one above the other, but it can be displaced to the right for up to one centimetre from the midline.

When opening a cone a crossbill always positions itself so the tip of the lower mandible turns in towards the cone. Therefore a 'left-directed' cross-bill has the cone on its left side, whereas a 'right-directed' bird has it on the right. Then the mouth is opened, and the lower jaw is displaced until the mandible tips lie one above the other. The bird then turns its head and presses the bill in under a cone scale. When the bill is pressed completely in the lower jaw is displaced and the head is turned. By this manoeuvre the cone scale is lifted and the two seeds are released so that they can be taken up by the sticky tongue. At the same time as the bill is closed, or while it is pulled back, the cone scale is torn lengthwise, and this gives cones stripped by crossbills a very characteristic appearance. However, the thick scales on a fir cone are not usually split (see plate on p. 115).

Anyone who has tried to bend back a scale on a Norway spruce cone will know what power the crossbill exerts when opening a cone.

While the crossbill mainly attacks cones of Norway spruce, white spruce, Sitka spruce, larch and mountain pine, the parrot-crossbill, which has a much more powerful beak, will also take the very hard cones of Scots pine.

These birds will most often bite off a cone and sit on a branch while stripping it, holding the cone firmly with one foot. However, the common crossbill usually strips Norway spruce cones while they are still attached to the tree.

Crossbills often forage in flocks, and they are usually noticed by the shower of seed wings and cones which floats down from the trees.

Nutcrackers frequently forage on the peculiar cones of the Arolla pine, from which they hack out the large seeds.

The fruits of yew are taken by many birds, which either eat the hard seed or the fleshy red aril.

Thrushes swallow the fruits whole but only digest the aril; the hard seed

asses through the body and is thus
ell distributed.

On the other hand, the hawfinch
tilises the seed itself, for it can easily
plit the hard seed covering with its
arge and powerful beak. When a flock
f hawfinches has been foraging in a
ew tree the ground underneath will
e strewn with seed husks and red arils.
hese remains from their feeding
ctivities are particularly striking when
he ground is covered with snow (see
late on p. 115).

The nuthatch is also very interested
n yew seeds, which it tackles after
aving wedged them in a bark crevice
see plate p. 115).

The marsh tit takes yew fruits and
ies with them in its beak to a suitable
eding place on a nearby horizontal
ranch. There it presses the hard fruit
ut of the fleshy aril, which being
icky usually remains hanging from
he branch. When the bird has ex-
acted the seed it lets the empty husk
ll to the ground (see plate on p. 115).

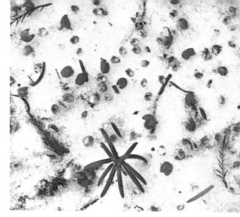

*A hawfinch's visit to a yew tree results in empty
seed cases and red arils beneath the tree.*

Yew seed wedged and emptied by a nuthatch.

ew seeds taken by marsh tits. Only the sticky arils remain behind.

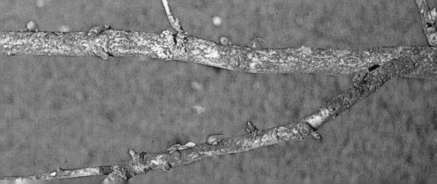

Hazelnuts

These are much sought after by many animals, and in particular by numerous rodents and birds.

The thick, hard shell renders this a difficult fruit to deal with, and animals often have to expend considerable energy in reaching the kernel. It is interesting to note the different techniques that are used to open these nuts.

Animals opening hazelnuts frequently leave clear signs of their activities in the form of beak and tooth marks, and because the shell has a smooth brown surface these signs are often very sharply defined. There is, therefore, no difficulty in deciding whether the nut has been attacked by the beak of a bird or the teeth of a mammal. With a little experience it is also often possible to identify accurately the species of animal concerned.

crowbar to crack the shell. The fragments of shell which are strewn on the ground under the tree where the squirrel has been feeding are easy to recognise and can scarcely be confused with those of other nuts handled by animals.

Experience teaches the squirrel how

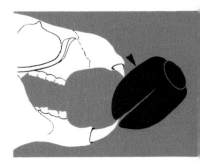

To crack the shell the lower incisors are inserted into the hole and the nut is pressed down until it splits.

Rodents

Identification of rodent tooth marks on nuts requires a knowledge of the ways in which the animals work when gnawing. A detailed account of rodent dentition and gnawing methods is given on page 93.

Squirrels are important consumers of nuts. When opening hazelnuts they use a method which corresponds closely to the way we open a nut with a knife, by cutting off the top, inserting the knife tip in the hole and then turning the blade round so that the shell cracks.

A squirrel holds the nut firmly with its fore-feet and gnaws a groove across the top, eventually producing a small hole. It then inserts the lower incisors into the hole and uses them like a

it can best open nuts. The young animals gnaw furrows at random on the shell of the nut, until by chance a hole appears, into which they can insert the lower incisors and break off a piece of shell. It is only after this that the animal learns where it is best to gnaw (see plate on p. 126).

Sometimes a squirrel will take nuts that are not yet ripe. The soft shell means that the animal can easily bite off the top and then fish out the small undeveloped kernel with the lower incisors (see plate on p. 126).

Like many other rodents, squirrels may also hide away any surplus in autumn when there is plenty of food. This is most often done with beechmast, acorns and nuts, which either singly or few together may be buried or put into odd cracks and crevices. There are seldom any records of really large reserve stores. The animal's collections bear the stamp of being unplanned and in fact it is often a matter of chance whether such food is found again. There have, however, been several observations from tracks in the snow, where a squirrel's trail led directly to a place where there was a buried depot. In such cases there seems to be no doubt that the animal was well aware of the location of the store (see p. 37).

A water vole has started to gnaw. The small marks made by the upper teeth above, and the long furrows left by the lower teeth below.

Mice

In principle, all the different species of mice and voles attack a hazelnut in the same way. They find a place on the surface of the nut which is slightly uneven or rough and which will provide support for the upper incisors. They then start to gnaw rapidly with the lower incisors.

There is a difference in exactly where the different species prefer to begin. Some start at one of the ends, while others gnaw in from the side. Thus, the water vole gnaws almost exclusively from the side, whereas the bank vole and the striped mouse gnaw from the end. In Germany, in a collection of 309 hazelnuts gnawed by the yellow-necked mouse some 46·8% had been opened from the side, whereas only 0·1% of 628 nuts gnawed by wood mice had been opened in this way.

Until they had actually pierced the shell the gnaw marks of the different mouse species look more or less alike, and it is usually difficult or impossible to identify the species concerned from an examination of the gnawing. In theory it should be possible to identify the gnawing by measuring the breadth of the tooth marks and comparing this with direct measurements on the mouse.

However, the lower incisors are all very pointed and this means that they leave marks of approximately the same breadth and appearance. In addition, the two halves of the lower jaw are not properly fused and can therefore move in relation to one another, so that the distance between the two teeth is not constant during gnawing.

The marks left by the upper incisors are really of more use in this respect, but they are often placed on top of one another and so close that it is impossible to take accurate measurements.

In adult water voles the combined width of the upper incisors is 3·5–4 mm, in the field vole about 2·5 mm and in the bank vole 1·5–2 mm. The corresponding figure for the wood mouse and yellow-necked mouse is about 1·5 mm, the measurement for the latter being often a little more than that for the wood mouse. In the rat the width is 2·5–3 mm.

Although, as already mentioned, all the mice and voles start to deal with nuts in the same way, it is an interesting fact that once they have made a hole they proceed in one of two different ways. These gnawing methods may be

126

Nuts and other fruits handled by animals

Adult Squirrel
see p. 124

Unripe cluster handled
by squirrels

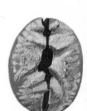

Young Squirrel
see p. 124

Wood mouse
see p. 125

Bank vole
see p. 128

Water Vole
see p. 129

Woodpecker, beak marks

Emptied
see p. 130, 13

Great tit
see p. 131

Nuthatch
see p. 131

Nutcracker
see p. 132

Magpie
see p. 131

WALNUTS

Wood mouse
see p. 132

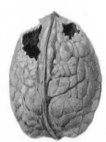

Great tit
see p. 132

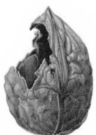

Jackdaw
see p. 132

Crossbill
see p. 132

BEECHMAST
× 1½

Wood mouse 2 types
see p. 133

ACORN   CHESTNUT
× 1½   × 1½

Wood mouse

Wood mouse
see p. 133

SLOE
× 1½

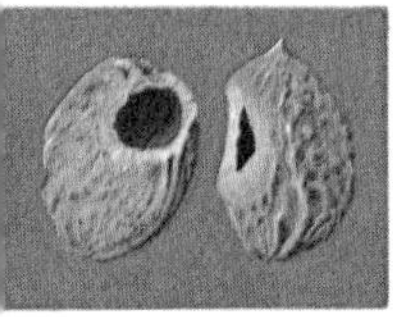

Wood mouse

Hawfinch

Bank vole

Wood mouse

Greenfinch

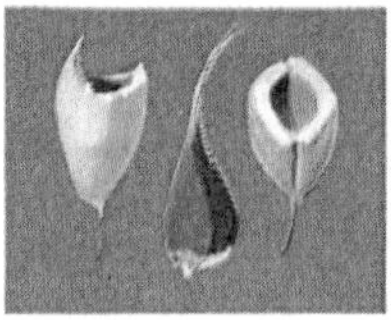

ROSE HIP
× 2

CHERRY × 1½

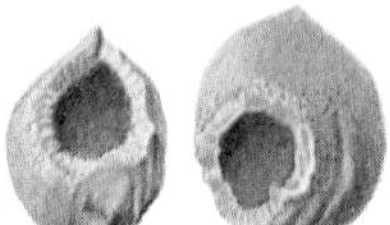

Wood mouse
see p. 135

Bank vole
see p. 135

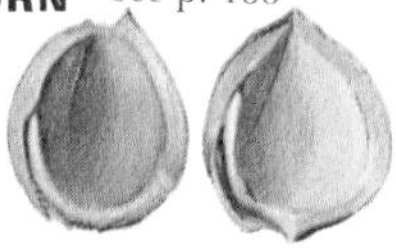

HAWTHORN
× 1½

Hawfinch
see p. 135

LIME
× 1½

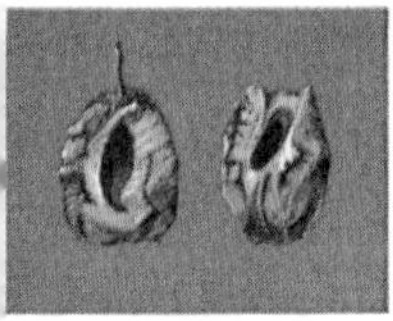

PLUM × 1½

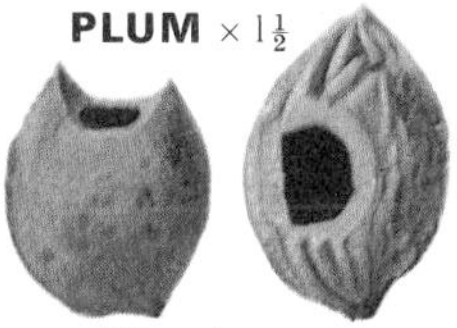

Wood mouse
see p. 135

HORNBEAM
× 1½

ALMOND × 1½

House mouse

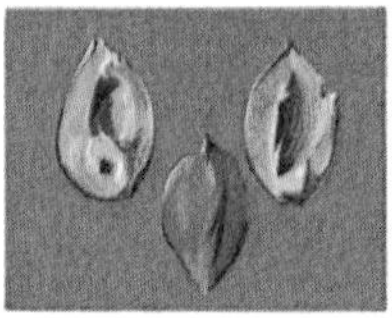

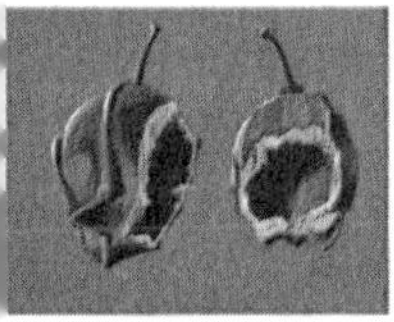

Squirrel see p. 136

Wood mouse see p. 136

OATS
× 2

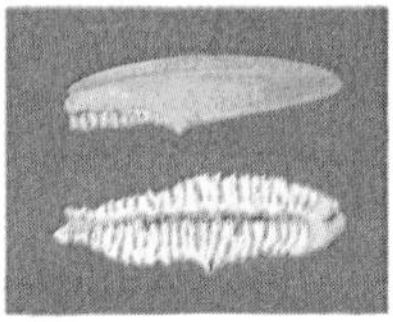

House mouse see p. 139

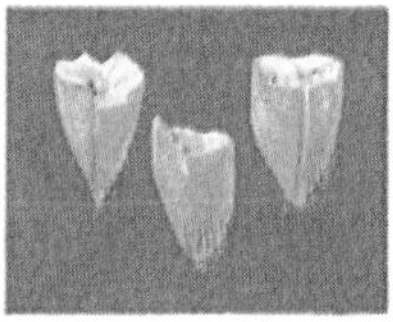

Rat see p. 139

MAIZE
× 1½

House mouse see p. 139

termed the wood mouse type and the bank vole type according to the species in which the behaviour was first noticed.

Wood mouse type: when gnawing, the wood mouse holds the nut pressed against the ground by the fore-feet, so that it is inclined obliquely in towards the breast. Once it has made a hole in the shell it inserts the lower incisors and, while holding the upper incisors against the outer side of the shell, gnaws at the side that is furthest from its body. Gnawing therefore proceeds in an outward direction, and as the mouse turns the nut round while gnawing, the upper incisors leave a row of marks, often in the form of a groove, on the outer side just below the edge of the hole; these show up as pale marks on the brown shell (see plate on p. 126).

Bank vole type: the bank vole also holds the nut pressed against the ground with the fore-feet, but in contrast to the wood mouse it holds the nut underneath itself, with the base under its

Wood mouse

Bank vole

chest and with the tip pointing obliquely away, so that the nut slopes away from the animal. Once the vole has made a hole in the nut, unlike the wood mouse, it inserts its snout and gnaws the side that is nearest. Gnawing therefore proceeds in an inward direction, and the gnawed edge is very clearly marked against the undamaged outer side. The marks left by the upper incisors on the inside of the shell are not very obvious on account of the loose brown lining of the shell (see plate on p. 126).

The yellow-necked mouse, the water vole and the hazel dormouse gnaw like the wood mouse, but remarkably enough the striped mouse, although closely related to the wood mouse and yellow-necked mouse, gnaws in the same way as the bank vole. The water vole, which is about the same size as a rat, has a very powerful bite, and the gnawed edge therefore acquires an irregular, serrated appearance. Nuts gnawed by a dormouse have a very regular hole, and the tooth marks are so weak that the gnawed edge is almost completely smooth (see plate on page 126).

As soon as a mouse has made a hole in the nut it starts to eat, picking out pieces of the kernel with the lower incisors. Usually they take these pieces in the fore-paws and hold them there while eating. The great mobility between the two halves of the lower jaw is an advantage as the two long incisors can be used almost like a pair of tweezers, for picking out the loose bits of kernel. When no more can be extracted through the hole the animal starts to gnaw again, enlarging the hole equally on all sides.

In its efforts to reach the kernel the mouse often sticks the lower incisors so far into the hole that the upper incisors come to scrape the outer side of the nut, producing long, pale scratches on it.

Mice and voles usually eat at special feeding places which may be under a tuft of grass, a pile of brushwood or in some other well sheltered site. Large collections of empty nut shells may be found in these places.

Some small rodents use nuts as winter stores. Thus, in autumn the water vole may gather large amounts into its system of underground tunnels, where they are used during the course of the winter. The empty shells are removed in the following autumn, when the store is due for refilling, and are thrown out in large piles in front of the holes leading down to the tunnel system.

Hazelnuts emptied by a water vole, lying outside the entrance to its burrow.

Birds open nuts by hacking the shell into pieces. Usually several blows are required before the shell is shattered, so hazelnut shells emptied by birds show numerous beak marks on the smooth brown surface. As the tip of the beak differs in form in nut-eating birds it is sometimes possible, from the appearance of the beak marks, to identify the species which has actually opened the nut.

In the *greater spotted woodpecker* the bill is laterally compressed and like a small chisel, and it leaves marks that are about 2 mm long (see plate on p. 126).

Before attacking a nut the bird wedges it into some kind of crevice. This may be a natural crack in an old post or a furrow in the bark, but the bird will often chip out a hole which exactly fits a nut. Such a place is sometimes known as a woodpecker workshop and as it may be used for quite a long time there will usually be several broken nut shells on the ground below.

It is interesting to note that the

'Woodpecker workshop' with a hazelnut wedged in a natural crack. Several emptied nuts lie on the ground.

A woodpecker has hacked a hole in the angle of a branch on a cherry tree in order to wedge a nut. The bird has been disturbed before it had eaten the whole kernel.

◀

Beak marks of:
1. *Woodpecker*
2. *Nuthatch*
3. *Magpie*
4. *Great tit*

woodpecker understands how to exploit the nut's structure, and that it is easiest to crack the shell longitudinally. The nut is always positioned with the base downwards, and the blows are delivered along the long axis of the nut, in the same way as a mason splits a block of stone.

The beak marks of a *nuthatch* are in the form of a half moon and thus easy to distinguish from those of a woodpecker. The marks are made only by the upper mandible, which extends a little beyond the lower mandible (see plate on p. 126).

The bird wedges the nut in a natural crevice which is only used once. When the nut has been emptied the shell is usually left where it is, so there is no pile of empty nut shells on the ground below.

The nuthatch, a considerably smaller bird than a woodpecker, is not capable of splitting nuts in the same way, but has to hack a more or less circular hole in the side.

In the late summer and autumn the nuthatch hides various kinds of seed, putting them in bark crevices and similar places, to serve as a food store in the winter. Hazelnuts are particularly popular for this purpose. It is probable that the nuthatches cannot distinguish one hiding place from another, but as, unlike most other birds, they maintain their territory in the winter, it is likely that the birds that find the seeds in winter are the same as those which hid them in the autumn.

The tip of a *magpie's* beak is shaped almost like a shallow three-sided pyramid with curved sides, and it leaves a relatively large, roundish mark. As in the nuthatch, it is only the tip of the upper mandible that makes a mark. The nuts are usually opened on the ground, where they are held in position by one foot (see plate on page 126).

The beak marks made by a *great tit* are similar to those made by a magpie, but are of course much smaller, and as the upper and lower mandibles are of equal length the tip of the whole beak has an almost square shape. This, however, is difficult to see in the beak marks on nuts. Great tits prefer nuts that are scarcely ripe, with relatively soft shells (see plate on page 126).

The *nutcracker* is a very active con-

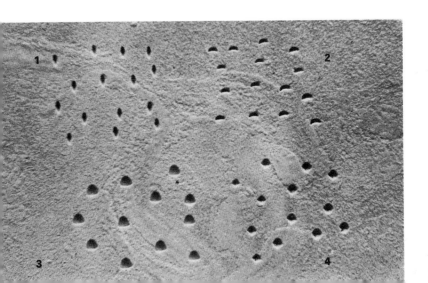

sumer of nuts and when it has the chance will collect stores which it hides in the ground for winter use. It can deliver a very powerful blow, usually aimed at the tip of the nut, which is thus split into two pieces. However, thin-shelled nuts are often shattered from the side. The nuts are opened at a special feeding place, such as a tree stump, and are held in position by one foot (see plate on p. 126).

into the shell it makes a hole by gnawing a deep furrow.

Mice have to open walnuts in a different way. They do not have the strength to split the shells apart and so they carefully gnaw their way in to reach the kernel. Often, but not always, a mouse starts by gnawing the thin-shelled area, producing a very regular pattern, which is easily recognisable by the numerous fine tooth marks left by the lower incisors (see plate on p. 126).

Walnuts

These are highly valued by many animals and walnut shells opened by animals are quite frequently found.

Because of the walnut's very hard shell and its knobbly surface tooth and beak marks are only rarely seen, and this naturally makes it difficult to determine the species of animal involved.

Quite often the animals have little difficulty in making a hole in the walnut, because there are two thin-walled areas near the point of the shell which are easy to break through; indeed, the shell there may be so incomplete that there actually is a hole leading into the kernel.

Rodents

When opening a walnut a squirrel presses the lower incisors in through one of the thin-walled areas, and splits the shells apart, using the teeth as a crowbar. If unable to insert the teeth

Birds

The *great tit* can only chip away the thin parts of the shell and therefore has to make do with as much of the kernel as it can reach through these rather regularly chipped holes. Great tits prefer to tackle nuts while they are still attached to the tree, but in doing so they often fall, and the process is then completed on the ground (see plate p. 126).

The *jackdaw* will usually take walnuts from the tree and carry them to a feeding place on the ground or on a branch. The nut is firmly held down with one foot while the powerful beak is used to hack a large, irregular hole in it. There are usually no clear beak marks to be seen on the shells (see plate p. 126).

Crossbills may attack walnuts in years when there is a poor supply of spruce seeds. But they can only deal with very thin-shelled or unripe nuts; they bite the shell and break it on each side of the strong joint (see plate p. 126).

Feeding place of a yellow-necked mouse with the remains of beechmast it had consumed.

Beechnuts and acorns

Rodents

Beechnuts (beechmast) and acorns are eaten by many rodents, particularly by wood mice and yellow-necked mice, and the remains of the gnawed shells are commonly seen at feeding places in beech and oak woods. The edges of the gnawed shells show clearly the marks left by the mouse's teeth, producing an uneven, scalloped appearance. Mice open beechnuts either by gnawing away two of the three sides, so that the remaining side falls away and the kernel can be removed, or by gnawing off the broad, lower end of the nut so that the kernel can be pulled out. With acorns, mice usually start by gnawing a hole in the lowermost, broad end which is uneven, so that the teeth can get a grip (see plate p. 127).

Birds

The chipped remains of beechnuts can often be found wedged firmly into bark crevices. Birds have brought them there to hack the kernels free. Distinct beak marks are usually not found so it

Beechmast wedged and hacked by a nuthatch.

is difficult to decide which species of bird is involved, but it is usually a woodpecker or a nuthatch.

Undamaged beechnuts can also be seen in bark crevices, and these are winter stores, not yet used, of the nuthatch.

During the winter, flocks of finches—particularly bramblings and green-finches—often forage on the ground in beech woods, and closer examination will show that the birds are eating beechmast; the husks, bitten apart irregularly, and small pieces of white kernel lie around in small heaps, each of which is the remains from a single beech nut.

Cherry stones emptied by a bank vole. The animal must have had a store in the hollow tree trunk and has thrown out the empty shells.

▼

Cherry stones cracked on the ground by a haw-finch. The two equal halves of the stone usually lie alongside one another.

▶

Cherries and plums

The fleshy fruits of cherries and plums are sought after by many animals, of which some eat the whole fruit whereas others take only the flesh or the kernel inside the stone.

Mammals which eat whole cherries include, for example, foxes and badgers. Martens take many fallen plums, but they may also take fruits up in the trees. Birds which take the whole fruits include the black-headed gull and many of the crows. In practice, all these animals digest only the fleshy part of the fruits, and get rid of the undamaged stones either in pellets or in the faeces. As these stones show no marks which might provide a clue to the identity of the animal, any identifi-

cation must rely on the other constituents of the faeces or pellets (see pages 171 and 194).

Rodents

Squirrels usually eat only the flesh, but sometimes also gnaw the stones.

The stones are utilised primarily by mice, whose gnawing is easy to identify by its regularity and by the numerous tooth marks which appear as fine furrows on the gnawed edges. As in the case of hazelnuts attacked by mice (see p. 128) it is possible to distinguish two types of gnawing on plum and cherry stones; the wood mouse type in which there are distinct tooth marks along the gnawed edge, and the bank vole type which lacks such tooth marks (see plate p. 127).

Birds

Starlings and thrushes are well known to forage in cherry trees. They eat only the flesh, and the completely exposed stone is often left attached to the stalk.

Hawfinches are also avid consumers of cherries, but they do not eat the flesh. They extract the stone, crack it with the extraordinarily powerful bill and then eat the kernel. They leave no bill marks on the stone, which is characteristically cracked into two halves of equal size, which usually lie side by side on the ground, together with the remains of the cherry. During the winter, hawfinches can be seen searching beneath cherry trees for the stones, and the cracked shells can be found quite commonly. Hawfinches deal with plum stones, sloe stones and many other hard-shelled seeds in a similar way (see plate p. 127).

Rose hips

Rodents

Rose hips are taken by squirrels and mice. Squirrels normally eat them on the ground, as they find it difficult to perch up on the slender, thorny branches. They bite along the seed to get at the kernel, whereas mice gnaw in from the broad, basal end and pull out the kernel (see plate, p. 127).

Birds

In winter the red, fleshy parts of the hips are eaten by many birds, particularly thrushes. These birds are only interested in the flesh and leave the

seeds, but finches hack away the flesh, small pieces of which can be seen smeared on branches and leaves, and then eat the seeds after having cracked them with the bill.

Apples

Rodents

Feeding signs left by small rodents can be observed on apples, both outside and in fruit stores. In most cases these animals eat both the flesh and the seeds, and the gnawing can be easily recognised by the numerous small tooth marks along the gnawed edge of the skin, and by the oblong depressions

Rose hip attacked by greenfinch.

Apples stored in a cellar have been plundered by house mice.

which the lower incisors leave in the flesh. It is often difficult to know from the gnawing alone which animal has been responsible. However, the size of the tooth marks will always show whether the gnawing has been done by an animal the size of a squirrel, rat or water vole, or by one the size of a mouse, for the tooth marks of the former are at least twice the size of those made by mice. A more exact identification can therefore only be made with the help of other signs.

Birds

Of the many birds that eat apples the signs left by thrushes are by far the commonest; these can be seen particularly on windfalls, and also on apples which are still on the tree. These birds are only interested in the flesh and as they remove as little as possible of the peel, the apple becomes hollowed out, leaving only the skin with the seed mass in the centre. The marks made by

Apple partly eaten by a blackbird.

Apples attacked by crossbills.

the pointed bill can be clearly seen on the inside of the skin.

In contrast to the thrushes, crossbills will attack apples for the sake of the seeds. By reason of the characteristic shape of the bill an apple attacked by one of these birds has a very characteristic appearance. They literally gnaw their way in to the core, biting off the flesh in pieces which often remain hanging in little clusters. Crossbills prefer small varieties of apple, such as pippins or crabs, as these have numerous seeds which are close to the surface.

Cereals

The different kinds of cultivated cereals attract many animals, whose foraging in arable land may cause damage of economic importance.

Deer

In fields bordering on woodland it is quite common for deer to move in at twilight or in the early morning and to nibble the shoots in a strip along the edge of the wood. This often takes place when the corn is still completely unripe.

Rodents

Maize fields are frequently invaded by rats and mice, which climb up the plants and gnaw off the soft sweet corn in the cobs after having first gnawed away the large sheathing leaves which surround the seeds, leaving clear tooth marks.

Feeding signs of small rodents can be easily recognised on ripe dry maize seeds, for by preference they eat the soft seed embryo, leaving the remainder of the seed as a characteristic half-moon shape (see plate p. 127).

Apart from a few species, such as the harvest mouse, most small rodents are too heavy to climb up the thin stems of cereals, so they fell them by gnawing through near the surface of the soil. They then usually gnaw off the seed head and carry it away to a suitable feeding place. House mice and rats gnaw oat seeds in different ways, so it is always possible from the remains of their meals to determine which species was involved. A house mouse gnaws the grain from the side, holding each end with a fore-foot. The remains are therefore oblong shavings, somewhat resembling bran. Rats, on the other hand, gnaw the seeds from one end, leaving only an end piece, of varying size (see plate p. 127).

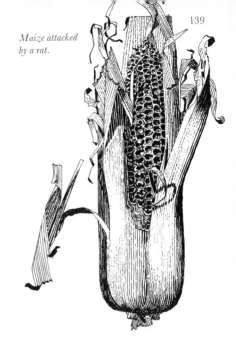

Maize attacked by a rat.

Birds

Cornfields are visited by flocks of house sparrows, particularly in the vicinity of towns, and in certain cases they may remove all the seed. The birds begin by eating the lowermost seeds and gradually move higher and higher up the stem. Under the weight of the birds many of the stems become broken and eventually the field takes on a quite characteristic appearance.

House sparrows frequently feed on maize cobs, but the sheathing leaves remain in position, although often frayed and torn.

Wheat stalks after a visit by house sparrows. ▼

A field vole has bitten off the dandelion flowers to get the unripe seeds. The white down remains at the feeding place.

Other seeds

Since all kinds of seed may serve as food for animals, innumerable feeding places with the remains of seeds will be found in the wild. When, for example, a goldfinch picks the seeds out of thistles during the winter or a siskin feeds on catkins, the snow around their feeding places will be covered with the remains of these plants. Mice will usually bite off the seed heads and bring them to a feeding place where the remains will be found gathered together. Thus, the wood mouse and the yellow-necked mouse bite off catkins up in the trees and bring them down to the ground before eating them.

Thistle attacked by a goldfinch.

Feeding signs on herbaceous plants

After a winter with much snow the reindeer's foraging can be detected in spring by the meandering belts of grazed lichen.

Herbaceous plants provide a very important source of food for a large number of animals. For the large herbivorous animals, such as deer, and for many of the rodents the leaves or roots of these plants yield their main food supply throughout the year. Some other animals, such as fowls and pheasants, only forage on herbaceous plants at certain times of the year.

Feeding signs on herbaceous plants are not usually very striking and are often difficult or impossible to identify with any degree of certainty. Nevertheless, by taking account of certain characteristic features of the different animal groups, together with observations on other signs such as faeces and footprints and some knowledge of the species that occur in the locality, it is usually possible to make a correct identification of the species concerned.

Deer

The feeding signs of deer are not at all noticeable during the summer, as these animals seldom crop the plants very closely, but nibble a little here and there as they move along. In winter, on the other hand, the feeding places are often very conspicuous, for the deer scrape away the snow with their fore-feet in order to get down to the ground vegetation.

During the winter, reindeer prefer to feed on areas below the tree line where there is plenty of lichen. When feeding conditions are good there may be little sign that reindeer have been in the area. On the other hand, if the conditions are poor, with deep snow the foraging is more concentrated and the lichen cover is gnawed off in meandering belts, which may remain sharply delineated for many years.

Scilla gnawed by a bank vole.

Rodents

Among the small rodents it is the voles, in particular, that feed on herbaceous plants, and feeding places with the remains of gnawed leaves and stems can always be found along the paths used by field voles and water voles. These animals like to be hidden away while feeding, and so the feeding places are always in the shelter of a tuft of grass, a fallen branch or something similar. After the snow has melted in early spring one can often see what appear to be completely fresh vole feeding places which are right out in the open, but this has a natural explanation. When they were in use these feeding places were sheltered by the snow, and owing to the low temperature and high humidity the faeces and food remains have been preserved in a fresh condition, so that one might well believe that such sites were still being used for feeding.

The feeding places are frequently a short distance from the gnawed plants, but if one lifts the hanging leaves of a grass tuft, one can often see that the lower and most succulent parts of the tuft's outer shoots have been gnawed away by field voles, while the uppermost part with the leaves is still in place on the tuft. During their foraging the mice make a well-trodden path strewn with faeces round the base of the tuft. The pieces of gnawed plant at the feeding places usually show distinct tooth marks. On leaves these can be seen as a row of small, curved indentations, which on the long narrow leaves of grasses lie at right angles to the long axis, for mice usually eat them from one end. In addition to the remains of food the feeding places always have large amounts of droppings. In general, the feeding places of the water vole and of the field vole are very similar, except in size. Thus, the water vole often gnaws much larger pieces of plant than the field vole, its tooth marks are at least twice as large and its droppings are also much larger (see p. 176).

A particularly striking feeding sign can often be observed when field voles, and probably also bank voles, turn their attention to rushes during the winter. The rush stems are gnawed through at the base and cut up into suitable pieces that can be held in the mouse's fore-feet while it gnaws off and eats the green outer layer. The spongy pith remains behind at the feeding place and its chalky white colour betrays the site from a long distance away.

In spring, fields with winter-sown corn and those with newly planted lucerne may also show signs that field voles have eaten the green leaves be-

New shoots of winter corn gnawed by hares.

neath the snow, often removing them completely over large parts of the field. Hares and deer also browse on such fields, but this usually takes place later

Rushes gnawed by field voles. Only the green parts are eaten.

Crocus flowers attacked by house sparrows, which seem to prefer the yellow varieties.

in the season when the plants have grown taller.

During winter, voles feed on the roots of herbaceous plants. In the autumn the water vole gathers winter stores which often consist of pieces of roots, tubers or bulbs, and in spring one can frequently see thistles, dandelions and similar plants with thick fleshy roots that have completely withered, and if they are pulled up it will be seen that the roots have been gnawed away. Many garden owners have had the bitter experience of seeing their carefully planted flower bulbs fail to come up or else to find them shooting in a crowded clump from a water vole's store, which for some reason the animal has not used. The gnawed roots and bulbs usually show distinct marks of the animal's teeth.

Birds

Many birds, particularly gallinaceous birds (fowl, pheasants, partridge etc.), feed during the spring on the fresh, green leaves of herbaceous plants, their beaks leaving wedge-shaped indentations on the edges of the leaves. Most gardeners will have seen the destruction of crocus flowers by sparrows. In such cases the birds are primarily interested in the stamens, but they also eat the petals, on which their beak marks can be clearly seen. The house sparrow prefers the yellow crocus flowers, although it will also take other colours.

Geese and some ducks are often seen grazing on winter-sown fields, where they bite off the new leaves and shoots, and in parks mallards may bite off sprouting crocus in spring just as they appear above ground. Sometimes they eat the shoots right down to the bulb, using the bill to bore a hole about 2 inches deep, which at the surface looks like a mouse hole.

Turnips

Turnip fields are particularly suitable for observing feeding signs, for various animals are very interested in these succulent roots, and the feeding signs are usually very conspicuous and easy to identify.

Deer

Deer often visit turnip fields, and red deer, for instance, pull up the plants long before the roots have grown, and as they only take a single bite from each turnip and leave the rest they destroy much more than they eat. When the turnips are fully developed deer only eat from the part above ground, and the marks left by their large lower incisors can be seen as broad furrows on the upper surface of the turnip.

Rodents

Hares also gnaw turnips, and like the deer species they often take only a little from each root, and as they also do not eat all that they bite off they always damage a relatively large number of plants. Their tooth marks are easy to identify on account of the groove on the front of the upper incisors (see p. 93), so that the gnawing looks as though it had been done by an animal with four small incisors in the upper jaw

Turnip gnawed by deer. Note the conspicuous broad tooth marks.

Turnips badly gnawed by hares.

and two large incisors in the lower jaw.

Water voles always gnaw turnips from below, as they work underground, excavating the root and leaving only a thin shell. From the farmer's viewpoint it is perhaps some consolation that the water vole does at least eat the whole turnip before starting on the next one. When a rat gnaws a turnip it starts from above and gnaws down into the root, so that the tip gradually disappears and the turnip root becomes hollowed out into a deep saucer.

Turnips hollowed out by a water vole.

Feeding signs left by predators

...emains found at a predator's feeding ...lace are generally those of warm-...looded prey.

When the prey is small, for example ...mouse or a small bird, it will usually ...e swallowed whole, being eventually ...roken up into quite small pieces, and ...o remains will be left at the feeding ...lace, or at the most there may be a ...ift of hair, a couple of feathers or a ...ttle blood. When the prey is large ...uite a lot will usually remain, and ...ere will be a chance to identify the ...redator from the method of killing ...nd any tooth marks. In the absence ...f such evidence it is normally rather ...ifficult or even impossible to identify ...predator's feeding place. Usually the ...osition of the feeding place, foot ...rints, droppings and possibly other ...gns may help, but even then an accur-...e identification may be difficult. Fur-...ermore, the task of identification ...ay be rendered difficult by the fact ...at the same prey may be exploited ...y several different animals. For ...xample, the remains of a hare at the ...eding place of a large bird of prey ...ill soon be visited by crows, gulls or ...xes, and various small rodents and ...rews will also take their pick.

Quite frequently it may happen that ...e animal whose remains are found ...t a predator's feeding place has not, ...fact, been killed by the predator ...oncerned, something that many ...unters forget when judging the extent ...f a carnivorous animal's depredations.

...predator will usually take whatever is easiest to get hold of, and in winter many will feed on carrion, which may remain fresh for a considerable time owing to the low temperatures. In addition, a predator will in many cases take sick or weak animals, which would in any case have died in a short time.

For most people there is something infinitely fascinating about carni-vorous animals, and apart from their attractive appearance, it is the fact that they feed on other animals that makes them so interesting. It is also particularly instructive to stand over a predator's feeding place and attempt to deduce from it the animal's choice of food, its method of feeding and also perhaps something about its hunting methods.

Carnivores

In practice, the remains of meals con-sumed by carnivorous mammals are relatively rarely found, because small prey is consumed whole and larger prey is usually taken to a more or less hidden feeding place, and the remains may be covered with leaves, mosses or snow or even buried—as the domestic dog buries bones.

The prey is often taken to the animal's home, and outside the en-trance to an occupied fox's earth one can often find the remains of many different kinds of prey. The organic matter which in this way reaches the soil will, together with urine and droppings, act as fertiliser. In fact, the vegetation around an old fox earth is much more luxuriant than in the surrounding area, and there are often plant species that require plenty of nutrient. The remains of prey can also be found in a loft or shed occupied by a beech marten. These are usually birds but sometimes there are eggshells and the remains of hedgehogs, in which case nearly everything will have been consumed except the skin and spines.

Birds are dealt with in a quite characteristic way, and the remains found at the feeding places of birds of prey can usually be identified (see p. 153). The brain is evidently a special delicacy, so the head is bitten off and eaten first. Then tufts of feathers are bitten off from the body, the feathers becoming more or less stuck together with saliva. The larger feathers may show signs of having been bitten over, and frequently the lower ends of the feather follicles are missing, but they can be found in the predator's droppings. The outer parts of the wing feathers are bitten off or the wing feathers may be bitten so close in to the wing that they are only attached by a narrow strip of skin. The tail is treated in a similar way. The remains of the bird's bones show clear signs of having been crushed or bitten.

Small rodents play a very large role in the diet of many of the smaller predatory mammals, and even though they are usually eaten whole with skin and fur so that nothing is left, the feeding places are sometimes betrayed in another way. Thus, in fields and on slopes it is not uncommon to find evidence that a fox has dug out the nest of a field vole or water vole and taken the young. The fox will probably have found the nest by scent or by listening, and the finely divided hay from inside it can be seen just on top of the upturned earth.

When the prey is a larger mammal or relatively fresh carrion, the predator will nearly always eat the viscera first, beginning by ripping the belly open. They are particularly interested in the

Tail feathers bitten off by a stoat. The lowermost parts of the quills have been chewed.

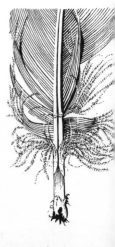

A fox has dug out a field vole's nest and eaten the young. The remains of the nest can be seen as a little ball of hay in front of the hole.

iver and lungs and will eat these organs before starting on the flesh itself. The size of the bones that have been crushed or bitten may provide an important clue to the size of the animal which has used the feeding place.

The different marten species kill large prey with a bite at the nape, just behind the head, but smaller animals such as small rodents are killed by a bite through the head itself. Sometimes when a beech marten has entered a

Carcase of a fallow deer (buck) partly eaten by a fox, which has marked it by spraying it with urine.

150

dovecot or a hen house it will kill many more birds than it wants to eat or to drag away. This has given rise to the belief that these animals suck the blood of their victims, but there is, in fact, no truth in this suggestion. Foxes may be responsible for similar carnage in colonies of nesting gulls.

Dead small mammals are found relatively rarely in the wild, because they are very quickly eaten by other animals. Shrews, however, form an exception for one will often find a dead specimen lying out in the middle of a road or on a tree stump. The explanation is that the shrews have a gland on each side of the body which produces a secretion with a strong musky scent which many animals cannot tolerate. Closer examination of the dead shrew will sometimes show that it has been killed by a predator, often a fox, a bird of prey or an owl. It has probably been confused with a mouse, and the mistake has not been noticed until it was too late for the shrew. However, some animals, for instance barn owls, will eat shrews.

At otter feeding places on the banks

Shrew killed by a carnivore.

of rivers and lakes one almost always finds the remains of fish, which form the animal's main food, and it also takes frogs and crustaceans. It usually eats the fish's head first and often leaves part of the tail. Some fishermen have observed that seals eat fish caught on lines, leaving only a part of the head attached to the hook.

The polecat eats many amphibians and one often finds the remains of frogs and toads at feeding places in marshes and along the banks of a lake. The heads of the toads are often left probably because they have large poison glands, and as the polecat kills amphibians by biting the head, it possible to find its tooth marks.

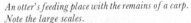

An otter's feeding place with the remains of a carp. Note the large scales.

Desiccated toad with the mark of a polecat's bite on the head. ▶

A polecat's feeding place among the reeds with the remains of frogs and toads.

A bird of prey has made a kill. Note the mouse track leading from the upper left corner of the picture.

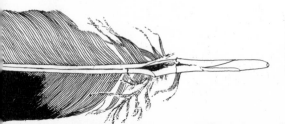

Pigeon feather torn off by a bird of prey. Unlike feathers bitten off by carnivores, the quill base is undamaged. Sometimes there may be beak marks a little higher up the shaft.

Birds of prey

In contrast to the feeding places of predatory mammals, those of birds of prey are very conspicuous, especially when the prey has been a bird; such sites are very common. Birds of prey handle their prey in quite a different way from predatory mammals (see p. 147), so there is usually no difficulty in deciding which type of animal has used the feeding place. Nevertheless, it should always be remembered that several different animals may utilise the same prey one after the other.

When a bird of prey has caught a bird it will often tear off the head and eat the brain, which is evidently a special delicacy, leaving the beak and the rest of the skull at the feeding place. Sometimes, however, the head is not eaten but is left untouched among the other remains.

A bird of prey will then start to pluck the prey, pulling out the feathers with its beak, so that the feeding place gradually becomes surrounded by a mass of feathers and down, which the wind may blow out in a long drift. The larger feathers are pulled out individually, so that the feather follicles are always undamaged, in contrast to what happens at a predatory mammal's feeding place. Closer examination of the feather itself will often show the place where it has been gripped by the beak, and sometimes there may be a bend at this point.

The breast musculature is usually the first part of the body to be eaten, and the predator's sharp beak removes wedge-shaped pieces from the keel of the breast bone, leaving very characteristic notches which provide a sure sign that the prey has been eaten by a bird of prey. These birds do not eat

Wedge-shaped marks on the keel of the breast bone are a sure sign that a bird has been eaten by a bird of prey.

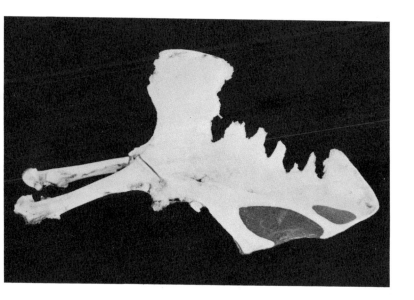

large bones, but they will swallow small pieces, which are later regurgitated together with any small feathers and down. The stomach and intestine are usually not eaten and they are left behind with the bones.

The appearance of the plucking place will naturally vary according to whether the prey is also eaten there or taken after plucking to another spot. If the prey is eaten where it was plucked there will be the remains of the skeleton as well as the feathers, beak, gut etc.

During the breeding season many birds of prey pluck the prey at some distance from the nest so as not to betray the presence of the latter, and then bring it to the incubating mate or to the young. In such cases the skeleton itself will not be found at the plucking place. When the birds in the nest have finished with the prey the remains are carried away and dropped elsewhere. It is only at the end of the nesting period when the birds have become less careful, that the remains are thrown over the side of the nest, so that old carcases can be found beneath the nest. Sometimes birds of prey will do the plucking up in the trees, and the feathers will then become spread over a large area, so that one does not immediately connect the widely distributed feathers with a plucking. From a knowledge of the feeding habits and hunting methods of birds of prey it is possible to identify with some degree of accuracy the originator of a new feeding place, by observing its position, the size of the prey and the way it has been handled. The following notes are intended to help in the identification of the most commonly occurring feeding places.

Among birds of prey the main hunters of other birds are the goshawk, sparrowhawk and the falcons, but not the kestrel which feeds mainly on small rodents.

The feeding places of the sparrowhawk and goshawk are very similar and usually they cannot be distinguished from one another with any degree of certainty. The prey is never plucked out in the open but is brought into some sheltered spot on the edge of woodland, and actually plucked on a tree stump or a rock.

The prey of sparrowhawks consists mainly of tits, sparrows and thrushes but the female, which is somewhat larger than the male, can also take birds the size of a pigeon or partridge. The prey is usually plucked at a favourite spot. Thus, during the breeding season one can often find within a limited area 50–70 or even more plucking places at some distance from the nest, which is usually built among dense vegetation. Even at other times sparrowhawks will pluck their prey at specially chosen sites.

The female goshawk, which is considerably larger and more powerful than the male, can capture and transport prey up to the size of a duck whereas the male can only manage prey of pigeon size. Within their breeding territory the plucking places are usually very widely distributed, but outside the breeding season the goshawk, like the sparrowhawk, often plucks at specially favoured spots.

In most cases the feeding places of the peregrine falcon are very characteristic. These birds can take large prey such as pigeons, gulls and ducks but these are always plucked out in the open, sometimes on a branch protruding from the crown of a tree. In most cases a peregrine falcon will only eat the flesh of the breast and leave the remainder. They do not, therefore, pull out the wing feathers, and the wing and breast skeleton remain attached

Blackbird killed by sparrowhawk. The head has been torn off and the breast partly eaten.

It is obvious that feeding places out in the open with carrion will very quickly be visited by other animals, such as foxes, gulls and crows.

Some birds of prey, for instance buzzards, Montagu's harriers and kestrels, feed primarily on small rodents, but others feed on carrion. When eating a mammal, goshawks and sparrowhawks will pluck off the fur, as they

Wood pigeon killed by goshawk.

Hare carcase almost completely eaten by buzzards. To the left are numerous tufts of fur which the birds have torn off the hare.

An osprey's feeding place with a partly consumed fish. The longish white streak in the right hand top corner is faeces squirted out by the bird.

do with the feathers on a bird, but the other birds of prey tear off the skin in shreds. Feeding places with the remains of fish can be found in areas where ospreys occur.

Little or no remains of prey will be found at feeding places used by owls. These birds usually pluck up in a tree but they do not pluck their prey thoroughly. They swallow small ro-

dents either whole or divided only into a few pieces. The eagle owl is an exception, because on account of its size it can overpower prey as large as a hare and there will often be the remains of prey at its feeding places. The many indigestible parts eaten by owls, such as feathers, fur and bones are regurgitated in the form of pellets (see p. 195).

Hare killed by crows which have eaten part of the hindquarters. Although crows can easily kill leverets, they can only overpower the adults when these are old, weak or sick. The hare shown here had had its eyes pecked out while still alive. The front paws became smeared with blood as the animal rubbed its eye sockets.

Other feeding signs

Animals that search for food in the ground often leave fairly conspicuous holes in the surface. In the section on predators (see p. 148) mention was made of the way foxes dig out the nests of small rodents, and here there is no doubt about the species of prey concerned. Often, however, there may be funnel-shaped depressions 10–15 cm deep, which do not immediately suggest the type of prey that was being sought. These will most frequently be places where a badger has been digging for worms or insects. On grassy fields and lawns that are attacked by cockchafer larvae, the badger will pull up tufts with its claws in order to get at the larvae which feed on the grass roots. Similar feeding signs, but on a much

A badger has torn up the grass while hunting for cockchafer larvae.

larger scale, will be found in places where wild boars have been rooting or ploughing up the soil surface with

A wild boar has been rooting in the ground for larvae; clear impressions of its snout can be seen at the back of the depression.

A wasp nest dug out by a badger which has eaten the larvae and pupae.

their snouts, in search of insects, roots and fungi.

Quite frequently the nest of a wasp or bee may be dug out and the remains left spread out on the ground. This will have been the work of a badger or a honey buzzard. The latter occupies a rather special place among the birds of prey, for it feeds largely on insects, particularly wasps and their larvae and pupae. It hunts especially for the nests of species that live in the ground, which it digs out with its claws and then pulls out the individual larvae and pupae with its beak. During the breeding season honey buzzards take the comb to their nest, and feed their young on the contents. The badger, which is not able to pick out the larvae and pupae individually, usually eats them with the comb. If it comes upon a bee nest the badger will be very keen to get at the stored honey, and indeed badgers have been known to turn over a bee hive to reach the honey.

During the autumn when the wasp colonies are dying out one frequently sees great tits, for example, making an opening in a free-hanging wasp nest in order to get at the remaining larvae and pupae. The same may happen in spring when adult wasps are killed by insecticide, but in this case the food, although plentiful, will not be very healthy.

During winter the large nests of the red wood ant may have large holes or even tunnels leading into their interior. This will be the work of a green woodpecker, searching for the ants and pupae which spend the winter deep inside the ant-hill.

Slightly old cow droppings often have their surface completely perforated by holes of various sizes. The small holes are made by insects, whose

An ant-hill with a hole dug by a green woodpecker searching for the ants.

larvae have developed inside the dropping and bored their way out when mature. The large holes are made by starlings, curlews or other birds which have inserted their bill to take the insect larvae. When searching for dung beetles the badger will also visit cow droppings, which it either turns over with its fore-feet or scatters in all directions in order to get at the beetles.

At low tide, in damp sand on the seashore and on mudbanks along the banks of rivers and lakes one very frequently finds numerous small holes which are made by various small waders inserting their bills to search for worms and small crustaceans. At the same time these birds leave foot-

A flock of foraging starlings has left numerous holes in the dry grass.

Beak marks made in the sand by a wader. ▲

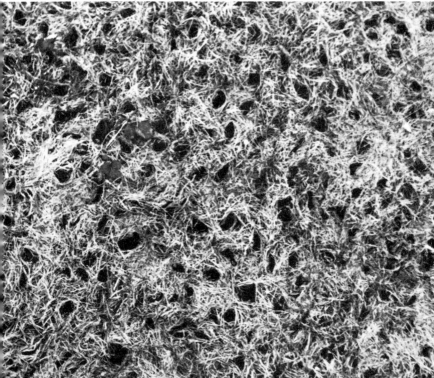

A song thrush's anvil. The bird bangs the snail shell on something hard, in order to crack it and thus get at the snail itself.

prints on the soft substrate and these can often be identified.

Sometimes there may be a large number of broken, empty snail shells lying on the ground around a rock or fallen branch or on a tree stump. These are the feeding places of song thrushes. This bird is not able to crack a snail shell with its bill, so it grips the edge of the shell's opening with the bill and hammers the shell against something hard until it breaks into pieces. The blackbird, which has not mastered this technique, may watch a song thrush doing it and then rush in and pick up the snail just as the shell breaks. Gulls and crows have another elegant method of opening animals that are encased in a hard shell. At low water they fly up with a winkle, a cockle or a crab in their bill and let it drop on to a rock so that it breaks. Rats and many other small rodents also take snails but this is seldom seen as they work under cover and not out in the open like the song thrush. They usually gnaw a piece out of the spire of the shell and follow the coils down as they gradually eat the snail. The last part of the snail is probably pulled out, as

Roe deer antler gnawed by mouse.

Snail shell gnawed by rat.

Spruce twig with galls attacked by a squirrel.

content. This is mainly done by small rodents, whose tooth marks show up as fine stripes.

In spruce forests one frequently finds branches on the ground showing gnawed galls, rather like miniature pineapples. These galls, which are caused by an aphid (*Adelges*), lie at the base of last year's shoots and are much sought after by squirrels. It is the aphids themselves that the squirrel is interested in, and to get at them it will bite off the shoot with the gall, gnaw it to release the little insects, and then let it fall to the ground.

Sometimes in spring, in meadows and marshland or along the banks of rivers and lakes one finds white slimy masses, and closer examination shows these to be the oviducts of a frog. Evidently some animal has eaten a frog but left the oviducts as being inedible. In the majority of cases these will have been left by a buzzard, but occasionally by an otter or polecat.

In some places sloe and hawthorn bushes will be seen to have large

most of the last and largest coil of the shell is usually quite undamaged.

Antlers and bones that have lain for a long time on the forest floor are often gnawed by various animals, probably on account of their calcium

A buzzard has eaten a frog leaving behind the oviducts.

insects or even mice and lizards impaled on their thorns. These are the feeding places or food depots of shrikes. It is primarily the red-backed shrike that has this habit of impaling its prey, but by no means all individuals actually do this. They may occasionally use barbed wire for the same purpose. The great grey shrike feeds mainly on small birds and mice as well as insects; it usually does not impale its prey but wedges it firmly in the angle between two branches or in a bark crevice.

Birds' eggshells are frequently found on the ground, particularly during the spring. In the majority of cases these are shells from eggs that have hatched, for the parent birds generally remove such shells from the nest by flying away with them in the bill and letting them drop elsewhere. However, some birds such as ducks, pheasants and gulls do not do this. These birds nest on the ground and the young leave the nest just after hatching. The broken, empty eggshells are left behind in the nest.

Complete eggs are, of course, very much sought after by many different animals, and many of the eggshells one finds will be the remains of some animal's meal. In most cases it is not difficult to decide whether an eggshell has come from a true hatching, or whether its contents have been eaten by another animal. Frequently it is also possible to identify the animal which has taken the egg by the way in which it has been handled.

At hatching time most chicks are provided with an egg-tooth, which is a hard horny spine situated near the tip of the upper mandible. During hatching the egg-tooth is used to make a circular cut across the blunt end of the shell. As this is being done, small pieces of shell break off and when the shell eventually splits in two, the tough lining extends beyond the edge of the shell. This lining gradually dries out

A dung beetle (above) and a mouse (below), impaled by shrikes.

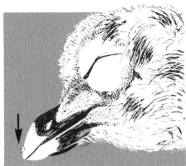

Head of newly hatched gull chick, showing egg tooth.

Blackbird's egg stolen and emptied by a magpie.

and in doing so rolls up into a kind of pad. The inside of the shell shows no trace of yolk or egg-white. Often the two halves of the shell will be found together, the parent bird having placed the smaller piece inside the larger before flying away with it.

When an egg is cracked or bitten open by an animal the lining does not come to extend beyond the edge of the shell and the pad mentioned above is lacking. On the other hand, there will nearly always be distinct traces of

Wood pigeon egg. The infolded membrane along the edge of the shell shows that the egg has hatched normally, with the help of the chick's egg tooth.

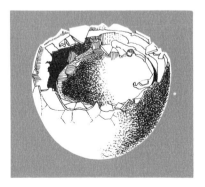

yellow yolk and a thin, shiny layer of egg-white on the inside of the shell, and if the egg has been near to hatching there may also be traces of blood.

The different members of the crow family are inveterate egg-stealers, and they will raid nests on the ground and up in the trees. They seize the egg in their bill and carry it to an open spot, where they put it on the ground and hack an irregular hole in its side. Gulls are also avid egg-eaters, but they only take eggs from nests on the ground, and usually do not carry the eggs away, but merely make a hole as they lie in the nest or possibly roll them a short distance away. It is interesting to observe that ducks, for example, which often nest near gull colonies, always cover the eggs with down or other nest material when they leave their nest, so that gulls and crows do not see the eggs. So, if one frightens the bird off its nest it is important to cover the eggs in the same way, otherwise the nest will almost certainly be

Sandwich tern nest after a visit from a gull.

In spite of the attached lead plate a great spotted woodpecker has hacked a hole in the nest box and taken the young birds.

plundered. Many garden-owners will know that the greater spotted woodpecker can raid a nest-box by hacking a hole in its side. These birds are not after the eggs, but the newly hatched chicks which they can hear cheeping inside the box. Such attacks can be prevented by covering the box with relatively strong sheet metal, but a woodpecker can, of course, hack through a lead plate without difficulty.

There are various mammals that take eggs. The most inveterate egg-eaters are the martens, as poultry farmers in some parts of Europe will know to their cost. The eggs are usually

removed from the nest, one at a time, and carried away in the mouth to be eaten in some secluded spot. Foxes and pine martens often bury the eggs under moss for future use. A marten opens an egg in a very characteristic way, by biting across it to produce an oblong, almost rectangular aperture, through which they lick up the contents. The hedgehog also likes eggs and in the vicinity of a colony of nesting birds, such as gulls, it may feed very largely on eggs and newly hatched young during the nesting season. It bites an irregular hole in the side of the egg and laps up the contents. A fox usually bites an egg so that the whole shell is broken, and then licks up the yolk and albumen.

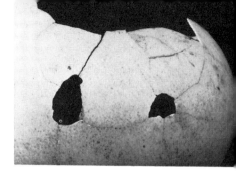

Eggshell with holes made by a polecat's canine teeth.

Polecat's feeding place with empty hen's eggshells.

DROPPINGS
natural size

MAMMALS

Bat

Serotine see p. 173

Hedgehog see p. 173

Beaver see p. 175

Hare see p. 174

Rabbit see p. 174

Squirrel see p. 175

Coypu see p. 177

Voles see p. 175   **True mice** see p. 177

Musk-rat see p. 176

Brown rat see p. 177

Water vole see p. 176

Black rat see p. 177

Lemming see p. 177

House mouse see p. 177

Field vole see p. 176   Wood mouse see p. 177

Fox, two types
see p. 178

Badger
see p. 179

Beech marten
see p. 181

Polecat
see p. 181

Weasel
see p. 181

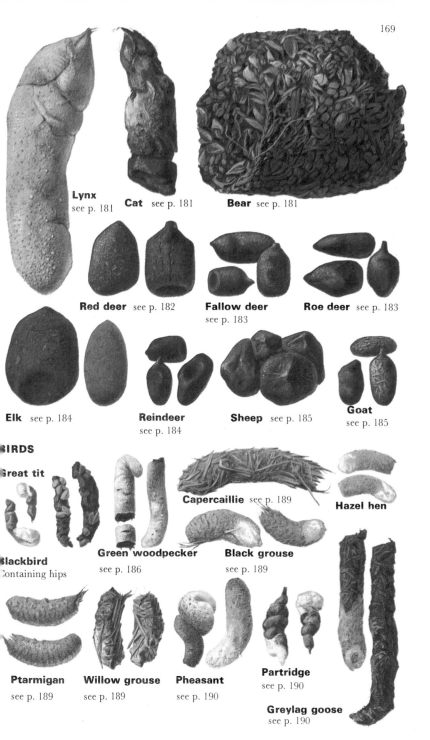

169

Lynx see p. 181

Cat see p. 181

Bear see p. 181

Red deer see p. 182

Fallow deer see p. 183

Roe deer see p. 183

Elk see p. 184

Reindeer see p. 184

Sheep see p. 185

Goat see p. 185

BIRDS

Great tit

Blackbird
Containing hips

Green woodpecker see p. 186

Capercaillie see p. 189

Black grouse see p. 189

Hazel hen

Ptarmigan see p. 189

Willow grouse see p. 189

Pheasant see p. 190

Partridge see p. 190

Greylag goose see p. 190

Winter droppings of fallow deer. Because of the nutritional value of their food, strict vegetarians such as the deer have to eat large quantities and therefore they also produce large amounts of droppings.

DROPPINGS

Mammals

Animal droppings provide important signs, and they are very widespread. Many people may regard this as a rather unattractive subject, but one does not have to study such things for long before realizing that droppings provide a great deal of interesting information, not only on the feeding habits of animals but also on their other activities.

Droppings consist of the indigestible parts of the food, such as hair, feather, bone splinters, pieces of chitin from insects, plant matter with more or less empty cells as well as mucus, cells shed from the alimentary canal and large numbers of living and dead bacteria. Mammal droppings have a scent, particularly when fresh, that is often so strong that even humans are aware of it. This scent plays an extraordinarily important role in the life of these animals, for not only each species but also each individual has its own special scent. In some mammals there are scent glands just inside the anus which transfer scent to the faeces as it is produced. These glands are only fully developed in the sexually mature animal, and they are particularly important at the breeding season, as the scent tells other members of the species that the animal is in rut or ready to mate. This is, of course, of great importance in bringing the sexes together. In some cases the droppings are used to mark the territory with scent (see also p. 225); this applies, for example, to the fox and the rabbit (see pp. 178 and 174).

Some rodents, and also shrews, produce two types of faeces. In addition to the normal droppings which one finds in nature, they also produce dark, soft, slimy droppings which are eaten again as soon as they have passed out through the anus. The significance of this is not completely clear, but it is thought to allow a more complete utilisation of the high content of vitamin B in the gut, this vitamin being produced by the bacterial flora in the alimentary canal.

A detailed examination of the droppings will produce much information on what an animal has been feeding on. From chitin fragments it may be possible to determine the kind of insects the animal has been eating, and from the cell structure of plant matter one may be able to say what plants the animal has been interested in. Simi-

172

larly, the bones, feathers and fur found in carnivore droppings may provide clear evidence of the prey species, but it is important to remember that because a predator has eaten an animal it is by no means certain that it has also killed that animal. Most carnivores are, in fact, avid carrion-eaters and this is one of the reasons why one relatively rarely finds dead animals in the wild. Naturally, only a specialist can accurately determine what an animal has been feeding on, but in most cases it is easy to decide whether the droppings have come from a herbivore or a carnivore, and whether the prey has been a bird or a mammal; indeed most people that are interested in natural history will be able to take the identification even further.

The amount of faeces produced by an animal depends upon the type of food and the extent to which this can be utilised by the animal. In general, plant food is relatively poor in easily accessible nutriment and herbivorous animals therefore have to eat large quantities, and subsequently they will produce large amounts of faeces, which always clearly betray the animal's presence. Flesh has a high nutritional value, and most of it can be utilised by carnivorous animals, which therefore produce much less faeces.

As a rule, the form and size of mammal droppings are fairly characteristic of an individual species. The size will, however, depend to some extent upon the animal's age. Thus, the droppings of young animals are naturally smaller than those of adults, and their shape may also depend upon the composition of the food. Lush grass will give soft, sometimes liquid faeces, whereas hay gives hard, dry droppings. In some cases one can also distinguish between an animal's summer and winter droppings. The droppings of

herbivores are generally small and round, while those of carnivores are often cylindrical or sausage-shaped, with a point at one end.

The colour of the droppings may also provide a clue to the animal's

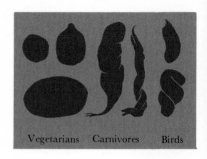

Vegetarians   Carnivores   Birds

Examples of different types of dropping.

food. Young mammals that are still suckling have pale, grey-brown faeces, and animals that have eaten brightly coloured berries, such as bilberries, produce droppings that are deeply stained.

In the identification of mammal droppings it is important to note not only their shape, size, contents, colour and smell but also their location. Many animals deposit their faeces at random, whereas others use special latrines, where large quantities may gradually accumulate. Certain animals, for example the badger and the domestic cat, dig a little hole in the ground for their faeces, and the cat, but not the badger, carefully covers up the hole after use. As already mentioned, some animals such as the fox use their faeces for scent marking their territory or home range, and in such cases these may be left in an elevated position—on a tree stump or a rock— so that the scent is effectively disseminated.

Hedgehog droppings.

Insectivores and bats

Hedgehog droppings are normally shiny black and cylindrical, usually with a point at one end. The size is very variable, but on average each dropping is 3–4 cm long and 8–10 mm thick. They consist very largely of the remains of insects, the fragments of chitin being clearly visible on the surface, to which they give a shiny appearance. Sometimes they may also contain hair, feathers and small pieces of bone. In late summer and autumn the droppings often contain the remains of berries. When a hedgehog has eaten a mouse or a bird the droppings will be dull, twisted and very thin and they may then be confused with the droppings of one of the smaller mustelid species (stoat, weasel).

The hedgehog deposits its faeces during its nocturnal foraging trips, and they can be found distributed at random on, for instance, lawns (see plate p. 168).

Shrew droppings are very small, 2–4 mm long and 1–2 mm across. They are usually dark brown or black and often pointed at each end. The contents consist very largely of insect remains. These droppings can be found under fallen timber or rocks and in similar places.

Bat faeces are rather similar to those produced by mice but they can be distinguished by their greater porosity and by the fact that they consist exclusively of finely divided insect remains. They are dark brown to black and the size varies according to the species of bat. The serotine, one of Europe's largest bats, has droppings that are usually 6–8 mm long and 3 mm across (see plate p. 168).

Such droppings are frequently found in large amounts in the bats' sleeping quarters in lofts and cellars or in hollow trees and caves. Many species also like to occupy bird nesting boxes.

Hare droppings in snow.

Hares and rabbits

Hare droppings are easy to recognise. In winter they are pale brown or yellow-brown, slightly flattened but otherwise spherical and firm, with a diameter of 15–20 mm. They consist of very coarse plant fragments, which can be clearly distinguished at the surface. The colour varies somewhat according to the type of food and becomes paler the longer the droppings have been exposed to the sun and rain. In summer, when the animal feeds on lusher food than in winter, the droppings are darker, almost black. Their consistency is softer than that of the winter droppings and one end may sometimes be drawn out into a small point (see plate p. 168).

The droppings are found particularly at the animal's feeding places, where they often lie in small piles, but it is also characteristic that hares defaecate shortly before they retire to their form, and droppings will frequently be found a short distance away, scattered among the tracks.

The droppings of the mountain hare are so similar to those of the brown hare that it is not really possible to tell them apart.

Rabbit droppings are also very similar to those of hares but are smaller, c. 10 mm in diameter, and more spherical (see plate p. 168). In contrast to the hares, the rabbit has a tendency to defaecate on slight elevations, such as grass tussocks and mole hills, and striking quantities of droppings may accumulate at such latrine sites. This is associated with the fact that rabbits use their faeces for scent marking their territory (see p. 224). On the outskirts of a rabbit warren there may often be latrines sited on runs, or at places where

Rabbit droppings deposited in heaps which serve to mark territory.

several runs meet. When a strange rabbit enters the area it will come across these piles of droppings and will be warned by their scent that the area is occupied. These latrines are usually used over a long period and as a result of their manuring action such places develop vegetation differing from that of the surrounding area.

Rodents

Squirrel droppings are quite short, almost spherical, often a little flattened at one end and with a small point at the other end. In summer they are brown, 5–8 mm long and 5–6 mm across, in winter dark brown or black and somewhat smaller. They primarily contain finely divided plant fragments, which can be distinguished at the surface of the droppings, and sometimes also the remains of insects (see plate p. 168).

It is very rare to find the droppings in summer, but in winter they can be seen on the snow, either on the surface or in the small holes they have formed when they were dropped. If they have lain for a time on the snow the latter will be stained yellow-brown and the droppings are then easier to find.

Beaver droppings are short and thick, often almost spherical and with a hint of a point at one end. They are dark brown, about 2 cm thick and 2–4 cm long. In consistency they are very similar to hare droppings, and like these they consist mainly of very coarse plant material, which can be clearly distinguished at the surface (see plate p. 168).

The beaver always defaecates in the water, but the droppings can sometimes be found floating in along the banks.

Among the *voles*, of which there are

several species, the droppings are cylindrical, usually with rounded ends. In summer when these animals feed largely on green vegetation the colour is often greenish, but in winter when they eat bark, roots and other plant material the droppings are brownish (see plate p. 168).

Apart from a few species, such as the musk-rat and water vole, whose faeces can be recognised by their size, it is impossible to distinguish between the droppings of the different vole species. Any identification must, therefore, rely on other signs, such as feeding signs, as well as on the location and a knowledge of the species which occur in the area concerned.

Musk-rat droppings are c. 12–14 mm long and c. 5 mm thick. They are found along rivers and lakes where in spring they are dropped very conspicuously on rocks and similar places (territorial marking). Later in the year

musk-rats defaecate mainly in the water (see plate p. 168).

Water vole droppings are 7–10 mm long and 3–4 mm thick, while those of the *field vole* are 6–7 mm long and 2–3

Field vole droppings at a feeding place; they are about half the size of those of the water vole.

Water vole droppings (scarcely 1 cm long) in front of the burrow entrance.

mm thick. Such droppings are found in small heaps at the animals' feeding places (see plate p. 168).

The droppings of the *Norway lemming* resemble those of the field vole. They are commonly seen on moors and heathland, where they occur in piles, which may become very large in the so-called lemming years when these animals occur in enormous numbers (see plate p. 168).

In the true mice, a family with numerous species, the faeces are not so uniform and regular as in the voles (see plate p. 168).

Brown rat droppings are cylindrical, usually with blunt ends, and are c. 17 mm long and 6 mm across, but the size is very variable. The animal has a tendency to have special latrine sites, but the droppings are often found more scattered, frequently several together (see plate p. 168).

Black rat droppings are shorter and thinner than those of the brown rat and are c. 10 mm long and 2–3 mm across; they are often slightly curved with a point at each end. When living in lofts, black rats quite characteristically leave their droppings scattered over the whole floor, whereas the brown rat, under the same conditions, places its faeces in corners or along the walls (see plate p. 168).

House mouse droppings are small and usually cylindrical, c. 6 mm long and 2–2·5 mm across. In comparison with these the droppings of the *wood mouse* and *yellow-necked mouse* are relatively shorter and thick (see plate p. 168).

Coypu droppings are 2–3 cm long and scarcely 1 cm across and have a characteristic finely grooved surface. They occur near rivers and in swampy areas (see plate p. 168).

Black rat droppings scattered over the floor of a corn loft.

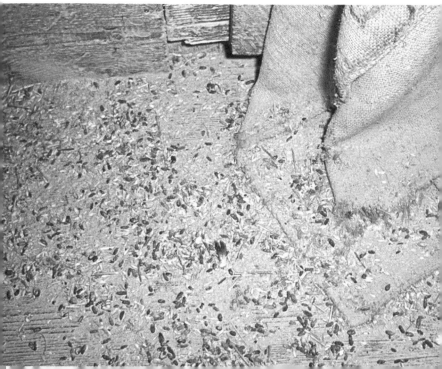

Carnivores

The faeces of carnivores are usually cylindrical and the end which last left the anus is almost always pointed. In some animals however, such as the badger and otter, the faeces are often liquid or semi-liquid. The colour is most frequently dark brown, but may vary according to the animal's diet. Many carnivores are avid consumers of berries and if these are brightly coloured, as for example bilberries, they will stain the faeces. Sometimes the surface of the faeces is covered with a white, friable layer, which may also extend into the faeces themselves. This consists of phosphate derived from fragments of bone which have been dissolved in the animal's alimentary canal, and it can be observed, for instance, in dogs which have been given a lot of bones.

The most striking parts of the faeces are hair, feathers, teeth and bone fragments, and in summer also the remains of insects, berries and other fruits. It is often possible to determine quite accurately from these remains what the animal has been eating. Fresh carnivore faeces always have a sharp, acrid smell, which is particularly strong at mating time, and many of these animals also use their faeces for scent marking.

Fox faeces are sausage-shaped, usually 8–10 cm long and c. 2 cm across and with a spirally twisted point at one end. Sometimes they fall apart into several pieces and then it is only the last part which is pointed. The colour varies from black to grey but in autumn when foxes eat many berries the faeces are often stained. They consist of fur, feather and bone fragments from small rodents and birds, but in summer the faeces commonly have fragments of insect chitin, particularly

A fox's faeces become whitish after it has eaten a lot of bones.

beetle elytra, and the remains of various berries and other fruits. Since the fox uses its strongly scented faeces to mark its territory they are often dropped on an elevation, such as a tree stump, a rock or a grass tussock, whence the scent is effectively disseminated, but they may also lie on roads or on paths used by the animals (see plate p. 168).

Wolf faeces are similar to those of a large dog. They are dark grey, 10–15 cm long and 2·5–3 cm across, and like those of the fox they are left in an elevated position and are sometimes rendered more conspicuous because the animal has scraped up the nearby soil with its hind-paws, just as dogs do.

The droppings of the *badger* may be sausage-shaped and dry or semi-liquid, depending upon what the animal has been feeding on. The sausage-shaped

faeces resemble those of the fox, but are more cylindrical and the surface is rough and uneven. They contain insect remains, the fur of small rodents, corn and berries (see plate p. 168).

The most characteristic feature is, however, the siting of these droppings. The badger has special latrines where the faeces are deposited in small oblong holes about 10 cm deep, which the animal scrapes in the ground with its fore-paws. The holes are not covered in after use and the same hole may be used several times. These latrines are often found quite near the badgers' set or in a special area near one of their paths. The holes may also be sited in more isolated places, but then nearly always on a frequently used path.

When fresh, an *otter's* faeces are black, tarry and slimy and have a

'ox faeces that are completely black because the nimal has been eating berries.

The badger digs a little hole in which it deposits its faeces.

characteristic and very persistent, oily smell. With time they become pale grey and crumbly. Their contents consist usually of fish scales and bones, crustacean carapaces and similar material.

These droppings are most frequently found—often in small portions—on elevated places along river banks, for example on a rock or tree stump near the shore. Sometimes they are deposited on the edge of a ditch where it opens into a larger stream, or on a small hillock of sand or grass which the otter has scraped together on a bare stretch of shoreline. This characteristic siting suggests that the otter uses the faeces as scent markers to orientate other members of its species.

Pine marten and *beech marten* faeces cannot be distinguished by their appearance but they can be identified by their scent and location. They are

Otter faeces deposited on top of a grass tussock. Here the animal has placed its faeces so that they can serve to mark territory.

A beech marten has chosen a pile of newspaper in a loft as its latrine.

normally sausage-shaped, 8–10 cm long and 1·2 cm across and usually twisted and drawn out to a point. They contain fur, feathers, bone splinters and in late summer and autumn they also have the remains of berries as well as flower seeds and cherry stones. The colour is dark grey or black (see plate p. 168).

Pine marten faeces have a marked and quite pleasant musky scent. They are usually deposited on an elevation, such as a rock, tree stump, wood pile or fallen tree trunk. On the other hand, the faeces of the beech marten are very evil-smelling, and where this animal occurs in lofts and outhouses one frequently sees that they have special latrine sites on boxes or similar objects, where large amounts of faeces may accumulate.

The droppings of *polecat* and *mink* are very similar to one another. When firm they have the usual marten shape, that is sausage-like, twisted and drawn out to a point; they are 6–8 cm long and c. 9 mm across, and thus somewhat smaller than those of the pine marten and beech marten. They normally contain fur, feather, pieces of bone and the remains of berries. If the animal has been feeding on fish or frogs the faeces will be loose and fairly liquid. Polecat faeces, in particular, have a very rank and unpleasant smell, but in spite of this they are not used for scent marking and are deposited very inconspicuously. The polecat usually has a special latrine associated with its lair (see plate p. 168).

Stoat droppings resemble the dry faeces of polecat, but are smaller, c. 5 mm across. They contain fur, feathers and bone fragments from small rodents and are usually deposited on elevated sites in the terrain. The faeces of the *weasel* and *least weasel* are like those of the stoat but even smaller, c. 2 mm across (see plate p. 168).

Cat faeces are sausage-shaped and usually 6–8 cm long and 1–1·5 cm thick, but they may also be more or less semi-liquid. They are deposited in a small hole which the animal scrapes out with its fore-paws in the soil or in snow, and afterwards the hole is carefully covered up again. The urine, which like the faeces has a very strong smell, is dealt with in the same way. In the wild cat it has been observed that it is only within the animal's territory that the faeces and urine are hidden in this way. On the outskirts of its territory the faeces are deposited conspicuously on a tree stump or rock in the same way as a fox does. Here, therefore, the strongly smelling faeces are used to warn other wild cats where the territorial boundaries begin (see plate p. 169).

Lynx faeces are similar to those of a cat, but larger. They contain fur, feathers and bone fragments. Like the cat, a lynx carefully covers up its faeces with soil or snow (see plate p. 169).

In summer, *bear* faeces are cylindrical and may be about 6 cm thick. They are deposited in large piles and consist of fur, pieces of bone and the remains of various insects and plants. During the autumn when the animal feeds on a variety of berries the faeces are semi-liquid (see plate p. 169).

Wild boar faeces.

Ungulates

Pigs

Wild boar faeces are normally in the shape of a sausage about 7 cm across, and made up of a series of oblong masses.

Deer

The faeces of deer are short, cylindrical or almost spherical, often with a small point. The surface is smooth and when fresh the droppings are usually black and overlaid with a thin, shiny layer of mucus, which however dries out very quickly. From the outside they give no clue to their contents but when broken up they will be seen to contain yellow-brown to greenish plant remains. In summer the droppings are sticky and soft and often more or less fused together. Deer droppings, known as fewmets, usually lie in quite large heaps at the feeding places, but they may also be deposited at random.

In a fully grown *red deer* the droppings are 20–25 mm long and 13–18 mm across. When fresh they are black and shiny, but they gradually become duller and more dark brown. The shape is cylindrical, often with a point at one end, but the other end is either rounded or slightly concave. The male's droppings are somewhat larger than those

Red deer fewmets.

Fallow deer fewmets in the spring, adhering to one another. See also the picture on p. 170.

of the female and are mainly of the type with the concave end, whereas the female's are mostly rounded. The summer droppings frequently have a very soft consistency, and they tend to coalesce (see plate p. 169).

Fallow deer droppings are like those of the red deer, but smaller, usually 10–15 mm long and 8–12 mm across. In summer the droppings tend to become fused together (see plate p. 169).

Roe deer droppings are 10–14 mm long and 7–10 mm across and are black or dark brown. In winter they are short and cylindrical, sometimes almost spherical, often with one end rounded and the other pointed. In summer the faeces are frequently deposited in large clumps with a furrowed surface. The droppings occur in heaps at the animal's feeding places, but quite commonly roe deer defaecate while on the move, so that the droppings can be found scattered individually along a trail. In general, a roe deer's drop-

pings are very similar to those of sheep and goat (see plate p. 169).

The droppings of an *elk* are easy to recognise by their colour and size. They are yellow-brown to blackish-brown depending upon the food. Thus, in

Roe deer droppings.

Elk droppings.

winter, they are pale, dry and firm whereas in summer they are darker, soft and wet with a tendency to coalesce. The winter droppings from a fully grown elk are 20–30 mm long and 15–20 mm broad. There are two main types: one is almost spherical, often with one end slightly pointed and the other end flattened or slightly concave, while the second type is more oblong with rounded ends, one of which may be slightly pointed. But there are all kinds of intermediates between these two main types. It is not the bulls that deposit the round droppings and the cows the oblong ones, as has been suggested. It is, in fact, impossible to distinguish between the droppings deposited by the two sexes (see plate p. 169).

The winter droppings of *reindeer* are 12–15 mm long and 7–10 mm across. At this time of the year they are very dark (black to blackish-brown), but in summer they are yellow-brown and also soft, indeed often semi-liquid (see plate p. 169).

In summer, reindeer droppings are often porridge-li

Mouflon droppings.

Sheep, goats and cattle

Mouflon droppings consist of spheres a centimetre in diameter which are deposited in compressed cylinders or clumps, and in this process they often lose their original shape and appear to be angled, or sometimes pyramidal.

Domestic sheep produce similar droppings (see plate p. 169).

Goat droppings are cylindrical, c. 1 cm long, and sometimes flattened at one or both ends. They often lie in small heaps (see plate p. 169).

In the *chamois* the individual droppings are almost spherical, c. 1·5 cm in diameter. They are often produced in compressed form, so that the individual droppings become somewhat flattened.

Cattle normally produce a brown semi-liquid circular mass of faeces. As this dries it forms a cohesive cake, in which the undigested plant material is visible.

Birds

In mammals the waste material from the gut (the faeces) and the waste liquid from the kidneys (the urine) leave the body by separate apertures. In birds, on the other hand, the ureters

Gull droppings on a statue that the birds have used as a roosting place.

Green woodpecker dropping. The dropping, which is enclosed in an ash-grey membrane, contains numerous fragments of the indigestible exoskeletons of ants.

open into the cloaca, an enlargement of the hind-gut, and the faeces and urine leave the cloaca more or less mixed together. Bird urine is normally a thick, whitish fluid, and the large amounts produced by cliff-nesting birds may form a striking feature of the landscape.

Many birds, such as birds of prey, owls, crows and gulls, get rid of a greater part of the indigestible part of their food by regurgitating it in the form of pellets (see p. 194). In these birds the droppings will not normally contain identifiable food remains, whereas the pellets naturally provide good evidence on the composition of the food. Conversely, investigation of the droppings of birds which do not produce pellets will usually give a good idea of what they have been eating. Thus, in many insectivorous birds, such as the green woodpecker (see plate p. 169), the droppings will contain the indigestible chitin of insects, and in birds which have been feeding on berries the actual seeds will pass undamaged through the alimentary canal and be found in the droppings. This process plays a very important role in the dispersal of many plant seeds, for the birds will often void the seeds far away from the place where they have been eaten. In cases where the berries are brightly coloured, for example bilberries and elderberries, the colour will stain the droppings, thus providing a good clue to what the bird has been eating. In purely herbivorous birds, such as swans, geese, many ducks and game birds, the fresh droppings will often be greenish and relatively firm, and their content of vegetable matter can frequently be clearly seen at the surface.

As regards shape and consistency, bird droppings can be grouped into three main types: liquid, roundish semi-firm and cylindrical firm droppings. There are, however, many intermediate types, and the droppings of an individual bird may also vary considerably in appearance according to the kind of food it has been eating. In fact, it is only rarely that one can with certainty identify a bird from its droppings alone, and so we can only describe the commoner types in general terms.

Birds of prey produce liquid droppings, which are deposited in a whitish stream; these birds actually lift the tail in the air and squirt the faeces and urine out backwards and horizontally. Such droppings can be seen at their feeding places (see p. 156) and at their roosting sites, but primarily at their nests, where the young birds defaecate over the edge of the nest so that the branches and ground below become splashed with white. The same type of excrement is found, for example, in herons and cormorants, and as these birds breed in colonies the nesting trees and the ground below become caked with droppings. These products are very acid, and the vegetation suffers from the continual splashing, and in the end the nesting trees and the ground vegetation may die, particularly in the case of a cormorant colony.

Among the *song birds* the droppings of the chicks are contained within an envelope of mucus and are relatively firm and almost spherical. The chick deposits a dropping immediately after being fed, and the parent bird which is

Cormorant faeces, which are very acid, kill the nesting trees and the ground vegetation.

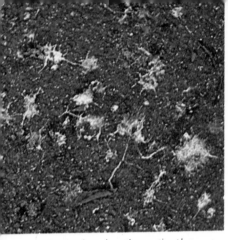

Starling faeces beneath a roosting place.

Capercaillie droppings. The semi-fluid part comes from the caeca.

waiting, perched on the edge of the nest, picks up the dropping in its beak and flies away with it. This procedure can be easily observed at a nest-box, where the parent bird will fly in with food in its beak, disappear for a moment and then leave the box carrying the whitish dropping. The removal of the droppings prevents the nest and the chicks' downy plumage from becoming fouled. When the young have reached a certain size the parent birds no longer wait for them to produce droppings. The chicks now defaecate on the edge of the nest and the droppings are either removed later on by the adults or simply pushed over the edge of the nest.

The adults' droppings do not have the envelope of mucus and are therefore more liquid. They usually produce a dropping consisting of an almost firm, oblong blob of faeces surrounded by the more or less liquid, white, slimy urine.

Game birds' droppings are slightly curved, cylindrical, dry and firm, particularly in winter. They usually consist of plant fragments and these can

be discerned at the surface. The colour varies but is usually yellow-brown to dark brown, often with a whitish cap of urine at one end. In summer and especially at berry time the droppings are softer and more lumpy. Single droppings may be found where the bird has been feeding or there may be little heaps on or under its roosting perch. In the latter case it is very common to see, for example in the capercaillie, that after having emptied the hind-gut of its firm, cylindrical droppings the bird has then evacuated its caeca, the contents of which consist of a semi-liquid, brownish mass, which flows out over the true faeces.

Game birds' faeces are firm and very resistant, particularly in winter, and it is often possible from their size and contents to identify the species that has produced them.

Capercaillie droppings are very large, the length of a little finger and c. 1·2 cm across, the male's being somewhat larger than the female's. In winter they consist almost exclusively of the remains of conifer needles, which can be clearly seen at the surface of the dropping. When fresh they are yellow-green, but gradually turn brownish or greyish (see plate p. 169).

Black grouse droppings are about half as large as those of the capercaillie and more compact. In winter they are pale yellow when fresh but gradually become brownish-grey. They usually contain the remains of birch buds, the dark scales of which can be distinguished among the other more finely divided matter (see plate p. 169).

Hazel hen droppings are 1·5–2 cm long and 6–7 mm across. In winter they are compact and consist largely of the remains of catkins from alder, birch and hazel (see plate p. 169).

The droppings of *willow grouse* and *ptarmigan* are approximately the same size as those of the hazel hen. In winter they often contain the remains of various buds and are very compact and fine-grained, but they may also have coarser plant fragments and their consistency may then resemble that of capercaillie droppings (see plate p. 169).

Black grouse droppings.

Pheasant droppings are about 2 cm long and 4–5 mm across and usually have a white cap of urine at one end. The colour varies according to what the bird has been eating, but is most often brownish-black or greenish. In winter the droppings are usually firm, often curved, but in summer they may

Ptarmigan droppings.

Pile of droppings at a pheasant's roosting site.

be more liquid (see plate p. 169).

The droppings of *partridge*, *red-legged partridge* and *rock partridge* are very similar to those of a pheasant, but only about half the size (see plate p. 169).

Ruff droppings can be found on water

meadows and at the birds' mating places (see p. 227). However, the dance of the male bird reduces the droppings to large white blotches.

Geese and *swans*, which are essentially herbivorous, usually produce firm cylindrical droppings which can be found in very considerable amounts in coastal marshlands, along the shores of lakes and in the case of geese on fields where they have been feeding. Goose droppings are 5–8 cm long and 10–12 mm across and consist of tightly compressed plant fragments, mainly grass. When fresh they are greenish but gradually turn grey-brown or grey-black (see plate p. 169). Swan droppings are similar to those of geese but are about twice the size.

Trodden faeces clearly mark the ruffs' display areas or 'hills'.

URINE

The whitish and often quite conspicuous urine of birds is produced together with the faeces and has therefore been discussed under the latter heading. In mammals, on the other hand, the urine is produced separately from the faeces and is usually a clear liquid which may vary from almost colourless to dark yellow.

During summer one can very rarely see where an animal has urinated, but one may become aware of it when the urine has a strong smell. When walking through an area that has foxes, one may suddenly be aware of a rank 'carnivore' smell, and this will nearly always be due to the strongly smelling urine of a fox. The fact that fox urine is frequently detected is because this animal uses it for scent marking, partly to define the limit of its home range to other members of the species and partly, during the mating season when the urine has a special scent, to advertise itself to the opposite sex (see also p. 225). The same process can be observed in male dogs, which rarely empty the bladder all at once, but release the urine in small portions on favourite places.

In winter, the yellowish urine can be more easily detected when the ground is covered with snow. At this time it is not only possible, with the help of the tracks, to identify the species from which the urine came but also its sex. When a dog fox urinates it lifts one of its hind-legs, like a domestic dog, and releases an oblique stream of urine which usually meets the ground somewhat beyond the three clearly marked footprints. A vixen, on the other hand, squats so that the urine is deposited

between the tracks of the two hind-feet. In the case of deer it is also possible to determine the animal's sex by the position of the urine in relation to the tracks. When a deer is about to urinate it assumes a characteristic position with the hind-legs straddled and at the same time slightly bent. Because of anatomical differences between the sexes the male's urine is deposited between the tracks of the fore-feet and hind-feet whereas the female's comes to lie between the hind-feet tracks or a little behind these.

Position of urine in relation to the track. Fox above, deer below.

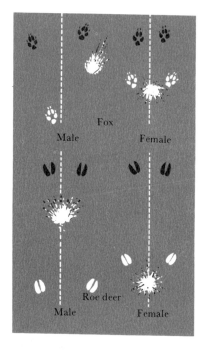

Fox

Male Female

Roe deer

Male Female

Pellets
natural size

Black-headed gull
Contents: fish bones
see p. 202

Berry remains

Beetles

Plant remains

Common gull see p. 202
Fish bones

Cherry stones

Beetles

Herring gull see p. 202
Ringed common gull chick

Mussel shells

CROW FAMILY

Crow, see p. 199
small rodents

Rook, see p. 199
plant remains, small stones

WADERS

Jackdaw, see p. 199
plant remains, small stones

Magpie, see p. 199
small rodents

Oystercatcher
Sand grains

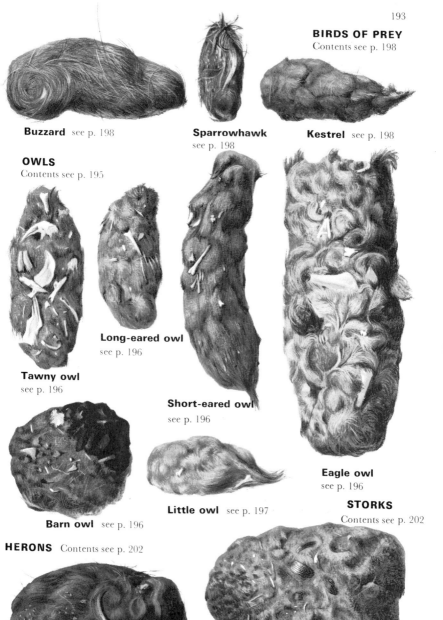

BIRDS OF PREY
Contents see p. 198

Buzzard see p. 198

Sparrowhawk
see p. 198

Kestrel see p. 198

OWLS
Contents see p. 195

Long-eared owl
see p. 196

Tawny owl
see p. 196

Short-eared owl
see p. 196

Eagle owl
see p. 196

Barn owl see p. 196

Little owl see p. 197

STORKS
Contents see p. 202

HERONS Contents see p. 202

Common heron see p. 202

White stork
see p. 202

PELLETS

Many birds get rid of those parts of their food which they cannot digest by regurgitating them in more or less compressed pellets. These may contain fur, feather, chitin from insects, bones, pieces of mollusc shell and various plant fragments which have not been broken down by the digestive juices in the alimentary canal. It is well known that owls produce pellets, but so do birds of prey, crows, gulls and many other birds. For these birds the process of regurgitation is a completely natural occurrence. It must not be confused with the vomiting which occasionally happens in animals which have eaten something that irritates the mucus epithelium of the stomach, and which therefore react by expelling the stomach contents through the oesophagus.

In birds, that part of the alimentary canal lying in front of the stomach proper is usually developed into a gizzard. In birds that produce pellets those parts of the food that are indigestible or difficult to digest gradually accumulate in the gizzard where they are pressed together into a lump which is regurgitated when it has reached a suitable size. A fresh pellet is covered with mucus which serves to ease its passage through the oesophagus and also helps to hold it together.

During its passage through the oesophagus the pellet assumes its final form. The diameter of the oesophagus therefore determines the calibre of the pellet, and as a large bird normally has a larger oesophageal diameter than a small bird, the diameter of the pellet is an important recognition character.

Kestrel pellet with a bird ring.

The shape of the pellets also varies somewhat according to the species. Thus, some birds produce almost spherical pellets whereas in others the pellets are cylindrical with one or both ends rounded or pointed. The consistency depends upon what the bird has been eating and may be more or less firm or so loose that the pellet easily falls apart.

Examination of the food remains contained in the pellets will provide much information on what a bird has been eating, and as each species has certain food preferences the pellet contents may also be a great help in identifying the species of bird concerned. In addition, of course, the different bird species also prefer certain habitats, and so it is also important to make a note of the exact location where the pellets were found, whether, for example, on a meadow, along the shore or in a wood, and also whether the latter consisted of deciduous or conifer trees.

Pellets are found primarily at the birds' roosting sites and nests, but they may be seen in feeding areas. In general, a bird produces about two pellets a day, and the actual regurgitation usually takes place just before it flies off to hunt for food.

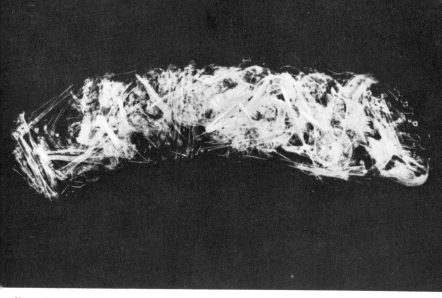

X-ray picture of an owl's pellet. The large content of almost undamaged bones makes it easy to distinguish from the pellet of a bird of prey (see p. 198).

Owls

When dry, owl pellets are usually grey and it is characteristic that they always contain well-preserved remains of the prey's bones. In most cases the skull itself will be broken, because owls normally kill their prey by a bite at the back of the head. Bones may likewise be bitten or broken, but the digestive juices have more or less no effect on them, so even the most delicate bones can be recovered from a pellet. This and the fact that owls usually swallow small mammals and small birds whole means that a careful examination of the pellet will tell exactly what the bird has been feeding on. Investigations of this kind can also be used to provide information on the occurrence of, for example, small rodents in a given area.

Apart from bones the pellets contain

fur, the remains of feathers and often fragments of chitin from insects, the wing-cases (elytra) of beetles being particularly striking. On the other hand, the horny sheaths from the prey's bill and claws will almost always have disappeared. It is, indeed, quite fascinating to unravel an owl pellet and see what it contains. After one has tried this for the first time it will be almost impossible to walk past a pellet without picking it up and breaking it apart to see what it contains.

Pellets from the different owl species can usually be distinguished on the basis of their size, shape and contents, as well as the location where they were found. The following section gives the characteristic features of the most commonly occurring pellets.

The pellet of a *tawny owl* is grey, cylindrical, usually 4–6 cm long and 2–3 cm across, and somewhat pointed at one or both ends. It is often slightly curved and usually has a very irregular surface. It normally contains the remains of mice and small birds and in some cases shrews and parts of insects. During the breeding period the tawny owl also takes medium-sized birds such as thrushes and pigeons, and the pellets will then contain their bones. These pellets are most commonly found in dense conifer forests, and also in churches, barns and similar places.

The *long-eared owl's* pellets are pale or dark grey, cylindrical, 4–7·5 cm long and 2–3 cm across and rounded at one or both ends. They appear to be more slender than those of the tawny owl and have a smooth surface. They contain the same type of material as the pellets of the tawny owl, and are also commonly found in dense conifer forests, where in winter they may occur in large numbers at places where these owls spend the day in small groups (see plate p. 193).

The *short-eared owl* produces pellets that are similar to those of the long-eared owl but may be somewhat longer, and the contents consist almost exclusively of the remains of voles. They can be found on or alongside tussocks in fields, meadows or similar places (see plate p. 193).

The pellets of the *eagle owl* are very large, 3–4 cm in diameter and often 10 cm long, and sometimes even longer. They contain the remains of small rodents and often also those of larger animals such as hare and capercaillie. They can be found in mountain forests and on talus slopes (see plate p. 193).

The *barn owl* has pellets that are cylindrical with blunt ends, or almost spherical, with a diameter of 2·5–3·5 cm. These pellets are very easy to recognise because they are covered with a blackish-grey crust which makes the surface quite smooth. It is also

Skull fragments found in pellets of the long-eared owl.

1. Bank vole **2.** Field vole **3.** Water vole **4.** House sparrow **5.** Harvest mouse
6. House mouse **7.** Wood mouse **8.** Rat **9.** Starling **10.** Common shrew
11. Water shrew **12.** Weasel **13.** Chaffinch **14.** Blackbird

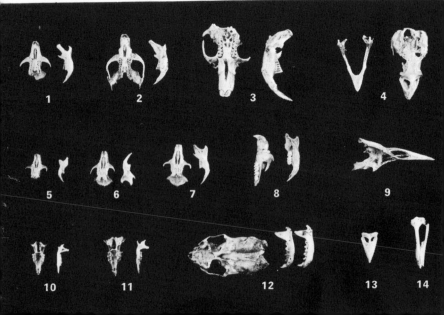

Pellets beneath the resting place of a long-eared owl.

typical that they contain the remains of shrews as well as of mice. They can be found in churches, barns, ruins and similar places (see plate p. 193).

The *little owl's* pellet is very small, 2·5 cm long and c. 1·5 cm across, and is usually rounded at one end, pointed at the other. In spring and summer this owl feeds largely on insects and earthworms, and this affects the pellets which may be completely blue-black from the remains of beetles and may contain particles of sand and earth derived from the guts of earthworms. At other times of the year the pellets are grey and contain the remains of mice and small birds. Found most commonly in churches, barns and hollow trees (see plate, p. 193).

Birds of prey

In contrast to the position in owls, the digestive juices of birds of prey can dissolve bones, and their pellets will therefore be found to contain no bones or only a few half-digested fragments. In addition, of course, a bird of prey divides its prey and avoids eating large pieces of bone. This, in turn, is associated with the fact that birds of prey have a crop, an enlargement of the oesophagus which fills up when the stomach is full. Once the crop is full the oesophagus is effectively blocked and regurgitation cannot take place. It is, therefore, important that the food should contain as few indigestible items as possible. In the case of birds of prey these are almost exclusively fur, small feathers and insect chitin and—in contrast to the owls—fragments of beaks and claws. The remains of food found in birds of prey pellets are mostly unidentifiable and, in contrast to owl pellets, they provide little information on the birds' food preferences. The pellets are found near the nests, at roosting sites and sometimes at their feeding places. They are usually difficult to identify, and are mainly distinguished by size.

Buzzard pellets are usually 6–7 cm long and 2·5–3 cm across, cylindrical with blunt ends or with one end pointed. They are grey and consist mainly of firm, matted fur from small rodents. They can be found under tall trees and near fence posts in fields (see plate p. 193).

Sparrowhawk pellets are 2–4 cm long and 1·2–1·7 cm across and consist of firmly compressed small feathers and mouse fur. They are found particularly along the edges of woods (see plate p. 193).

Goshawk pellets are similar to those of sparrowhawks but are larger, up to 6–7 cm long. They contain feather shafts and fur, usually from larger types of prey than those taken by the sparrowhawk (see plate p. 193).

Kestrels produce pellets that are 3–3·5 cm long and c. 1·5 cm in diameter. They are rounded at one end and pointed at the other and in addition to mouse fur and small feathers they may also contain insect fragments (see plate p. 193).

X-ray picture of a bird of prey pellet. In contrast to an owl pellet (see p. 195) it only contains a few bone fragments.

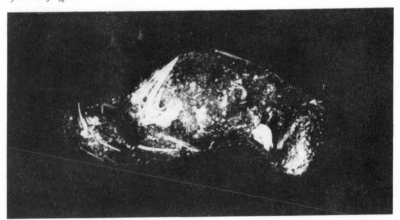

A kestrel has roosted on a drainpipe. The bird's pellets can be seen to the right, its faeces to the left.

Crows

The pellets produced by the various members of the crow family are usually elliptical or oval and contain much plant material, particularly chaff from different grasses, and also insect chitin. In addition, they nearly always have a number of small stones swallowed by the bird, which have helped to crush seeds and other material in the gizzard. These pellets are usually yellowish and very loose, so that they tend to fall apart. When the diet has contained small mammals, mostly taken in the form of carrion, the pellets will be dark and much firmer and will contain bones.

The pellets of the *carrion crow* are 4–4·5 cm long and c. 2 cm across. They are to be found at the nest, in fields and along the seashore (see plate p. 192).

The *rook's* pellets are 3–3·5 cm long and scarcely 2 cm across. They are most commonly found below the nesting colonies and on fields where the birds have been feeding (see plate p. 192).

The pellet of a *jackdaw* is c. 3 cm and 1–1·5 cm across, and can be found mainly at the nesting sites (see plate p. 192).

Magpie pellets are 3–3·5 cm long and 1·5–2 cm in diameter. They are commonly seen near the nest, but may be found almost anywhere (see plate p. 192).

Gulls

The pellets of gulls are generally spherical or cylindrical, sometimes slightly pointed at one end. The contents are very variable and consist either of animal or plant remains, or more usually a mixture of both. The pellets are normally very loose when they consist of the remains of animals, such as fish bones, small pieces of snails, bivalve molluscs and crabs. They will then fall apart very easily and are usually seen as small piles of more or less loose material. When the pellets consist exclusively or primarily of plant remains, for example chaff or berry skins, they will have a firmer consistency. This type of pellet frequently contains numerous insect parts, especially from beetles.

In gull colonies close to large towns where the birds do a lot of foraging at the municipal refuse dumps it is not uncommon to find the most astonishing things in the pellets, for instance, fragments of glass, elastic bands, plastic bags, silver paper and much else, which demonstrates the blind greed of gulls foraging in flocks. In some colonies of this type there have been reports of pellets containing cutlet bones.

Examples of herring gull pellets.

Above, with broken gastropod and bivalve shells.
Centre, with chaff and corn husks.
Below, with broken bivalve shells and fragments of crab.

Herring gull nest surrounded by paper, plastic bags and so on, which the birds have swallowed at a refuse tip.

In gull colonies close to refuse tips one often finds the most remarkable objects in the pellets. In colonies around Copenhagen the pellets contain large numbers of cutlet bones.

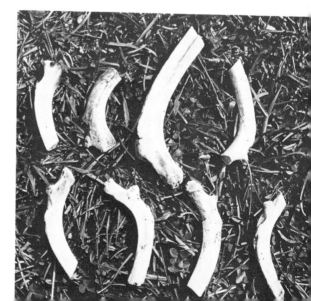

Gull pellets are found primarily at the breeding colonies and at places along the shore where the birds congregate and rest, but in the case of the black-headed gull and common gull the pellets can also be found in fields where the birds have been feeding.

Black-headed gull pellets are 2·5–4 cm long and 1·5–2 cm across. They may contain fish bones, the remains of various shore animals and, when the birds have been feeding on land, chaff and other plant material such as bilberries and crowberries which stain the pellets blue-black. Quite often the pellets also contain the remains of insects, particularly beetles (see plate p. 192).

Common gull pellets are 5–8 cm long and c. 2 cm in diameter and contain much the same as those of the black-headed gull. In areas with cherry orchards it is not uncommon to find pellets that consist entirely of cherry stones (see plate p. 192).

Herring gull pellets are 3–5 cm long and 2·5–3 cm across and they contain the remains of fish, crabs, snails and bivalve molluscs as well as some plant material (see plate p. 192).

Storks

The digestive juices of storks are, like those of birds of prey, capable of dissolving the bones of their prey, so these are more or less absent from the pellets. On the other hand, fur, feathers and insect chitin are well preserved.

White stork pellets are usually 4–5·5 cm long and 2·5–3·5 cm across, and more regular than those of the heron. They frequently have a sweetish, sickly smell and they contain fur, feathers and insect remains. Storks also take many earthworms and the large content of sand found in the pellets probably comes mainly from the worms' alimentary canals (see plate p. 193).

Herons

The pellets produced by the *common heron* vary considerably in shape and size. They may be regularly spherical or ovoid masses of closely packed mammal fur or very irregular and made up of small more or less cohesive balls of matted fur. Sometimes they consist of a loose mass of feathers. In general, the greater part of the pellet consists of fur from small rodents, particularly field voles and water voles, with some from shrews and moles. Frequently there is also some chitin from insects, but there is usually no sign of the numerous fish which herons catch.

The pellets are commonly found at the birds' roosting places and in coastal meadows and similar places where the birds feed (see plate p. 193).

A fallow deer's lair.

HOMES AND SHELTERS

When animals set up a home it is usually in a well sheltered or inaccessible place and it will very often be very inconspicuous and therefore difficult to find. By following an animal's trail one will eventually reach its home or shelter. The position of its home may be betrayed during the breeding season by the lively traffic of the adults bringing food for the young, and in autumn by the fall of the leaves.

Only a few animals have a permanent home which they use throughout the year. The great majority only have one during the breeding season for the protection of the young, and possibly winter quarters to protect themselves against damp and cold, but most animals continually move their sleeping quarters. Certain animals do not have a fixed home even during the breeding season but are constantly shifting the places where they sleep.

Birds' nests are by far the commonest homes found in nature. While in use these are generally well sheltered in ground vegetation or among the leaves of trees and bushes, but by winter time many of them will have become very conspicuous. Nests vary considerably in appearance, and are characteristic of the different species by reason of their position, size, structure and the materials of which they are built. It is not possible, within the scope of the present book, to discuss the many

Pit used for sleeping by a willow grouse. Note the droppings at the bottom of the pit.

different kinds of birds' nests in greater detail. Those who are interested in this subject may be referred to the very numerous bird books which give good descriptions and often also good illustrations of the main nest types. Game birds often have roosting or sleeping places on the ground, which are in the form of saucer-shaped depressions and these generally contain a little pile of droppings (see page 190). In cold climates where the night temperatures in winter are so low that it is dangerous for game birds, for instance, to spend the night up in the trees they will often bury themselves in the snow to seek shelter from the cold.

Mammal homes are also very variable and the following section contains descriptions of the different types of home and shelter that are most commonly found in the wild.

Homes on the ground

Deer and hares have no permanent home, but sleep in any suitable place, which may exceptionally be used more than once; deer sleep in a 'lair' and hares have a 'form'. Even during the breeding season these animals have no fixed abode, but the young are capable of leaving their place of birth very soon after they have been born and from then on they are continually shifting their quarters.

Most deer pay little attention to the construction of their lair. They merely lie down to rest in a more or less sheltered place. On account of their weight the vegetation in such places will be noticeably flattened and this betrays the fact that they have been there long after they have moved off. In most cases there will also be drop-

An elk's lair.

pings near the lair and these, together with the size of the lair, should enable one to identify the species of deer. In snow the lair is naturally more clearly marked and often there will be distinct impressions of the animal's limbs as well as its body.

The lair of a *roe deer* is rather different from those of other deer, for here the animal carefully scrapes away

A roe deer's lair. Before lying down the animal has scraped away the leaves etc.

A hare's form. When in use the hare sits with its hindquarters innermost and its fore-feet on the loose earth.

loose leaves and twigs and often even growing vegetation with its front hooves, before lying down to rest on the bare earth.

A *hare's* form is a shallow, often natural depression which is roughly like that produced when a man kneels in soft earth, and is a little deeper and broader behind than in front. The hare usually scrapes away leaves and so on and then lies down on the bare earth. However, hare forms in which young have been born are often lined with fur, which the doe hare has plucked from her own pelt. The form normally lies alongside a grass tussock or a rock which provides shelter from the wind. The animal always lies with its hind end over the deepest and broadest part of the form, resting on the thick fur of the hind-limbs which are tucked in under the body while the fore-legs are extended forwards.

A hare lying on its form is very difficult to see, and it usually sits very close until one almost treads on it. By carefully approaching the animal from in front, that is, from the direction in which it will jump, it is often possible to get very close to it, sometimes so close as to be able to touch it before it leaps away.

In winter a hare's form is usually only a depression scraped in the snow. Often the warmth of the animal's body will have melted the snow a little, and clear impressions of the long hind-legs can be seen in the centre of the form. In deep snow, the *mountain hare* often digs a short, curved tunnel in the snow just at the side of the form. As there is no form in the tunnel itself this is probably made as a refuge in which the animal can quickly take shelter when threatened by an owl or a bird of prey.

Homes above ground

Some mammals build their homes in vegetation and seen from a distance these may look somewhat like birds' nests.

Thus, *squirrels* build their homes or drays in trees, usually close to the trunk, where they have the support of one or more side branches. A squirrel's dray is spherical, with a diameter of 20–50 cm, and with an entrance hole c. 5 cm across on one side; this hole is blocked up by the animal when the weather is inclement or when it has to leave its young while it goes in search of food. Externally the dray consists of loosely plaited twigs and it is lined with a thick layer of grass, moss or plant fibre which the animal has torn from dead branches. Internal to this

A squirrel has torn the bark off a dead branch for use in making its dray.

A squirrel's dray.

there is a lining of soft material, such as fur or feathers.

A squirrel will build several drays: a solidly constructed main dray which is used for breeding and as winter quarters, and two or three more simple drays which are used occasionally as sleeping quarters. Sometimes squirrels build drays in hollow trees or nest boxes.

A squirrel's dray is rather like the spherical nest of a magpie which consists of a solid nest cup, made of twigs,

A nest box used as winter quarters by a squirrel which has had to enlarge the hole in order to get in.

mud and thin roots, covered by a domed roof of dry twigs. A magpie's nest is, however, considerably larger than a squirrel's dray and is normally out among the branches rather than close in to the trunk of the tree.

Harvest mice make two kinds of nest, namely summer nests and winter nests. The summer nests are built high up in vegetation, usually 30–40 cm above the ground, and are very artistic structures. Each nest is spherical with a diameter of 8–10 cm and a circular entrance hole at the side. The nest material consists almost exclusively of grass leaves which the mice split longitudinally with their incisors and carefully weave together. To support the nest they weave in all the nearby leaves and stems, but do not bite these off and so they retain their green colour throughout the summer and serve to camouflage the nest. When, however, the vegetation withers in autumn the nests become very conspicuous as tiny spheres of hay. The harvest mouse builds several summer nests, of which one is used for breeding. This is a little larger than the others and is lined with the fluff from seeds. Summer nests are commonly built in tall grass or among other tall herbaceous plants, but they may also be found in dense bushes, such as hawthorn or blackthorn, or even on one of the lowermost branches of a conifer tree.

The summer nests can often be confused with birds' nests, for example the spherical nest of a wren, but the latter will always contain down.

The winter nests are built down on the ground, in a grass tussock, under a tree root or rock, or the mouse may dig a short tunnel underground and construct its winter quarters there. In general, the winter nest resembles the summer nest but is not built so carefully and skilfully. In mild winters harvest mice will sometimes use

Grass frayed by a harvest mouse for use in nest building.

The summer nest of a harvest mouse. The nest is very delicate and has not been used for breeding.

summer nests that have been specially lined, but in such cases they always use those that have been built in bushes or small trees.

Several of the dormice, which are well known for their long period of hibernation, build nests in trees or bushes during the summer. Among these the *hazel dormouse* is an absolute master in the art of construction, and its elegant nest is just as artistic a creation as the spherical nests of the wren and long-tailed tit. This nest is spherical or ovoid, with a diameter of 10–15 cm and an entrance hole at the side, and it is built 1–4 m above the ground. The nest material may vary considerably according to what the animal can find. They commonly use hay, dry leaves, bark fibre, moss and lichen which they skilfully interweave, and then line the

interior with fine plant fibre and similar soft material. The winter quarters of the hazel dormouse, in which it hibernates, are usually in a cavity in the ground, under a rock or a root, but they may also be found in hollow trees and not uncommonly in nest boxes.

As the name suggests the *garden dormouse* often occurs in gardens, parks and orchards (but not in Britain), where it builds a spherical nest out of twigs, leaves and moss, lined with grass, wool and other soft material. The summer nest may be found free in a tree or bush, but is more commonly built in a pile of brushwood, an old birds' nest, a squirrel's dray, a hollow tree or a nest box. The winter quarters are in the same type of place as those of the hazel dormouse. In certain parts of Europe it is quite common, particularly in the autumn, for the garden dormouse to enter buildings where it lives in cellars and store rooms, and under such conditions it does not need to hibernate.

Homes in the ground

Many mammals make their home in the ground, usually in association with a more or less branched system of burrows. In the construction of these homes the animals get rid of the soil they excavate, either by pressing it sideways or, at suitable intervals, by pushing it up to the surface, as in a mole hill, or they may scrape the earth out of the entrance hole where it forms an often very conspicuous flat, fan-shaped pile.

Since any one species uses only one of these methods of removing the surplus soil, this will provide a good clue for identifying the occupant of the burrow. A note should also be made of the size of the entrance hole, its position and any tracks and droppings seen in front of it. Examination of the roots which protrude from the roof of the burrow will often reveal hairs which again provide a clue to the identity of the occupant.

In deciding whether a burrow is still in use or is deserted, one should note whether the entrance hole shows fresh signs of having been used and possibly new footprints, or whether it is overgrown, more or less filled with fallen leaves or possibly even closed by spiders' webs.

Small mammals such as *shrews* and many *small rodents* often build a home that consists of a spherical nest of hay, moss or other plant material in a natural cavity, as for example a decayed tree stump, under rocks and fallen trees or on the ground in among dense vegetation. They may construct very simple short runs in the uppermost layer of soil, which is so loose that it can be pressed out to the sides, and they then build their nests there. On the surface such runs are only marked by a small entrance hole. In general, it is difficult to distinguish the homes of the different species from one another.

The *mole* makes three different types of underground burrow. Two of these lie quite close to the surface, namely the ordinary shallow burrows and those made in spring when the male is looking for a mate. The third type, the true hunting burrows, which also contain the nests, lie deeper in the soil and it is only in association with these that one finds molehills. The burrows are slightly oval in cross section, c. 5 cm broad and c. 4 cm high.

The mating season burrows are open, surface runs, rather like a small ditch with upturned soil on each side. They are produced, not only when the animal is looking for a mate, but also

A field vole's nest. This may also be built above ground in winter.

when, for some reason or another, it is highly excited. When a mole digs down into the ground from the surface, it brings the fore-paws in front of its snout and by pressing them downwards and outwards pushes the soil aside, at the same time pressing its snout into the hole it has just made. If the mole now continues in this way along the surface of the ground instead of going downwards, it will produce a burrow of the type made at mating time.

The surface burrows are formed by the mole digging just below the surface of the ground and displacing the soil by pressing it upwards with the fore-paws, so that the roof of the burrow is lifted up and appears as a ridge at the soil surface.

The deeper hunting burrows consist of more or less horizontal tunnels from which oblique passages lead up to the soil surface, and through which the soil excavated by the mole is passed up-

wards to form molehills. When pushing the earth up it uses the right and left fore-paw alternately. These movements can be detected for the soil is heaved up in a series of small jerks and it appears in the middle of the mole-hill and then falls out to the sides. In

Surface runs made by a mole in a newly rolled field.

A molehill in which some of the earth has retained the shape of the tunnel from which it has been expelled.

Molehills. Some idea of the layout of the tunnels can be deduced from the position of the hills. There will be a nest beneath the large molehill.

winter when the mounds freeze rather easily the earth emerges as a cohesive column having the same diameter as the tunnels. In very loose earth, as for example in deep woodland litter the mole tunnels by pressing the soil out to the sides, so in such places there are no molehills at the surface.

The spherical nest of the mole, which consists of hay and leaves, is normally made in connection with the deep burrows. In low-lying, water-logged areas, however, the nest is often found in a gigantic molehill which may be 0·5 m high and about 1·5 m in diameter.

When a mole leaves its system of burrows to hunt for food on the surface it always does so through one of the oblique tunnels, through which it has pushed out soil. Its exit hole will therefore always be associated with a molehill. These holes are rarely seen, but this is probably because the animal

closes the hole after it, probably when it returns.

The *water vole* has its home in a system of deep burrows that is often extensive, and very similar to that of a mole, and it also gets rid of the excavated soil by pushing it up to the surface. These piles of earth are very variable in size and are more irregular both in form and distribution than true molehills. In summer, when the water vole feeds on the green parts of plants, one frequently comes across large holes that lead down to the system of tunnels. These holes have a diameter of 6–8 cm, and the vegetation has usually been grazed up to a certain distance from the opening. The holes are nearly always unconnected with the piles of earth (compare the mole), and normally there is no loose soil in front of the hole, as there is in the case of rat holes. In loose soil the water vole does not produce earth piles but

The mole leaves its tunnel system through an oblique burrow. On its return it closes the hole behind it.

The hills or mounds of earth made by a water vole are more irregular, both in size and positioning, than those of a mole, and the holes are usually not connected with the hills.

The vegetation around the entrance to a water vole's burrow has usually been grazed.

presses the soil to each side.

The water vole's large, spherical nest is normally made in a special nest chamber within the tunnel system, but in very damp areas it may be above ground, e.g. in a reed tussock. The nest material is usually grass or rushes.

In spring, after the snow has melted, one sometimes sees large, branched sausages of soil on the surface. These have a diameter of 6–8 cm and may be several metres long and they are made by water voles. During the winter the animal will have had burrows in the lowest stratum of snow and when subsequently extending its underground tunnel system it will have disposed of surplus soil by pressing it against the walls of the snow tunnels. These sausage-like structures are particularly likely to survive for a time when there is a slow thaw in clear frosty weather.

A *fox's* earth is easy to recognise and very often conspicuous. It is usually

Large sausages of earth are produced when a water vole has filled a tunnel in the snow with loose earth.

A fox's earth, newly dug. These earths are usually very conspicuous as the animals spread the surplus soil in a fan-shaped heap in front of the entrance hole.

positioned on a south-facing slope with sandy or gravelly soil, but may also be found in flat terrain. The earth varies considerably in construction from a simple excavation with a single entrance under a large rock or tree root to a large complex system of tunnels with numerous holes, of which only a few are in regular use. During excavation the fox transports the loosened soil to the exit holes where it is spread out in all directions, and gradually forms a fan-shaped pile. In newly established earths the entrance hole is very narrow, 20–25 cm in diameter, but large earths which have been used for decades, perhaps for centuries, have very large holes. As the earths are continually being enlarged by new tunnels the piles of soil in front of the holes may become enormous and on slopes may even form large terraces.

The fox has a sharp, acrid 'carnivore' smell, so it is often possible to decide whether or not a den is occupied by sticking your head in and sniffing. If there are young in the earth there will usually be food remains, such as bones and feathers, spread about in front of the hole, and as the animals like to lie out and sunbathe in good weather the vegetation near the entrance will be trampled and worn. The faeces and urine of the foxes and the food remains act as manure, so the vegetation close to a fox's earth, or to a badger's set, is considerably more luxuriant, particularly in spring than it is in the surrounding area; also the actual plants often belong to species with high nutritional requirements.

A *badger's* home, known as a set (or sett), is similar in general appearance to a fox's earth and it is made in a comparable site; in fact the two can easily be confused. However, a badger's set can usually be distinguished from a fox's earth by the fact that when a badger scrapes out the excavated soil it takes it a short distance away so that there is a furrow of varying depth in front of the entrance to the set. Also, unlike the fox, the badger uses hay, dry leaves and moss as nest material, and scraps of these will often be seen outside the set where the badger has dropped them. Furthermore, the badger does not have the strong smell of a fox, and around the set there will usually be characteristic small holes, which the animal has scraped in the soil for use as latrines (see also p. 179).

Unlike the hare, the *rabbit* has an underground burrow, which consists of a nest chamber c. 40–50 cm beneath the surface of the earth, and around it an extensive and complex system of burrows with numerous holes. The soil is loosened with the front paws and then pushed out backwards with the hind paws to form a pile outside the hole. However, some of the burrows are dug inwards and these will have no excavated soil in front of them. The holes are connected on the surface by paths or runs which are usually well marked, and the rabbit's small round droppings will always be very conspicuous on these and also around the holes (see p. 175). In contrast to hares, rabbits are social animals which

An old badger set. The badger moves the surplus soil further away from the entrance, so that a furrow is formed in front of the hole.

Wild rabbits often live together in large numbers, and they have an underground warren with many holes. The surplus soil accumulates in heaps in front of the holes. Some holes are, however, dug from inside and these have no piles in front of them.

normally live in colonies, known as warrens, in which the burrows of the different animals intercommunicate.

The dominant females in a rabbit warren make special breeding nests in blind alleys within the colony itself, whereas the nests of subordinate females are often in a blind alley at a depth of c. 1 m on the outskirts of the warren. The nest is lined with hay or with fur which the doe rabbit plucks from her own pelt. The female only remains in the breeding nest when the young want to suckle, and when she leaves it she closes the entrance with soil and marks it with urine or faeces. This marking is respected by the other animals in the warren.

When living in buildings the *brown rat* usually makes a nest under the floor, in hollow masonry or in among stored goods. It will use almost any available material for nest building, but mainly hay, plant stems, paper and scraps of cloth. Out in the open, brown rats live in an underground system of tunnels, the extent of which varies considerably according to the conditions, but it usually does not go deeper than 40–50 cm. There may often be several holes to each system and on the surface these are joined by distinct, well-trodden runs. The rat is essentially a social animal which usually lives in groups with common tunnel systems.

Rat holes vary considerably in size

A brown rats' burrow out in the open. The surplus soil lies in front of the hole (compare with water vole).

but are usually 6–8 cm in diameter and they can be distinguished from those made by water voles—which are the same order of size—by the fact that a rat leaves the excavated soil in a heap outside the hole. As an exception to this, when a rat digs its way up from a broken drain the hole is made from below and the excavated soil will fall down into the drain and

Rat hole in a drain. The soil surface has sunk because the rats have excavated the underlying earth.

be washed away by the current. The amount of earth removed in this way by rats may often be so great that the surface of the ground starts to subside.

The *black rat* does not dig tunnel systems and in northern and central Europe it does not occur out in the open.

In spite of its name the *wood mouse* is not particularly associated with woodland, but commonly occurs on open land, where it has its home in a system of burrows which normally lie fairly deep, often 1 m or more below the surface. Associated with the burrow system there is a large nest chamber, filled with finely comminuted grass. The excavated soil forms a large conical pile in front of the holes, which are 3–4 cm in diameter. It is also not uncommon to find holes without soil in front, and these will have been made by a mouse that has dug itself out from below. When the burrows extend down into paler soil beneath the leaf mould, the excavated soil will be very conspicuous on the dark soil surface. The deep, branched burrow systems are mainly used in winter. In summer wood mice often dig more superficial and simpler burrow systems and sometimes the nest will be found above the surface in, for example, a dense tussock of grass.

The *musk-rat* lives near lakes and ponds and along rivers where the current is not too strong. It builds its home in the banks, excavating branched systems of tunnels, with a diameter of 15–20 cm. It often also builds a free-standing structure of rushes and reeds in among the vegetation in shallow water. This nest has a diameter of c. 1·5 m and may rise 1 m above the water surface. The entrance is under the water. As the plant stems used in its construction are hollow sufficient air enters the nest for the animal to breathe, even in winter when the water surface is frozen.

The *beaver* is the master builder among the mammals, well known for

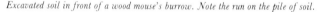

Excavated soil in front of a wood mouse's burrow. Note the run on the pile of soil.

Musk-rat 'lodge' on a frozen lake. The entrance to the nest is below the ice.

its dams and for its skilfully constructed lodge. A solitary or wandering beaver may build tunnels in the banks of a lake and make a home there, but a pair of beavers will normally construct a true lodge. This is made of lengths of branch (see p. 102), packed together with soil, aquatic plants and other plant material. As the branches are closely entangled the lodge is an extremely solid structure and may be very large—up to two metres high and c. 15 m in circumference. When built out of the water a beaver lodge is usually circular, but when on a bank it is oblong. This is because the entrance must lie below the water surface and so the lodge has to have an extension out into the water. Inside the lodge there is a spacious nest chamber lined with dry grass and wood shavings.

A beaver's lodge on the banks of a lake. The nest chamber itself is on land, but the entrance is below the water at the end of the lodge than extends out into the lake.

Feeding area

Nest chamber

Diagram of a beaver's lodge.

OTHER SIGNS

Tree fraying

The fraying of trees by deer produces a rather special type of sign which is very striking and easy to recognise. These are the marks which are produced when deer rub their antlers on trees and bushes and sometimes also on rigid herbaceous plants.

Antlers are carried only by male deer, except in the reindeer where the female also has them. These impressive structures are used for fighting, but they probably also provide external, visible evidence of the owner's strength, and may serve to warn an adversary and attract the females.

The antlers of a deer comprise two variously branched bony structures which are cast once a year and replaced by a new set of usually larger antlers. The cast antlers are nearly always found singly and they are normally quite easy to identify as the antlers of each deer species have a characteristic shape.

When growing each antler is sur-

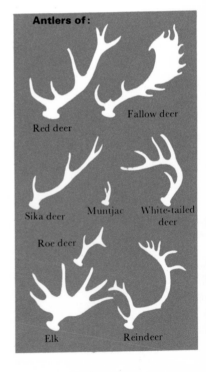

Antlers of:

Red deer

Fallow deer

Sika deer

Muntjac

White-tailed deer

Roe deer

Elk

Reindeer

rounded by a highly vascularised layer of skin known as the velvet. Once the antler is fully formed and completely ossified the blood vessels in the velvet break up and at the same time the velvet becomes loosened and can be easily removed. In practice the deer gets rid of the velvet by rubbing or fraying the antlers against thin, springy trees or bushes. In doing so the tree bark is torn off in long strips and side branches may also be broken. As the velvet is quite loose at this time it does not take the deer very long to rub it all off, and indeed it usually only takes a few hours to clean the antlers by fraying. The deer eats the frayed velvet so it is very rare to find any of it at the fraying sites. The antlers are completely white when the velvet has been rubbed off, but they very quickly acquire a brownish colour, the intensity of which probably depends primarily on the sap of the tree or bush which the deer has used for fraying. Red deer, fallow deer, sika and elk fray in late summer or early autumn, but roe deer fray in spring.

Deer produce another type of sign, particularly during the rutting season, by striking the antlers against bushes and even large trees so that the bark is ploughed into large furrows or torn off in strips. It has been observed that this behaviour occurs in deer which have just met a rival, and can possibly be regarded as a method of working off excess aggression. In fact from the striking damage done it looks as though the deer had been actually fighting the tree, and it is characteristic that the attacks are made from all sides, whereas in true fraying the antlers are always rubbed against one side of the tree only.

The *roe buck* behaves rather differently from the other deer, for after having cleaned the velvet off its antlers it still continues to rub its antlers against

Fraying by a red deer on a young pine tree.

trees throughout the summer. This is part of the animal's method of marking its territory.

Many animals establish a territory, that is an area which they defend against the incursions of other members of the species; this happens mainly during the breeding season, but frequently also at other times. An animal will mark its territory in various ways in order to show that the area is occupied and to warn other individuals of its species not to enter. However, some of these methods of marking leave no visible sign. Thus, birds mainly mark their territory by song or by some other sound. Woodpeckers, for example, drum with the bill on a dry branch or some other resonant object, such as the metal cap on the top of an electric or telephone pole.

Scent marking

Mammals, which have an extremely fine sense of smell, use scent marking and many species have special glands which produce a secretion with a scent which is not only specific to the species but also to the individual animal. These glands may be concentrated in special scent organs which can be found on the animal's feet, whence the scent material is transferred to the tracks. They may also occur on the head or body, often around the tail region, whence the scent may be deposited on specially strategic places, for the animal rubs scent on to vegetation or directly on to ground. These scent organs include, for example, the musk glands at the base of a badger's tail, the anal

A roe deer has frayed the bark off an alder tree, as part of its system of marking territory. Note the deep scratches in the bark and wood caused by the tips of the antlers.

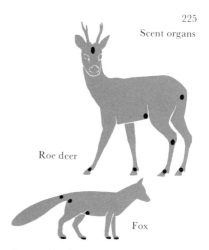

Scent organs

Roe deer

Fox

glands of martens, the frontal glands of roe deer, and the glands in front of the eye in red deer (preorbital glands).

Some scent organs function continually throughout the year, whereas others are functional only in sexually mature animals, and mainly during the rutting period.

Scent marking can also be carried out with urine and faeces, which deposit special scents in association with the excretory products.

Man has a poorly developed sense of smell and so we almost never notice the scent marks left by animals, unless they are particularly striking, as for example, the urine markings left by foxes. As already mentioned in the sections on faeces and urine, one can deduce from the siting that in certain animals, e.g. the fox (see pp. 178 and 191) and the rabbit (p. 175), these products have been used for scent marking. This applies particularly, for instance, to the roe buck which carefully marks the boundaries of its territory with some very conspicuous fraying and also by rubbing scent on to the frayed sites; this scent comes from scent glands situated on the forehead at the base of the antlers (frontal gland). At the same time as the fraying the animal usually scrapes the earth, using each fore-foot alternately and thus produces further conspicuous signs. The roe buck therefore marks its territory not only with scent but also visually by fraying and scraping the ground. In fact the majority of roe deer frayings seen are actually territorial and not associated with the removal of the velvet.

During the roe deer's rutting period one sometimes comes across some peculiar, much trampled circular paths, the so-called fairy rings or roe rings. These are produced during one of the last stages in the roe deer's courtship, during which the doe moves

Scent marking by a roe buck. The dark stripe on the tree trunk shows where the scent secretion from the frontal gland has been deposited. The antlers have scratched the bark on either side.

in a circle closely followed by the buck. These roe rings, which usually run round a bush, a tree stump or a rock, are normally circular or elliptical and relatively small but may vary both in shape and size according to local conditions. In some cases the animals use the same ring year after year. When playing a roe fawn may also run round in a circle and this would be difficult to distinguish from the rings of the adults if there are no tracks.

Wallows

During the rutting season, red deer fallow deer and elk have what are known as wallows. These are made by the males who turn the soil aside with the antlers and fore-feet, thus producing a depression into which the animals shed urine and semen. As it rains this is gradually transformed into an evil-smelling slush which the deer trample around and wallow in. The animals are then said to soil. The smell from the wallows is so strong that even man is aware of it from some distance, and it attracts and excites the females which sometimes also soil in the wallow. In deer parks with a crowded stock of red deer or fallow deer, these (and particularly the latter) may make wallows close to one another, and fights between the males will then be quite common.

Outside the rutting season red deer have another type of wallow, where they take mud baths. These occur in swampy places, along the banks of lakes and in similar sites and are used extensively by both sexes throughout the greater part of the year. The significance of these mud baths is not clear but it is most likely that they are associated with care of the skin. It is also possible that the mud may serve as a protection against stinging insects. These wallows are mostly in places where the animals could well have a bath in clean water, and so it is unlikely that the mud baths are taken as a means of cooling off. The elk may use comparable wallows, but these have not been observed in the case of the roe deer and fallow deer.

The *wild boar*, and also the domestic pig, are both very fond of wallowing, and the wallows are not uncommonly seen in areas with wild boar. In the vicinity of the wallow there will often be a tree which shows clear signs of the animals having rubbed themselves very thoroughly against it. Something similar to this can also be seen at deer wallows.

The numerous tufts of *hare* fur which can be found on certain fields during the spring have nothing to do with the animals' moulting, but stem from the very strenuous fights between males, during which they tear large tufts out of each other's pelts.

Ruff

In coastal meadows, usually on a slightly elevated area with rather dry earth, one sometimes sees a number of circular patches, with a diameter up to 50–60 cm, where the vegetation has been trodden down or completely worn away and scorched by a thin layer of white excrement (see p. 190). These are the display areas of the *ruff*, the so-called 'hills'. As the breeding period approaches, the males congregate at these places, where each one has its own stand, on which it hops and dances about, making sham attacks on its neighbours. Now and again a female appears, selects a male with whom she mates and then disappears.

At a ruff's display area the vegetation has been worn away, and the ground is covered with trodden faeces.

Great snipe

Similar social courtship displays occur in the *great snipe*, which lives in swamps and marshes. Here the display area is on a knoll or in tussocky terrain. Other species showing similar behaviour include the *black grouse*, which has its display areas or leks in open heathland and moorland, and the capercaillie with similar areas in woodland clearings. In many places these birds, and particularly the black grouse, start displaying before the snow has gone, and they will then leave tracks showing where they have danced with trailing wings and fought each other.

House sparrow

The *house sparrow* can often be seen taking a dust bath in dry, powdery earth, in the vicinity of human habitation. After having loosened the soil with its beak the bird lies down and flaps its wings, so that the dust

During courtship display black grouse run around in circles, dragging their wings, which make a furrow on each side of the footprints.

penetrates in among the feathers, and gradually a hemispherical depression forms. This type of behaviour which is part of the bird's method of keeping its plumage in good condition can also be observed in other birds, e.g. larks. It also occurs very commonly in game birds and fowls in which the feet as well as the beak are used to form the dust bath. Wild jungle fowl commonly make such baths in south-facing, sun-drenched sites with fine dry earth.

Signs associated with the moulting

A pheasant's dust bath, in the form of a saucer-like depression in the ground.

of fur or feathers are often found in nature. These are usually single feathers or tufts of fur, which lie around here and there, but sometimes they may occur in large numbers. Thus, many *ducks* have special moulting places along the coast, which they move to at the moulting season, and often each species has its own area. Large masses of feathers may be driven ashore at such moulting sites. Quanti-

ties of feathers can also be found in areas with colonies of breeding birds and on coastal meadows and similar places which gulls use for roosting.

On the edges of partially dried-out ponds the mud may show a mass of small bird tracks and broad beak marks. These have been produced by *swallows* which have come down to fetch material for their nests which are constructed of mud and straw.

Beak marks made by swallows collecting mud for their nests from a partly dried-out puddle.

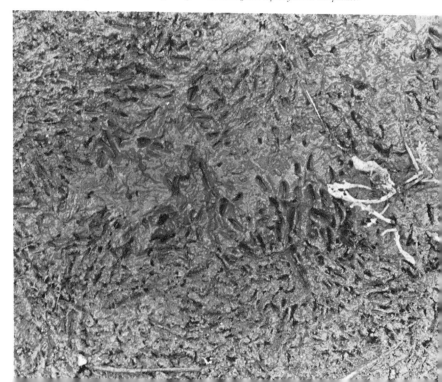

A river dammed by beavers. These animals often build two or three dams quite close to one another.

Beavers living in running water build dams so that the water is held back, and thus floods neighbouring flat ground; this gives the animals easier access to trees in such areas (see also p. 24). These dams, which may be over 100 m long, are constructed of branches, earth and water plants, and they are extraordinarily firm and solid (see also p. 102). Quite frequently two or three dams may be built one after another, with only a short distance between them.

Cats sharpen their claws on some fairly soft material in order to keep them in good condition. They often use tree trunks and appear to prefer elder. They tend to use the same place for quite a time so the bark soon becomes torn. It is important for cats always to have their claws pointed and sharp and they scratch the bark in order to loosen the outer horny layer of the claws. A careful search will usually reveal these horny fragments of claw.

Elder tree with bark scored by a cat sharpening its claws.

COLLECTING AND PRESERVING

For anyone who wants to identify tracks and signs accurately it is an advantage to make a collection of the various objects to be found in the wild. By collecting, one comes into closer contact with such objects and is better able to observe and appreciate the characteristic features of each find. A collection also allows one to make comparisons and it is an invaluable help in identifying new finds.

The collection may consist of photographs, casts of tracks, pellets, droppings or food remains. To derive most advantage from a collection it is quite essential, right from the start, to prepare a label for each individual find, giving details of the locality, the date, the species of animal and any other observations made at the time.

A photograph has the great advantage that it provides an actual picture of the location of the find and its immediate surroundings. In many cases this may be of great interest, as for example when a feeding place has been found. As a rule it is best to use colour film and to provide some sort of scale, particularly with photographs of tracks. The value of the collection is increased if, at the same time, measurements are taken of the stride length and the straddle and of a complete group of tracks (see p. 19).

Casts of animal tracks can be made in paraffin wax or plaster of Paris. Paraffin wax is easier to work with but it requires heat to melt it and the cast is fragile and easily damaged, so plaster of Paris is usually preferred.

Before making a cast, choose a track that appears to be characteristic and has a well-defined outline. Any loose leaves or small lumps of earth that have fallen into the track should be removed, but do not try to take away a trodden grass stem or anything similar as this might easily change the contours of the track. The track is then surrounded by a suitable strip of cardboard or metal foil which is folded to form a rectangular frame; this is carefully pressed into the ground, using the flat of the hand. A jug or similar receptacle is then filled with a suitable volume of water and small portions of the plaster of Paris are added, taking care to avoid lumps. As the plast absorbs water it sinks to the bottom. This process is continued until the plaster reaches the water surface, and only after standing for a few more minutes should it be carefully stirred to ensure that it is evenly mixed and without lumps.

The plaster is now ready for use and it should be carefully poured over the track, taking care that it flows into all the depressions. After an interval of 10–20 minutes the plaster will have hardened and the cast can be taken up. There will usually be some earth adhering to the cast, but this can be removed later under running water, possibly with the help of a soft brush.

Plaster casts are relatively fragile and may easily break if jolted during transport. It is, therefore, advisable to reinforce casts of large tracks or groups of tracks. This can be done by embedding suitable pieces of steel wire or hessian in the plaster before it sets.

One now has a negative impression of the track and can—usually without difficulty—take a positive impression in plaster of Paris. Just before doing this the negative cast should be rinsed with an aqueous solution of potash to prevent the two plaster mixtures from adhering. If this is not available, the negative can be smeared with vaseline or soap lye.

The finished plaster cast can be painted with a couple of dullish colours in order to emphasise the track itself. A little powdered red iron oxide can also be mixed into the plaster for the positive impression; this will produce an attractive red-brown cast which brings out the track itself and produces a more natural effect that the greyish-white plaster of Paris.

In some cases the shape of the plaster negative may be such that it is impossible to take a positive in plaster, because the two blocks become locked together and cannot be separated without damaging the track impressions. In such cases a positive impression can be made in silicon rubber, a plastic material which sets on the addition of 2–3% of hardener, and gives a rubber-like cast, which because of its elasticity can be separated from the plaster negative without damaging the cast impressions. To ease the separation of the two impressions the negative can be smeared with a thin layer of a fast-drying celluloid varnish (shellac cannot be used).

As with plaster casts—and with the same effect—a little red iron oxide (c. 0·5%) can be added to the silicon rubber when the hardener is stirred in.

The plaster casts are best stored in flat boxes, and to save space it is a good idea to use cast frames that are rectangular with the following standard measurements: 5 × 7·5, 7·5 × 10, 10 × 15 and 15 × 20 cm, all with a height of 5 cm. Frames with these measurements can be fitted into the same size of storage box in many different combinations. If the internal dimensions of each box are 22 × 32 cm (i.e. a couple of cm larger than the total dimensions of the casts), it should be possible to remove the casts without difficulty. The frames should be made in advance and folded up for ease of transport.

In collecting objects that have been handled by animals it is often annoying to find that many of them do not tolerate room conditions. The greatest problem is desiccation, which may cause deformation or the object may gradually fall apart, so that it completely loses its original appearance.

It may, therefore, be necessary to preserve the material in some way and this can often be done quite simply.

Cones handled by animals provide a typical example of objects that need

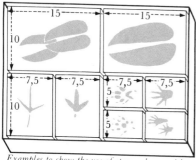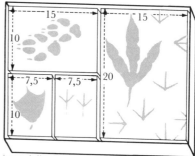

Examples to show the use of storage boxes with an internal diameter of 22 × 32 cm.

some attention before they can be incorporated into a collection. As they dry out the scales bend backwards giving the cones a completely different appearance from what they had in the wild. In most cases this problem can be solved very satisfactorily by wrapping gauze round the cones and then allowing them to dry slowly.

Pieces of wood that have been gnawed may gradually develop cracks as they dry out. This can be prevented by drying the pieces slowly, a process which is best achieved by placing them in a deep freeze so that they freeze-dry.

Many types of pellet are so loose that they very quickly fall apart. This can be avoided by dipping them one or more times in a solution of celluloid in acetone. As the acetone evaporates, which happens very rapidly, a thin skin of celluloid is left behind, which binds the individual components of the pellet together, and at the same time gives it a natural, slightly damp appearance. This method of preservation can also be used when collecting very friable pellets, such as those of gulls which may consist of fish bones or crushed mollusc shells. The celluloid solution can be dropped directly on to the pellet as it lies, using a small drip bottle; the skin formed will allow the pellet to be transported.

The celluloid solution is also very suitable for preserving droppings. These must be dry before they are placed in the solution. Small droppings can be merely put into the solution for a few minutes, but it is best to process larger droppings in a desiccator, a container in which the air pressure can be reduced by means of an air pump. A dish with the droppings and the solution is placed in the

Preservation of cones handled by crossbills. The cone on the right has been wrapped in gauze before drying, as shown in the centre. The cone on the left has been dried without gauze.

desiccator and when the air pump is put into operation the air in the droppings will be evacuated. When the pump is stopped and air is allowed into the desiccator the solution will be sucked up into the droppings which thus become thoroughly impregnated.

In addition to reinforcing the droppings and preventing them from falling apart the celluloid impregnation also protects them from the attacks of insects.

These preparations are best kept in flat boxes of the same size as the plaster cast boxes, i.e. 22 × 32 cm, a size that fits into most bookcases. Instead of partitions one can use plastic boxes, which can be obtained in all sizes, and these must have dust-proof lids. Finally, remember the labels with description, locality and date.

Index

Numbers in italics indicate pages with illustrations.

Bibliography

BRINK, F. H. van den. 1973. *A field guide to the mammals of Britain and Europe.* London.

ENNION, E. A. R. and TINBERGEN, N. 1967. *Tracks.* Oxford.

HARRISON, C. 1974. *A field guide to the nesting of British and European birds.* London.

HEINZEL, H., FITTER, R., and PARSLOW, J. 1972. *The birds of Britain and Europe with North Africa and the Middle East.* London.

LAWRENCE, M. J. and BROWN, R. W. 1967. *Mammals of Britain, their tracks, trails and signs.* London.

LEUTSCHER, A. 1960. *Tracks and signs of British animals.* London.

MURIE, O. 1954. *A field guide to animal tracks.* Boston.

MUYBRIDGE, E. 1957. *Animals in motion.* New York.

PETERSON, R. T., MOUNTFORT, G., and HOLLOM, P. A. D. 1973. *A field guide to the birds of Britain and Europe.* London.

SOUTHERN, H. N. (ED.) 1964. *A handbook of British mammals.* Oxford.

Photographers

BOLDT, KAJ: page 216

CHRISTIANSEN, ARTHUR: page 7, 79 below, 110, 156 below, 161 below.

CLARK, MICHAEL: page 68

ERIKSSON, OLOF: page 54, 141, 204

ERLINGE, SAM: page 51 left

FRANZMANN, NIELS E.: page 82 left, 161 above

GERELL, R.: page 47 below

HAARLØV, NIELS: page 104 right

HANSEN, ELVIG: page 140 below, 151, 167

HOLLAND, P. D.: page 22 below

ISAKSON, ERIK: page 43, 53, 59, 70, 72

JENSEN, ANNELISE: page 180 above

JENSEN, BIRGER: page 50

MARTIN, OLE: page 111

NIELSEN, JØRGEN: page 195, 198

NIELSSON, EDVIN: page 44, 56 right, 57, 80, 83 below

OMMEN, F. VAN: page 150 below

PULLIAINEN, ERKKI: page 205

QUEDENS, GEORG: page 60, 200

SCHÜNEMANN, H., BAVARIA: page 164 below

SEEGER, BURT: page 14

SIIVONEN, LAURI: page 38, 228 above

STENMARK, A.: page 152

STRANDBAEK, E.: page 160, 186

YAN-DIEUZAIDE: page 5

ZOOLOGICAL MUSEUM, COPENHAGEN: page 6 below

The remaining photographs were taken by PREBEN BANG

Artiodactyls

Wild boar

Fallow deer

Red deer

Sika deer

White-tailed deer

Muntjac

Roe deer

Elk

Reindeer

Chamois

Mouflon